# Bob Vila's Guide to
# Historic Homes of New England

*Bob Vila's Guides to Historic Homes of America*

# Bob Vila's
# Guide to Historic
# Homes of
# New England

# LINTEL PRESS

QUILL
WILLIAM MORROW
New York

ISBN: 0-688-12493-3

Library of Congress Catalog Card Number: 93-083605

Printed in the United States of America

First Quill Edition

1  2  3  4  5  6  7  8  9  10

MANAGING EDITOR— SUSAN RYAN
LAYOUT AND DESIGN BY EVA JAKUBOWSKI

# Acknowledgment

$\mathcal{I}$ would like to acknowledge all of the people who helped make the idea of this book become a reality. To my wife Deborah who shares my enthusiasm for everything about history and whose idea of a vacation is incomplete without visiting every historic house along the way. Her encouragement and determination to see every room in every house gave me the idea for this series of guides.

To Ron Feiner who brought us all together long ago and by doing so enriched us all. To Bob Sann and Hugh Howard whose path findings led us to our publishers, a special thanks for enabling us to be spared the normative agony of attempting to get published. Through Hugh's excellent relationships we hope to benefit all.

To my brother, whose expertise in the publishing business facilitated my limited understanding of the industry.

To Susan Ryan and Kim Whelan who worked so tirelessly and professionally to make this a reality. I could not have found more skillful people whose strengths complemented my weaknesses.

To my partner Barry Weiner, whose unfailing support allowed us to open the checkbook when the possibility of returns were vague.

To Eva Jakubowski, who makes books and computers come together. If I ever figured out what you do I'd probably thank you even more.

And finally, to my mother, who aside from being a librarian demonstrated to me at a very early age that a universe of knowledge could be found between the covers of that most marvelous and wonderful of all things...books.

— *Jonathan Russo*
**Lintel Press**

# Table of Contents

# Publisher's Note

*W*e hope that this book will serve as more than a conventional guide to historic homes. For while we set out to create a detailed, informative, and unique guide, devoted exclusively to historic houses, we also had higher goals. For those among you who enjoy, and are devoted to, preservation, architecture, decorative and fine arts, what we have attempted will be self-evident. For those who are first becoming interested in the world of historic Americana, we will try to give you a helping hand. For all those venturing across these historic thresholds, we invite you in, knowing that you will not be disappointed.

The following pages contain a wealth of information on the fascinating people—both the famous and not so famous—who lived in these houses, as well as descriptions of the houses and their remarkable collections. What can also be found within this book, beyond the listings of locations, hours, and tour information, is the most elusive of all things—wonder. For behind each and every house listing lies a world of wonder. Not the manufactured kind, packaged and sold to replace the imagination. Not the superficial kind which manipulates the emotions at the expense of the intellect. But wonder on a higher plane.

The first wonder is that any of these houses still exist and that anyone cares at all. Our society has often achieved its enviable position of affluence by focusing on the new and disposing with the old. The desire for the latest architectural styles, furnishings, and conveniences has often meant a bulldozing of the past, to the point where even the recent past is endangered. Of course, this has always been so; Colonial homes were remodeled into Greek Revivals at the expense of their original architecture. But the changes are far more devastating now, instead of remodeling the houses, we are tearing them down altogether. Time after time, when we went to a historic house in a small city or village, our guide's first statement was that the historic society had been formed to prevent the house from being torn down, often to make room for a parking lot. Historic houses have been made into rooming houses, beauty parlors, or high rises. As we walked through a fifteen room, four-story house built in 1840, complete with irreplaceable architectural details, the enormity of the "let's tear it down" mentality became overwhelming.

Of course the houses themselves possess more wonder than anything else. It is a sorrowfully calloused person who cannot experience the past in a historic house. To tour the prosperous ship captain's house in historic Newport, Rhode Island is to wonder at the riches of furniture, decorations, textiles and food stuffs that ships and winds provided. To tour the 18th-century stone houses of Washington, Pennsylvania with their two-foot thick walls is to wonder at the fortitude of their inhabitants as they struggled against attacks and defended themselves against the cold winters. The very cosmopolitanism of mercantile families in Greenwich Village, New York permeates the air of the historic houses there. One can sense the refinement these people must have felt when they sipped brandy and smoked cigars in their impressive parlors. To be told why people used fireplace screens —so that the wax women used as a cosmetic to fill in their pockmarked faces would not melt—is an explanation of a common object that brings the past alive in a personal and wonderful way. The treasures of art, architectural details, furniture, household implements, and costumes contained in these homes also makes us pause in reflection. Things were viewed very differently when they were made by hand and scarce. There is an education for all of us living in a throw away culture.

So it is to the individuals, organizations and societies who are saving, preserving and displaying historic America that our sense of wonder and gratitude is directed. Sometimes, we would drive by a mall and see endless cars, stores and shoppers, and know that the energy of the town was now clearly centered at the mall. Then we would arrive at our destination, the local historic house, and find we were the only visitors. Despite this daunting competition from today's faster paced entertainments, our guide was cheerful, patient and full of enthusiasm for the wonder of the house.

We admire the volunteers who fundraise, lobby, catalogue, lecture, and guide their fellow citizens. As visitors, we enrich ourselves because of the efforts of the organizations and individuals who have labored to restore and revitalize these fine houses. We wish to thank the individuals who have given us their time and energy on these tours, and have given us their cooperation in putting this book together. If, in some small way, this guide helps you in your efforts, please consider it a thank you.

— *Jonathan Russo*
**Lintel Press**

# Editor's Note

Thanks to everyone who filled out our questionaire and sent the vast amounts of brochures and booklets which provided the basis for the book. All of the information about the houses has been supplied by the historical organizations and societies themselves; we have tried to reproduce the descriptions, biographical information, and schedule information as accurately as possible. Since many of the houses are subject to uncertain funding, and their hours and activities for visitors vary from season to season, we encourage people to call in advance to verify the information. Wherever possible, we have mentioned other houses located in the same town or village for which we do not have a complete listing. Finally, please contact us if there are other houses you would like to see listed in the next edition.

# *Introduction*

All buildings have character, some seem friendly while others have a forbidding feel. Many big buildings demand your attention, while more than a few small ones seem content to let you pass by them unnoticed. Buildings can be eccentric, exotic, familiar, unassuming, warm and welcoming, or cold and sinister; but their individuality is there for all who choose to recognize it.

Since the Bicentennial celebration, millions of Americans have come to appreciate another element of the architectural personality. Like people of a certain age, antique buildings have survived wars and changes and visitors, wanted and unwanted alike. Their very characters are reflections of times past. Some buildings, like some people, have aged gracefully; some have seen happy and sad times, but all of them have something to teach us, about their histories and even ourselves. The truth is that all old houses have something in common with your house and mine.

I fell in love with houses and buildings early in my life—I studied architecture long before *This Old House* and *Bob Vila's Home Again* introduced millions to some intriguing rehabilitation jobs with which I've been involved. My fondness for buildings in general and my experience with old houses in particular only heightens my appreciation of the houses you'll meet in these pages, and the uncompromising approach the many historical societies, community organizations, individuals, and groups have taken to getting the houses restored just right.

These houses represent an immense range of the American experience. Every one has a story to tell, whether it's of the people who built the house or those who lived there; the community that is the context for the place; or even the events that led to its preservation; which so often involve battles with developers or others insensitive to the value and merit in a tumbledown, antique structure.

Each of these houses provides a unique opportunity to step back in time, to learn about how our ancestors lived. Which is another way of saying, these houses offer a glimpse of history, that wonderful state of mind that explans, in part, why and who we are today. I hope in some way we can help inspire you to visit these houses and those other eras that have so much to teach us.

*—Bob Vila*

# Connecticut

1. **Canterbury**
   *Prudence Crandall Museum*

2. **Cos Cob**
   *Bush-Holley House*

3. **Coventry**
   *Nathaniel Hale Homestead*

4. **Darien**
   *Bates-Scofield Homestead*

5. **Fairfield**
   *Ogden House*

6. **Farmington**
   *Stanley-Whitman House*

7. **Guilford**
   *Henry Whitfield State Historical Museum*
   *Hyland House*
   *Thomas Griswold House*

8. **Hamden**
   *Jonathan Dickerman House*

9. **Hartford**
   *Butler-McCook Homestead*
   *Harriet Beecher Stowe House*
   *Isham-Terry House*
   *Mark Twain House*

10. **Lakeville**
    *The Holley-Williams House*
    *Museum*

11. **Litchfield**
    *Tapping Reeve House and Law*
    *School*

12. **Moodus**
    *Amasa Day House*

13. **New Canaan**
    *Hanford-Sillman House Museum*

14. **New Haven**
    *The Pardee-Morris House*

15. **New London**
    *Joshua Hempstead House*
    *Nathaniel Hempstead House*
    *Shaw-Perkins Mansion*

16. **Newington**
    *Enoch Kelsey House*
    *Kellogg-Eddy House*

17. **Niantic**
    *Smith-Harris House*

18. **Norwalk**
    *Lockwood-Mathews Mansion*
    *Museum*

19. **Norwich**
    *Leffingwell Inn*

20. **Old Lyme**
    *Florence Griswold Museum*

21. **Old Saybrook**
    *Gen. William Hart House*

22. **Ridgefield**
    *Keeler Tavern Museum*

23. **Simsbury**
    *Capt. Elisha Phelps House*

24. **Stamford**
    *Hoyt-Barnum House*

25. **Stratford**
    *Judson House*

26. **Suffield**
    *Hatheway House*
    *King House Museum*

27. **Torrington**
    *Hotchkiss-Fyler House*

28. **Wallingford**
    *Samuel Parsons House*

29. **Washington Green**
    *Gunn Historical Museum*

30. **West Hartford**
    *Noah Webster House*

31. **Westport**
    *Bradley Wheeler House*

32. **Wethersfield**
    *Buttolph-Williams House*
    *Silas Deane, Joseph Webb &*
    *Isaac Stevens Museum*

33. **Wilton**
    *Sloan-Raymond-Fitch House*

34. **Windsor**
    *1640 Lt. Walter Fyler House*
    *1765 Dr. Hezekiah Chaffee House*

35. **Woodbury**
    *Glebe House Museum*
    *Hurd House*

36. **Woodstock**
    *Bowen House, Roseland Cottage*

# Prudence Crandall Museum

P.O. Box 58, Routes 14 and 169
Canterbury, CT 06331
(203) 546-9916

**Contact:** Connecticut Historical
Commission

**Open:** Jan.16-Dec.14, Wed.-Sun.
10 a.m.–4:30 p.m.

**Admission:** Adults $2; children (6-18) and
seniors $1; groups (10 or more with appt.):
adults $1; children $.50. Guided tours.

**Suggested Time to View House:** 1 hour

**Facilities on Premises:** Gift shop, library
for in house study, by appointment only

**Description of Grounds:** The museum
grounds and a picnic table are available
for public use.

**Number of Yearly Visitors:** 4,000

**Year House Built:** c. 1805

**Number of Rooms:** 16, 7 open to the public

**Style of Architecture:** Federal

**On-Site Parking:** Yes **Wheelchair Access:** Yes

## Description of House

The Prudence Crandall House was the site of New England's first black female academy, an important landmark for the struggle for racial equality in education. Crandall was born in Rhode Island in 1803 and moved to Connecticut at the age of nine. In 1831, the town of Canterbury approached her about opening a school for local children. The school flourished until the fall of 1832 when Crandall admitted Sarah Harris, a young black woman. After losing community support, Crandall dismissed her students and reopened the academy on April 1, 1833 as one solely for black women. With courageous perserverance, she managed to keep the school open until Sept. 9, 1834. She faced strong opposition, and news of her work spread across the country. Her years here were crucial to both the abolition movement and to black and women education.

The house is a notable example of what has been termed the "Canterbury type" because of several similar examples in the vicinity. It has a peculiar roof form of gable on hip with twin chimneys, and a triangular pediment roof at the eaves above a projecting pavilion at the center of the facade. A Palladian window lights the stair hall on the second level above an elaborate entrance doorway.

The three period rooms on the first floor are appropriately furnished for the period Prudence Crandall operated her academy, 1832 to 1834. No original furnishings remain. The building is the only example of "Canterbury style" of architecture open to the public.

## Notable Collections on Exhibit

Furnishings on display date to pre-1840. There is a portrait of Prudence Crandall painted by Carl Henry, a Connecticut artist. The painting is a copy of the original, now owned by Cornell University.

# Bush-Holley House

39 Strickland Road
Cos Cob, CT 06807
(203)869-6899

**Contact:** Historical Society of the Town of Greenwich

**Open:** Tues.-Fri. 12–4 p.m.; Sun. 1–4 p.m.

**Admission:** Adults $3; senior citizens and students $1.50. Guided tours; occasional special exhibitions.

**Suggested Time to View House:** 1 hour

**Description of Grounds:** Grounds open to the public: berb, rose and flower gardens. Some on-site parking, with limited wheelchair access.

**Best Season to View House:** Spring, summer and fall

**Number of Yearly Visitors:** 2000

**Year House Built:** 1732

**Style of Architecture:** New England saltbox

**Number of Rooms:** 10

**On-Site Parking:** Yes **Wheelchair Access:** Yes

## Description of House

This was the home of David Bush, a prominent Greenwich landowner of Dutch descent, who played a leading role in local history until the 1850s. In the 1890s, the Holley family opened their home to the young artists and writers who formed the Cos Cob art colony, the first impressionist art colony in America. Artists J. Alden Weir and John Henry Twachtman founded the colony in 1892, and taught the first summer class. Frequent visitors and residents of the house included Ernest Thompson Seton, Willa Cather, Jean Webster, Rose O'Neil, Theodore Robinson, and Childe Hassam. Hassam thoroughly documented the house and site with his paintings, pastels, and etchings.

The Bush-Holley House is a classic central chimney saltbox located beside the Mianus River in the historic district of Cos Cob. The building was declared a National Historic Landmark in 1991.

There are few original furnishings of the Bush family, but numerous family portraits. The house maintains an outstanding collection of late-18th-century Connecticut pieces. The house also contains furnishings from the Holleys and MacRae families and paintings of artists who visited the house.

## Notable Collections on Exhibit

Permanent exhibits include late 18th century Connecticut furniture and antiques as well as paintings by Childe Hassam, Elmer Livingston MacRae, John Henry Twachtman, sculpture groups by John Rogers, and pottery by Leon Volkmar.

# Nathaniel Hale Homestead

South Street
Coventry, CT
(203) 742-6917

**Contact:** Antiquarian and Landmarks Society
**Open:** May 15-Oct. 15, 1–5 p.m.
**Admission:** Adults $2; students $1. Guided tours, outdoor antique show in July, special programs.
**Suggested Time to View House:** 30–45 minutes
**Facilities on Premises:** Gift shop

**Description of Grounds:** Rural setting with stone-walled fields and some outbuildings
**Number of Yearly Visitors:** 6,000
**Year House Built:** 1776
**Style of Architecture:** Colonial
**Number of Rooms:** 9 open to public
**On-Site Parking:** Yes    **Wheelchair Access:** No

## Description of House

The house was built by Richard Hale, a successful farmer and father of Nathan Hale, Connecticut's state hero, and a nationally recognized patriot.

The center passage of this five bay house reveals its awareness of new architectural styles. Typical of New England homes, the interior was finished over the course of years and includes woodwork removed from an older structure. A long service ell now houses caretaker's quarters.

Some furnishings are original to the house, the remaining items were collected for the museum.

## Notable Collections on Exhibit

The house displays many pieces of Hale family memorabilia, including Nathan Hale's Bible and army trunk.

# Bates-Scofield Homestead

45 Old Kings Highway North
Darien, CT 06820
(203) 655-9233

**Contact:** Darien Historical Society

**Open:** Thurs. and Sun. 2-4 p.m.

**Admission:** Free

**Suggested Time to View House:** 30 minutes

**Description of Grounds:** 18th-century herb garden

**Best Season to View House:** June-July

**Year House Built:** 1736-37

**Style of Architecture:** Saltbox

**Number of Rooms:** 8

**On-Site Parking:** Yes

**Wheelchair Access:** No

## Description of House

John Bates occupancy of this Colonial saltbox dwelling dates from 1736. Local town meetings were held at the house until a meetinghouse was completed in 1740. Bates and his family of nine children continued to live in the house until his death in 1759. After his death, the property went to his son, Ebenezeer, until he sold the house and it changed hands many times. The house's other namesake, Ezra Scofield, purchased it in 1822, and for the next century Scofields occupied the dwelling.

The Darien Historical Society moved the house to its present location in 1964. The building is built around a massive chimney, with a huge fireplace and beehive oven. The restoration after the house's change of location, restored it to its original saltbox shape.

The Bates-Scofield Homestead is furnished according to the inventory taken at the time of John Bates's death with collected furnishings. They span the period from the late 17th century to around 1820.

## Additional Information

To the rear of the house is an 18th-century herb garden maintained by the Garden Club of Darien. The property is also planted with antique roses and 18th century plants.

# Ogden House

1520 Bronson Road
Fairfield, CT 06430
(203) 259-1598

**Contact:** Fairfield Historical Society
**Open:** Mid May-mid Oct., Thurs.-Sun. 1–4 p.m. Closed on holidays. Groups by appointment.
**Admission:** Adults $2; children $1. Docent-led guided tours of houses and site.
**Suggested Time to View House:** 45 minutes
**Facilities on Premises:** gift shop

**Description of Grounds:** Approximately 2 acre site with demonstration 18th-century kitchen garden and wildflower trail along the banks of "Brown's Brook."
**Best Season to View House:** May-Oct.
**Number of Yearly Visitors:** 1,500
**Year House Built:** circa 1750
**Style of Architecture:** Vernacular Colonial (saltbox)
**Number of Rooms:** 6
**On-Site Parking:** Yes **Wheelchair Access:** No

## Description of House

The original residents, David and Jane Ogden, were members of well-to-do farming families and descendants of the earliest settlers in Fairfield. Two sons, David and Sturges, served in the Revolutionary War. The house was passed on to Sturges and his daughter, Ellen, who married retired sea captain Ebenezer Silliman. The structure was restored under the leadership of the Standard Oil heiress, Miss Annie B. Jennings of New York and Fairfield, and Cameron Clark, the Colonial-Revival architect, in 1935. The house was also home to the noted antiques dealer, Mary Allis, until 1975.

The house is a center chimney saltbox-style farmhouse built c. 1750 for a prosperous family. The Ogden House is one of the few 18th-century coastal Connecticut houses to survive without major alterations. The interior paint colors were restored in 1991.

The house is furnished with pieces from the Fairfield area dating back to the period of 1750 to 1775 and reflects the contents of the house as listed in the inventory of David Ogden's estate in 1776.

## Notable Collections on Exhibit

The most comprehensive collection of 18th-century Fairfield furniture in existence is housed here, including chairs, tables, case pieces, and beds. There is also a collection of household objects such as kitchenware, textile tools, glassware, and pewter on display.

# Stanley-Whitman House

37 High Street
Farmington, CT 06032
(203) 677-9222

**Contact:** Stanley-Whitman House

**Open:** May 1-Oct.31, Wed.-Sun. noon–4 p.m.; March, April, Nov., Dec., Sun. noon–4 p.m.

**Admission:** Adults $3; seniors, AAA members and children (6-18) $2; under age 6 free. Guided tours, educational programs, special events.

**Suggested Time to View House:** 30–45 minutes

**Description of Grounds:** Dooryard garden, small orchard, herbs, flowers and trees.

**Best Season to View House:** Spring and fall

**Year House Built:** 1720

**Style of Architecture:** Saltbox, wood framed with overhang

**Number of Rooms:** 7

**On-Site Parking:** Yes  **Wheelchair Access:** Yes

## Description of House

The exact date of construction for the Stanley-Whitman House may never be known but evidence suggests that it was built in 1720 by John Stanley, the son of one of the founders of Farmington. Very soon after the house's construction, it was sold to the Captain Ebeneezer Steel and it remained with Steel family members until 1734 when it was sold to Reverend Samuel Whitman, a Farmington minister. He bought the house for his son, Solomon Whitman, who married and lived there with his family of six children until 1772. The house continued to be owned by Whitmans into the 20th century.

The Stanley-Whitman House is one of the best existing examples of colonial New England overhang style of architecture. Solomon Whitman added the house's lean-to, giving the structure its classic saltbox shape. The interior plan is typical of the early central chimney house, with the great chimney flanked by a room on either side and two chambers above. The house was opened as a museum in 1935 and named a National Historic Landmark in 1961. The Stanley Whitman House is furnished with collected period furniture and decorative objects, none are from the original residents.

## Notable Collections on Exhibit

A display of tables, chairs, chests and textile production equipment, including a bench loom, represents the period of occupancy from 1722 through 1750. The second half of the 18th century is shown through Queen Anne and country furniture including a clock made in Farmington by L. Curtis.

## Additional Information

Special theme tours, teas and luncheons, are available by prior arrangement. There are family activities in the summer.

# Henry Whitfield State Historical Museum

Old Whitfield Street, P.O. Box 210
Guilford, CT 06437
(203) 453-2457

**Contact:** Connecticut Historical Commission

**Open:** April 1-Oct. 31, Wed.-Sun. 10 a.m.–5 p.m.; Nov.1-March 30, Wed.-Sun. 10 a.m.–4 p.m.

**Admission:** Adults $3; seniors and children (6-16) $1.50; no fee for school groups. Guided tours.

**Suggested Time to View House:** 45 minutes

**Facilities on Premises:** Herb garden, gift shop, restrooms

**Description of Grounds:** Public access dawn to dusk, herb garden, orchard, and lawns surrounding house

**Best Season to View House:** Spring for garden and flowers, fall for the foliage

**Number of Yearly Visitors:** 5,000 for house; 10,000 for grounds

**Year House Built:** 1639

**Number of Rooms:** 6

**Style of Architecture:** English medieval

**On-Site Parking:** Yes  **Wheelchair Access:** Yes

## Description of House

Henry Whitfield, the first owner of the house, was one of the leaders of the settlement at Guilford. He was also the town's minister. Whitfield lived in the house for about twelve years and then moved back to England during the little-known Counter Migration.

Also known as Old Stone House, the structure is the oldest building in Connecticut, the oldest stone house in New England, and the first museum operated by the state of Connecticut (1899). In addition to serving as a residence, the house aslo served as a defensive structure and meeting hall. The two-story stone house is a unique example of English medieval architecture and features massive chimneys and a corner window.

The house and its collection are original objects from circa 1640 to 1740 with some earlier and later items. None of the objects were in the house originally.

## Notable Collections on Exhibit

There are many unique 17th and 18th-century pieces from Guilford and from Connecticut including a Governor William Leete chair, the first tower clock in the colonies (1729), and a weaving and textile collection.

# *Thomas Griswold House*

171 Boston Street, Box 363
Guilford, CT 06437
(203)453-3176

**Contact:** Guilford Keeping Society
**Open:** June-Sept., Tues.-Sun. 11 a.m.–4 p.m.
**Admission:** Adults $1; children (6-12) $.50, under 6 free. Guided tours.
**Suggested Time to View House:** 45 minutes
**Description of Grounds:** Several acres of open field, some woods, and a garden near the house with period flowers

**Best Season to View House:** Spring and summer
**Number of Yearly Visitors:** 300
**Year House Built:** c. 1774
**Style of Architecture:** Saltbox
**Number of Rooms:** 7
**On-Site Parking:** Yes **Wheelchair Access:** No

## *Description of House*

The house reflects the lifestyle and season functions of a a late 18th-century to mid 19th-century household. A major restoration in the 1970s restored the house to its original saltbox shape.

The Thomas Griswold House is a classic saltbox house dwelling standing along a commanding knoll along the old Post Road in Guilford. Thomas Griswold III built the house for his two sons, Ezra and John, circa 1774. It was a two family dwelling for a number of years until 1805 when John Griswold Jr. sold his interest in the property. Four generations more of the family occupied the house until it became the property of the Guilford Keeping Society in 1958.

The house is furnished with many Griswold family heirlooms which include an antique cherry lowboy (1760), a ladderback "Pilgrim Chair", and a round-backed Guilford cupboard.

## *Notable Collections on Exhibit*

The house's distinctive features include a rear double batten door, and many Griswold heirlooms.

# Hyland House

84 Boston Street
Guilford, CT 06437
(203) 453-9477

**Contact:** Dorothy Whitfield Historical Society
**Open:** June-Labor Day, 10 a.m.–4:30 p.m.;
Labor Day-Columbus Day, weekends
only; closed Mon. and holidays
**Admission:** Adults $2; seniors $1.50;
children (under 12) free (must be
accompanied by an adult).
**Suggested Time to View House:** 45 minutes

**Description of Grounds:** Herb garden and
small yard
**Number of Yearly Visitors:** 700
**Year House Built:** 1660
**Style of Architecture:** Saltbox
**Number of Rooms:** 7
**On-Site Parking:** Yes

## Description of House

Built in 1660 by George Hyland, this was the home of his family and descendants for many years. In danger of demolition, the Hyland House was bought, restored, and furnished by the Dorothy Whitfield Historic Society in 1916.

The simple saltbox structure has been altered over the years. In 1720, the rear lean-to kitchen and attic were added. What was the original outside wall then became an inner wall, with all of the hand-spit clapboards with wrought iron nails preserved. The interior also features five great fireplaces and hand-hewn floors and walls.

Some of the furnishings belonged to the original occupants and include old family chests, four-poster beds, and primitive utensils. Others were collected, such as a William and Mary high boy with original brasses, several Guilford chairs, and a rare decorated Guilford chest.

## Notable Collections on Exhibit

The house exhibits the homely furnishings, the primitive utensils, the four-posters, the rope bedsteads, old family chests, tables and chairs. Conspicuous among the furnishings of the parlor is a remarkable Bible-box on its own standard, the gift of Dr. Park in Philadelphia. Pieces of fine antique furniture displayed, including a pencil post bed with hangings, and a rare Guilford chest with original brasses.

# Jonathan Dickerman House

105 Mt. Carmel Avenue
Hamden, CT 06518
(203) 288-2466

**Contact:** Hamden Historical Society

**Open:** July-Aug., Sat.-Sun. 12–3 p.m.

**Activities:** Guided tours for school children (by appointment)

**Suggested Time to View House:** 30–45 minutes

**Description of Grounds:** Herb Garden from the 18th and 19th centuries

**Best Season to View House:** June-July

**Number of Yearly Visitors:** 200-400

**Year House Built:** 1792

**Style of Architecture:** Cape in the Dutch style

**Number of Rooms:** 5

**On-Site Parking:** Yes

**Wheelchair Access:** No

## Description of House

In 1792, Jonathan Dickerman II (1747-1821) moved his family eastward from their original farm on the rocky hills of western Hamden to this new home near the river. His father and uncle had settled in Mount Carmel some fifty years earlier and their descendants for more than a century were major landowners with leading roles in town affairs. In the mid-19th century, after Jonathan's death, his widow and then the subsequent owners took in boarders, some of whom worked in nearby mills. In 1875, ownership passed to an Irish immigrant family and the house became known as the "Grogan Place."

This small house, with its sweeping roofline and deep front overhang, was the home of a moderately prosperous farming family in the late 18th century. It reflects the conservative tastes and plain living of Hamden farmers in that era. The simply-designed rooms, with few adornments other than the paneling fireplace walls, are today much as they were when the Dickermans lived here. In its two centuries of existence, the house has never had plumbing or central heating. The furnishings are from the same period as the house.

## Additional Information

The Hamden Historical Society maintains the house's gardens with its many examples of culinary and folk medicine herbs and herbs used by Connecticut physicians as documented in the 1811-1830 diaries of Dr. William Beaumont of Lebanon.

# Butler-McCook Homestead

**396 Main Street
Hartford, CT
(203) 522-1806**

**Contact:** Antiquarian and Landmarks
Society

**Open:** May 15-Oct. 15, Tues., Thur. and
Sun. noon–4 p.m.

**Admission:** Adults $2; students $1.
Guided tours, "Christmas on Main
Street" in Dec.

**Suggested Time to View House:** 45 minutes

**Description of Grounds:** The formal
garden beds behind the house were
designed by Jacob Weidenmann in 1865.

**Best Season to View House:** June

**Number of Yearly Visitors:** 1,000

**Year House Built:** 1782

**Style of Architecture:** Colonial

**Number of Rooms:** 9 open to public

**On-Site Parking:** No  **Wheelchair Access:** No

## Description of House

The Butlers and McCooks were average middle class families and this house reflects their livestyles. McCook was a minister and professor at Trinity College; his sons were a lawyer and a doctor. One daughter went to China as a missionary in 1899.

This simple frame building was home to four generations of the same family. Shifts in fashion over the years are reflected in changes in the physical fabric of the house and furnishings, all of which are original to the house and represent the accumulated possessions of 200 years. The house is interpreted for the period 1900 to 1910. The Butler-McCook Homestead is unusual in that it has survived  amidst a high-rise urban area.

## Notable Collections on Exhibit

Particularly noteworthy are the collections of Victorian toys, Japanese armor and weaponry, 19th-century landscape paintings and late-18th-century portraits on display. The collections also include extensive family archives and photographs.

# *Isham-Terry House*

**211 High Street**
**Hartford, CT**
**(203) 522-1984**

**Contact:** Antiquarian and Landmarks
Society
**Open:** By appointment only
**Admission:** Adults $2; students $1.
Guided tours.
**Suggested Time to View House:**
30–45 minutes
**Description of Grounds:** Small house lot
**Number of Yearly Visitors:** 200
**Year House Built:** 1854 with tower
added c. 1896
**Style of Architecture:** Italianate
**Number of Rooms:** 9 open to public
**On-Site Parking:** No
**Wheelchair Access:** No

## Description of House

The house was built by Ebenezer Roberts, a successful wholesale grocer. In 1896, the property was purchased by Dr. Oliver Isham; his two maiden sisters bequeathed it to the society.

The house is a good example of the solid Italianate dwellings built for middle class Americans before the Civil War. The distinctive tower was added by the second owners about 1896. The interior retains much of its mid 19th-century appearance, including untouched gas lighting fixtures, as well as decorative wall finishes from the early 20th century. All the furnishings are original to the house and the family.

This house has a frozen-in-time quality because its original contents appear much as they did at the time of original ownership. The building itself is a good study collection of architectural features with an early water closet, gas fixtures, and original decorative finishes.

## Notable Collections on Exhibit

The museum rooms are furnished with the eclectic possessions of a typical family of the mid 19th century. The on-site garage houses the Isham's 1902 Oldsmobile and 1907 Mitchell.

# Mark Twain House

351 Farmington Avenue
Hartford, CT 06105
(203) 247-0998

**Contact:** Mark Twain Memorial
**Open:** Year round, Tues.-Sat.
9:30 a.m.–4 p.m., Sun. 12–4 p.m.;
June 1-Columbus Day, open Mon.; closed
major holidays
**Admission:** Adults $6.50; students (6-16)
$2.75; under 6 free, seniors and AAA
$5.50. Guided tours, special programs.
**Suggested Time to View House:** 1 hour

**Facilities on Premises:** Gift shop-book store
**Description of Grounds:** 1½ acre house site
with carriage house
**Best Season to View House:** April-Oct.
**Number of Yearly Visitors:** 50,000
**Year House Built:** 1874
**Style of Architecture:** High Victorian Gothic
**Number of Rooms:** 18
**On-Site Parking:** Yes **Wheelchair Access:** Yes

## Description of House

The American literary icon Samuel Clemens, better known as Mark Twain, purchased land on the outskirts of Hartford known as Nook Farm in 1873. He and his wife worked together with New York architect Edward Tuckerman Potter to design this Gothic structure so that the best views of the countryside could be seen. The house was completed in 1874; Twain lived and worked here—writing some of his major works—from 1874 to 1891. His family lived here until 1910.

The exterior of the house is particularly striking. The architect exploited the decorative possibilities of brick by changing the direction, angle, or projection of various courses, then further embellished the surface with a bold pattern of black and vermillion paint. He extended the bay windows up to form turrets, the top floor of which became open porches for a relaxed enjoyment of the view. The elaborate treatment of the wood structural members and railing is characteristic of the "stick style" of the 1870s. Potter's interest in ornament derived from natural forms is shown in the waterleaf brackets of the "Ombra" or porch, and in the butterfly and lily pattern of the porte-cochere. He also provided for living plants both within and outside the house.

The interior of the house is equally impressive. In 1881, following the success of *The Adventures of Tom Sawyer* and a several lecture tours, the kitchen was enlarged and the major rooms completely redecorated by Associated Artists, a distinguished firm of interior designers which included Louis Comfort Tiffany, Lockwood deForest, and Samuel Colman. The Twain House has the only interior designed by Associated Artists open to the public on a regular basis. The furnishings are a mix of Clemens family possessions and period pieces.

## Notable Collections on Exhibit

In addition to the exquisite interior decorations, the house also exhibits Mark Twain materials and thematic exhibitions which change annually.

# Harriet Beecher Stowe House

77 Forest Street
Hartford, CT 06105
(203) 525-9317

**Contact:** The Stowe Day Foundation
**Open:** Tues.-Sat. 9:30 a.m.–4 p.m.,
Sun. 12–4 p.m., Open Mon.
June 1-Columbus Day and Dec.
**Admission:** Fee is charged for the joint tour
(with Mark Twain House). Group tours
by reservation at a reduced rate. Guided
tours daily; Special events take place
regularly throughout the year, but change
annually.
**Suggested Time to View House:**
45–60 minutes

**Facilities on Premises:** Gift Shop in
Victorian Garden
**Description of Grounds:** Variety of gardens
with 19th-century varietals including
formal and informal, flower and kitchen
**Best Season to View House:** Late
spring-early summer
**Number of Yearly Visitors:** 15,000
**Year House Built:** 1871
**Style of Architecture:** Gothic Cottage
**Number of Rooms:** 12
**On-Site Parking:** Yes  **Wheelchair Access:** Yes

## Description of House

Harriet Beecher Stowe (1811-1896) is best known for writing the abolitionist novel, *Uncle Tom's Cabin* (1852). She penned some thirty volumes of works during her career. Stowe lived in this restored Hartford home from 1873 to her death in 1896. Her husband, Calvin Ellis Stowe (1820-1886), and twin daughters also resided here.

Built in 1871, the house is typical of 19th-century pattern-book designs with an assymetrical floor plan, two-story bay windows, three side porches, in an overall Gothic mode. Further indications of the style are found in the triangular forms of the hip roof, dormer windows, bays and by the pierced bargeboards and brackets. The furnishings are all appropriate to the period; a significant number belonged to the Stowe family.

## Notable Collections on Exhibit

The core furnishings of the Harriet Beecher Stowe house are on permanent exhibition and include artwork collected by and produced by the author. In addition, seasonal and thematic exhibits, staged throughout the year, attempt to present a variety of other artifacts . Past displays have included "The annual move to Mandarin,""Travel Reminiscences,"a 19th-century wedding reception, and Easter and Christmas settings.

## Additional Information

In addition to the Stowe house, the foundation also opens the nearby Katharine S. Day House to the public on an occassional basis.

# The Holley-Williams House Museum

15 Main Street
Lakeville, CT 06039
(203) 435-2878

**Contact:** The Salisbury Association

**Open:** July-Oct., Sat. and Sun. 1–4 p.m.; also by appointment

**Admission:** Adults $3; student groups (10 or more) $2; children (under 12) free. Workshops in winter, guided tours, monthly exhibits, concert series.

**Suggested Time to View House:** 1 hour

**Description of Grounds:** A walled Victorian garden

**Best Season to View House:** June-Aug.

**Number of Yearly Visitors:** 1,200

**Year House Built:** 1768

**Style of Architecture:** Classical-Federal

**Number of Rooms:** 12, 8 open to public

**On-Site Parking:** No  **Wheelchair Access:** No

## Description of House

This impressive structure that vistors see today was enlarged and enhanced in 1808 by John Milton Holley, one of Lakeville's leading citizens. Holley was a partner in the family iron business at the Mt. Riga Furnace which produced cannons and cannonballs. The building then became a pocket knife factory (the first in the nation) after the iron industry went into decline. Holley's descendents lived in the house until 1971.

A fine example of Classical Revival and Federal architecture, the house stands on a knoll overlooking the site of the Furnace Village Forge where the Holley Manufacturing Company was established several years later. The original pre-revolutionary structure was built in 1768 and the newer section in 1808. The interior features many examples of superior design and craftsmanship including hand-carved woodwork, spiral staircase, archways, and original window treatments. Family furnishings encompass the 173 years of the Holley family's residence and include fine furniture and mirrors, silver, glass and china, several portraits by itinerant painters and a Clementi piano.

The outbuildings feature a complex of original buildings including a carriage barn with an iron industry exhibit and a seven hole outhouse.

## Notable Collections on Exhibit

The permanent exhibits include Holley Manufacturers pocket knife items; Thesorian greeting cards; wedding gowns and accessories (1870-1920s); family diaries; and portraits of family members and local contemporaries by Edwin White, Ernest Sherman Pease, Erastus Salisbury Field, and Ammi Philips. Also on display are 127 pieces of governor Alexander Hamilton Holley's inaugural dinnerware made of porcelain from Paris (c. 1850).

## *Tapping Reeve House and Law School*

82 South Street, P.O. Box 385
Litchfield, CT 06709
(203) 567-4501

**Contact:** Litchfield Historical Society
**Open:** Mid May-mid Oct., Tues.-Sat.
11 a.m.–5 p.m., Sun. 1–5 p.m.
**Admission:** Adults $2; children free.
Guided tours, videotape, special
programs.
**Suggested Time to View House:** 40 minutes
**Facilities on Premises:** Museum shop
**Description of Grounds:** Lawn and garden

**Best Season to View House:** Summer and
fall
**Number of Yearly Visitors:** 4,000
**Year House Built:** 1774
**Style of Architecture:** Federal
**Number of Rooms:** 8
**On-Site Parking:** No
**Wheelchair Access:** No

### Description of House

Tapping Reeve, a lawyer and legal scholar, built this home in 1774. In 1771, Reeve had begun his apprenticeship with a lawyer in Hartford, Connecticut and was admitted to the bar of Litchfield County in 1772. Once established with his career, he married Sally Burr, a young girl whom he had met while working as a tutor in New Jersey. In 1773, Reeve purchased land, built a house, and moved with his young wife to Litchfield. Soon after arriving, he agreed to oversee the legal training of his brother-in-law Aaron Burr. This began his work in legal training; soon he was so popular, attracting students from all over the country, that he was forced to build the adjoining one-room schoolhouse in 1784 to accomodate the increased enrollment.

The house was restored in the 1930s and now contains many Colonial Revival features. The house has five rooms and an entrance hall furnished to show the late 18th-century and 19th-century periods. The three bedrooms, parlor and dining room illustrate the Reeve family's use of these rooms and how they've changed over time. The house was designated a National Historic Landmark in 1966.

### Notable Collections on Exhibit

Furniture on exhibit includes twelve faux bamboo chairs made by Litchfield cabinet maker, Silas Cheney; a Federal sideboard and two bow front chests.

# *Amasa Day House*

**33 Plains Road**
**Moodus, CT**
**(203) 873-8144**

**Contact:** Antiquarian and Landmarks Society
**Open:** Memorial Day-Labor Day,
   Wed.-Sun. 1–5 p.m.
**Admission:** Adults $2; students $1. Guided
   tours, special programs.
**Suggested Time to View House:** 30 minutes

**Description of Grounds:** Lawn with a small
   cutting flower garden in the rear
**Number of Yearly Visitors:** 1,000
**Year House Built:** 1816
**Style of Architecture:** Federal
**Number of Rooms:** 7
**On-Site Parking:** Yes  **Wheelchair Access:** No

### Description of House

A farmer, Julius Chapman, built this modest house in 1816. The house is named after businessman Amasa Day who purchased it in 1843. Descendants of the Day family lived here until 1967 when the building was aquired by the Antiquarian and Landmarks Society.

The entrance to this simple frame five-bay house is marked with a portico. Stencilled designs have survived on the floors in two rooms of the house as well as on the stair risers. Many Day family artifacts are displayed along with other furnishings acquired to complete the period rooms.

### Additional Information

The East Haddam Historical Society administers this property for the society; they maintain a museum of local history in the property barn with a small gift shop.

# Hanford-Silliman House Museum

13 Oenoke Ridge
New Canaan, CT 06804
(203) 966-1776

**Contact:** The New Canaan Historical Society
**Open:** Tues.-Sat. 9:30 a.m.–12:30 p.m. and 2–4 p.m. Groups by appointment. Closed Thanksgiving and Christmas.
**Admission:** $3 per student. Guided tours, special activities.
**Suggested Time to View House:** 2 hours
**Facilities on Premises:** Gift shop

**Description of Grounds:** About 2 acres with 5 buildings
**Best Season to View House:** Spring
**Number of Yearly Visitors:** 5000-6000
**Year House Built:** 1764
**Style of Architecture:** Center Chimney Saltbox with additions
**Number of Rooms:** 7
**On-Site Parking:** Yes **Wheelchair Access:** No

## Description of House

The Hanford-Silliman House was built by Stephen Hanford, a weaver, and one of the early licensed tavern keepers in the community. Hanford brought his bride Jemima to the recently completed house in 1764. After his death (1784), his widow sold the property to Elisha Leeds, who gave it to his daughter, Martha, and her husband, Dr. Joseph Silliman. Succeeding generations of Sillimans occupied the house until the 1920s.

The original structure is a typical Colonial dwelling with one room to either side of the front door. The tavern room had been on the left, a bedroom was on the right, and across the back a keeping room or kitchen. The roof was raised in the 1790s to make room for the extra bedrooms needed by the Sillimans. The Greek Revival pediment and the small Greek columned porch were added later, perhaps in the 1830s. Other notable features of the interior include three original fireplaces and some of the original fine paneling.

## Additional Information

The New Canaan Historical Society administers a number of other museums at this site: the Town House, with a costume museum and recreation of a drug store from 1845; a recreation of a 19th-century printing press office; and an extensive tool museum.

# The Pardee-Morris House

325 Lighthouse Road
New Haven, CT 06512
(203) 562-4183

**Contact:** The New Haven Colony Historical
Society

**Open:** June-Sept. 1, Sat. and Sun.
11 a.m.–4 p.m.

**Facilities on Premises:** Gift shop

**Year House Built:** 1779

**Admission:** Adults $2; children $1.
Guided tours, Autumn Harvest Festival.

**Number of Yearly Visitors:** 1,200

**On-Site Parking:** Yes

## Description of House

This substantial 18th-century farmhouse, located on the east shore of New Haven harbor, has seen its share of historic events. Originally built by Amos Morris in 1750, the Pardee-Morris House was burned by the British during the raid on New Haven in 1779 and completely rebuilt. Listed on the National Register of Historic Places, the structure today houses significant permanent and special exhibitions which present a panorama of New Haven's past.

## Notable Collections on Exhibit

Visitors to the Pardee-Morris House will see a variety of exhibits ranging from fine art (paintings, including landscapes by local artists and portraits from the 18th and 19th centuries) to decorative arts, with many fine examples of regional furniture from the 17th to 19th centuries as well as pewter, silver, clocks, textiles, glass and ceramics. In addition, the nearby New Haven Colony Historical Society houses comprehensive exhibits related to maritime history, technology and manufacturing (including an original model and full size working version of Eli Whitney's cotton gin, an early milling machine from the Whitney Amory, one of the first Morse Code receivers, and a reconstruction of the first telephone switchboard), and a photographic archive with more than 75,00 images ranging from daguerrotypes to modern prints on paper.

# Joshua Hempsted House

11 Hempstead Street
New London, CT
(203) 443-7949

**Contact:** Antiquarian and Landmarks Society
**Open:** May 15-Oct. 15, Tues.-Sun. 1–5 p.m.
**Admission:** Adults $3; students $2. Guided tours, special programs.
**Suggested Time to View House:** 45 minutes
**Description of Grounds:** Lawn

**Number of Yearly Visitors:** 1,300
**Year House Built:** 1678 and expanded in 1728
**On-Site Parking:** No
**Wheelchair Access:** No

### Description of House

Nine generations of Hempsteds, a family of farmers and teachers, lived in this unpretentious house. This is the oldest structure in New London and one of the oldest, documented houses in Connecticut. The house was lived in continuously by the Hempsted family until its acquisition by the society.

The Hempsted House's exterior frame structure reflects the two periods of construction; the steep pitched roof and casement windows of the 17th century and the sash windows of the early 18th. The entrance is through a two-story porch.

The museum rooms are furnished appropriate to the period with some original family artifacts. There are some fine examples of early New England furniture.

### Additional Information

Visitors to the Joshua Hempsted House and the adjacent Nathaniel Hempstead House are able to study three generations of the same family. The diary of Joshua Hempstead, which he kept for over forty years, from 1711 to 1758, has been published by the New London County Historical Society.

# Nathaniel Hempsted House

corner Jay and
Hempstead Streets
New London, CT
(203) 443-7949

**Contact:** Antiquarian and Landmarks Society
**Open:** May 15-Oct.15, Tues.-Sun. 1–5 p.m.
**Admission:** Adults $3; students $2 (combined admission with Joshua Hempstead House). Guided tours, special programs.

**Suggested Time to View House:** 30 minutes
**Description of Grounds:** Lawn
**Number of Yearly Visitors:** 1,300
**Year House Built:** 1759
**Style of Architecture:** Colonial
**Number of Rooms:** 7

## Description of House

The Hempsted family were an established family of tradesmen in the New London community. Nathaniel Hempsted, who built this house, held the unusual occupation of ropewalker. His grandson, Joshua Hempsted, was a silversmith.

This gambrel roofed house is built of cut stone, unusual for 18th-century New England. The interior is simply finished and furnished to reflect period lifestyle, and features a projecting bake oven.

A few artifacts belonged to the Hempstead family, the remainder were acquired for display in the museum.

## Notable Collections on Exhibit

The house is adjacent to the Joshua Hempsted House, which permits the visitor to trace the lives of three generations of the same family through their homes and possessions.

# *Shaw-Perkins Mansion*

**305 Bank Street**
**New London, CT 06320**
**(203) 443-1209**

**Contact:** New London County Historical
Society

**Open:** Wed.-Fri. 11 a.m.–4 p.m.,
Sat. 10 a.m.–4 p.m. Closed major
holidays and the month of Jan.

**Activities:** Guided tours, exhibitions,
special programs, research library,
publications

**Suggested Time to View House:**
45-60 minutes

**Facilities on Premises:** Gift and book store

**Description of Grounds:** Flower gardens,
1840s summer house and root cellar

**Best Season to View House:** June-Aug.

**Number of Yearly Visitors:** 2,000

**Year House Built:** 1756 with major
renovations in the 1840s

**Style of Architecture:** Georgian

**Number of Rooms:** 18, 9 open to the public

**On-Site Parking:** No **Wheelchair Access:** No

## *Description of House*

Located on the west bank of the Thames River, the Shaw Mansion was
built in 1756 for Captain Nathaniel Shaw and his family. Shaw was a
successful and prominent businessman in New London and his home
reflected his wealth and social position. Ownership of the house eventually
passed to the Perkins family in the late 1790s. Descendants of the family
lived in the house until 1907 when it was purchased by the historical society.

The Shaw-Perkins Mansion was built of stone quarried from the granite
ledge upon which the house was built. One unusual architectural detail is
the paneled cement fireplace walls in the major rooms of the house. Many
changes were made to the house by occupants during the 19th century. The
front porch was added along with a stone wing on the north end where the
wooden one had burned. The floors on the first floor were lowered in order
to obtain the high ceilings admired during the Victorian era. Other additions
include a summer house and root cellar in the back yard.

The mansion also holds the distinction of being one of the few surviving
structures built before 1781 when the city was burned by British troops led by
Benedict Arnold. Furnishings extend from mid-18th century to late 19th century.

## *Notable Collections on Exhibit*

The New London furniture on display includes an 18th-century
secretary, card table, sofa, and wingback chair. There are also six portraits
by Ralph Earle (c. 1790s). In addition, the society has an extensive
manuscript collection which the public may view featuring letters from
George Washington, John Hancock, and Benedict Arnold.

# Kellogg-Eddy House

679 Willard Ave
Newington, CT 06111
(203) 666-7118

**Contact:** Newington Historical Society

**Open:** Jan.-Feb., Sun. 1–4 p.m.; March-Dec., Sat. and Sun. 1–4 p.m.

**Activities:** Guided tours, special programs to be announced

**Suggested Time to View House:** 30–45 minutes

**Facilities on Premises:** Gift shop

**Description of Grounds:** Large lawns

**Best Season to View House:** Spring

**Number of Yearly Visitors:** 250-300

**Year House Built:** 1808

**Style of Architecture:** Federal

**Number of Rooms:** 7 period, 3 additional open to public

**On-Site Parking:** Yes

**Wheelchair Access:** No

Kellogg - Eddy House, 1808
Newington, Conn.

## Description of House

The Kellogg-Eddy House, built by General Martin Kellogg in 1808, was lived in by Kellogg and his wife Mary. The house also was birthplace to Roger Eddy, a former Senator from Connecticut.

The house is noted for its many ornate architectural and design features. Elaboratedly detailed exterior and interior woodwork distinguish the home of one of Newington's most prominent early residents. Today this distinguished dwelling is decorated with furnishings originally owned by several of Newington's oldest families. The parlors of the Kellogg-Eddy House provide a glimpse of Newington long ago.

## Notable Collections on Exhibit

Changing exhibits are on display in the meeting room and the second floor exhibit room.

# Enoch Kelsey House

**1702 Main Street**
**Newington, CT 06111**
**(203) 666-7118**

**Contact:** Newington Historical Society &
Trust, Inc.

**Open:** May-Oct., Sat.-Sun. 1–4 p.m.

**Admission:** Free. Guided tours, special
programs to be announced.

**Suggested Time to View House:**
30–40 minutes

**Facilities on Premises:** Gift shop

**Description of Grounds:** Large lawn with
sitting area, herb garden

**Best Season to View House:** May and June

**Number of Yearly Visitors:** 200

**Year House Built:** 1799

**Style of Architecture:** Center-chimney

**Number of Rooms:** 5 open to the public

**On-Site Parking:** Yes

**Wheelchair Access:** No

## Description of House

This modest home was built by farmer and tinsmith Enoch Kelsey in
1799. Although common in design, this center-chimney style dwelling features rare free-hand painted wall decorations which imitate wallpaper. The
house is sparsely furnished so as not to detract from the wall paintings. The
house was threatened with destruction in 1979. Through the efforts of the
society, the house was relocated, thus saving its irreplacable interiors.

## Notable Collections on Exhibit

In addition to the *trompe l'oeil* paintings and free-handed painted wall
decoration, the house exhibits an operational 19th-century loom (with
demonstrations and sales); an operating spinning wheel; artifacts recovered
during archeological investigations of Kelsey House grounds; and various
items representative of those listed on the probate inventory of Enoch
Kelsey.

# Smith-Harris House

**33 Society Road**
**Niantic, CT 06357**
**(203) 739-0761**

**Contact:** Town of East Lyme

**Open:** July-Aug., daily (except Tues.)
1–5 p.m.; Sept.-Dec. and April-June,
Sat.-Sun. 1–5 p.m.; Jan.-March, by
appointment

**Admission:** Free, donations appreciated.
Private tours by arrangement, annual
Wassail Party in December, the house is
also available for public functions.

**Suggested Time to View House:** 1 hour

**Description of Grounds:** Picnic facilities
available

**Best Season to View House:** Summer

**Number of Yearly Visitors:** 800

**Year House Built:** 1845

**Style of Architecture:** Greek Revival

**Number of Rooms:** 5 plus barn

**On-Site Parking:** Yes

## Description of House

The house was built in 1845 by Thomas Avery, a descendant of the Averys of Groton, Connecticut. When he died in 1869, the house and accompanying farm (known locally as the Brookside Farm) were inherited by his son, William. Later the house was sold to William H. H. Smith, a native of Niantic who lived in Washington, D.C. He used the farm as a summer home until his death in 1927. In the late 1890s, William Smith's younger brother, Herman, and his nephew took over the management of the farm, and married two sisters who lived in the area. Together, the two couples shared the house and worked the farm for over sixty years.

The Smith-Harris House was built in the popular Greek Revival style which was common in America in the early 19th century. Few changes have been made in the house over the years. It was restored in 1973 by the Town of Lyme. At that time, the ground floor was turned into a museum with an apartment for the curator on the second floor.

The furnishings in the Smith-Harris House have been carefully selected to represent the mid-1800s, the period when it was lived in by the Averys.

# *Lockwood-Mathews Mansion Museum*

295 West Avenue
Norwalk, CT 06850
(203) 838-1434

**Contact:** Lockwood-Mathews Mansion Museum

**Open:** Feb.-mid Dec., Tues.-Fri. 11 a.m.–3 p.m.; Sun. 1–4 p.m.

**Admission:** Adults $5; seniors and students $3; children (under 12) free. Guided tours, A/V presentation, Victorian Valentine's Dance Party, Ice Cream Social, Antiques show, Christmas boutique and educational programs.

**Suggested Time to View House:** 1½–2 hours

**Facilities on Premises:** Gift shop

**Description of Grounds:** Public park with 3 acres, picnic tables, playground, tennis courts

**Best Season to View House:** Spring-fall

**Number of Yearly Visitors:** 25,000

**Year House Built:** 1864-68

**Style of Architecture:** Victorian

**Number of Rooms:** 50

**On-Site Parking:** Yes  **Wheelchair Access:** Yes

## Description of House

This was the summer home of Legrand Lockwood and his wife, Ana Louisa; both were Norwalk natives. Lockwood made his fortune at the brokerage company of Lockwood and Co. in New York City. After Lockwood's death, the mansion was purchased by Charles Mathews, an importer from Staten Island, New York. The building remained in the Mathews family until 1938.

The mansion was the first major estate built in America after the Civil War. The Lockwood Mansion stands four stories high, and features a magnificent octagonal rotunda surrounded by fifty beautiful rooms. This unique Victorian palace features stenciled walls and inlaid woodwork. Artists and artisans were brought from Europe to create the rich variety of gilt, fresco, and etched glass found throughout the building. Room interiors were designed by Leon Marcotte, Herter Brothers, George Platt and E.W. Hutchings.

The furnishings are all appropriate for the period. Many are original; others have either been donated or acquired through purchase. The mansion was designated a National Historic Landmark in 1971. The mansion and its furnishings constitute an important and unique collection and has great importance for both the local community and for a national audience. The building itself is the one remaining example of a time when sumptuous estates crowded into Norwalk's borders.

## Notable Collections on Exhibit

Exhibitions change several times each year. There is a permanent exhibition of mechanical music boxes on loan from the Musical Box Society of America.

# Leffingwell Inn
## (Christopher Leffingwell House)

348 Washington Street
Norwich, CT 06366
(203) 889-9440

**Contact:** Society of the Founders of Norwich
**Open:** May 15-Oct. 15, Tues.-Sat.
  10 a.m.–12 p.m. and 2–4 p.m.; Sun.
  2–4 p.m.; winter by appointment
**Admission:** Adults $3; children $1; school
  tours $.75. Guided tours.
**Suggested Time to View House:**
  60–90 minutes

**Best Season to View House:** Spring and
  summer
**Number of Yearly Visitors:** 1,500-2,000
**Year House Built:** 1675
**Style of Architecture:** Colonial
**On-Site Parking:** Yes
**Wheelchair Access:** No

### Description of House
William Backus, Sr. was one of the original settlers of Norwich in 1659. On his death he gave his home lot to his son, Stephen, who built a house in 1675. In 1700, the house was sold to Ensign Thomas Leffingwell, who, in 1701, was granted a license "to keep a publique house for the entertainment of strangers." Only the leading men of the community were granted the coveted innkeepers license, and it was handed down in the family as an inheritance. The inn's most prominent resident was Christopher Leffingwell who lived here during the late 1700s and into the early 1800s. He was a leading citizen, a prosperous industrialist, and an ardent patriot. By 1770 he had established the first paper mill in Connecticut, as well as a stocking factory, a chocolate mill, and other businesses.

The Leffingwell Inn is considered one of the most outstanding Colonial dwellings in Connecticut. The two-story structure consists of two small saltbox houses brought together with an addition made to the rear. The oldest section dates from 1675, another section was added in 1715, and the third between 1730 to 1765. The interior, however, was never remodeled, and it is rare to find so ancient a building in its original form. The property was authentically restored and furnished from 1956 to 1960 by the Society of the Founders of Norwich. The furnishings are of the same period as the house and are primarily from, or associated with, Norwich.

### Notable Collections on Exhibit
There is an extensive collection of locally crafted silver pieces of the colonial period; at one time Norwich had more than forty silversmiths. Much of the furnishings and accessories originated in, or were associated, with Norwich and include a Thomas Harland grandfather clock, Oriental imports, and Chippendale and Queen Anne-style furniture.

# Florence Griswold Museum

96 Lyme Street
Old Lyme, CT 06371
(203) 434-5542

**Contact:** Florence Griswold Museum
**Open:** June-Oct., Tues.-Sat. 10 a.m.–5 p.m.,
   Sun. 1–5 p.m.; Nov.-May, Wed.-Sun.
   1–5 p.m.

**Admission:** Adults $3; children (under 12)
   and members free.
**Description of Grounds:** 2 landscaped acres
**Year House Built:** 1817
**Style of Architecture:** Georgian

## Description of House

The Florence Griswold Museum portrays an extraordinary era in our nation's history, when a group of the country's most accomplished artists gathered at "Miss Florence's" house to record their impressions of Old Lyme's natural beauty. Together they forged a flourishing colony that became America's best known center of impressionist painting.

The museum is housed in an architectural landmark of national importance. Designed by Samuel Belcher, this late Georgian mansion is situated on two beautifully landscaped acres in the heart of the Old Lyme historic district. Through the period furnishings and the art on display, visitors will be able to experience the setting where the artists once lived and worked.

## Notable Collections on Exhibit

Period rooms interpret aspects of the region's history; exhibitions of impressionist paintings and other works of art are held in the galleries.

# General William Hart House

305 Main Street
Old Saybrook, CT 06475
(203) 388-2622

**Contact:** Old Saybrook Historical Society
**Open:** June 12–Sept. 13, Fri.-Sun.
  12:30–4 p.m.; Nov. 27-Dec. 13,
  Fri.-Sun. 12:30–4 p.m.
**Admission:** Adults $2; seniors $1.50;
  children (under 12) free. Six historical
  programs a year.
**Suggested Time to View House:** 30 minutes
**Facilities on Premises:** Gift Shop
**Description of Grounds:** Colonial garden
  and antique rose garden
**Best Season to View House:** May-Sept.
**Number of Yearly Visitors:** 400
**Year House Built:** 1767
**Style of Architecture:** Early Georgian
**Number of Rooms:** 8

**On-Site Parking:** Yes  **Wheelchair Access:** No

## Description of House

General William Hart (1746-1817), in addition to being a prosperous merchant and a shipper, was an officer in the American Revolution. He was deeply engaged in Connecticut politics, and also prospered as a real estate entrepreneur in the western reserve of Connecticut. The Hart family was prominent in state affairs, and its members married into other prominent families.

The Hart House is early Georgian style made airy by a nine window facade with twelve-over-twelve panes. Special attention to detail is apparent in their molded cornices, wide cornerboards topped with columnar capitals, and clapboards of upwardly increasing width designed to create an impression of geometric perfection.

There are eight corner fireplaces, one decorated with a set of Sadler and Green transfer-print tiles, unusual for New England. The Hart House was opulent for its time as visitors can see in the beautiful waved molding on the staircase, and the elegant paneling in the four downstairs rooms. The furnishings are collected and appropriate to the period 1767 to 1830.

## Notable Collections on Exhibit

The house is best known for exhibiting the Saybrook Chest and the imported tiles illustrating Aesop's fables which decorate the library fireplace. There is an outstanding costume-textile collection from which exhibits are periodically created. One large room houses periodic exhibits such as World War I posters, wedding dresses of different eras, art by local artists, and the West Indian trade.

# Keeler Tavern Museum

132 Main Street, P.O. Box 204
Ridgefield, CT 06877
(203) 438-5485

**Contact:** Keeler Tavern Preservation
Society, Inc.

**Open:** Sat., Sun. and Wed. 1–4 p.m.

**Admission:** Adults $3; seniors $2; under 12
$1. Guided tours, concerts, lectures,
special events. Annual Christmas
luncheons.

**Suggested Time to View House:** 30–40
minutes

**Facilities on Premises:** Gift shop (with
books)

**Description of Grounds:** The garden
house, designed by Cass Gilbert, has
brick walled garden open to the public
except when in use for outside functions.

**Best Season to View House:** Spring
through early fall

**Number of Yearly Visitors:** 2,000

**Year House Built:** Tavern: 1713-23, Garden
House and Barn: 1915

**Style of Architecture:** Classic New England
with many alterations

**Number of Rooms:** 13 open to the public

**On-Site Parking:** Yes

**Wheelchair Access:** Yes

## Description of House

The Keeler Tavern is Ridgefield's most significant structures located on
one of the town's original home lots. Timothy Keeler, who lived here as well
as worked here as innkeeper, was active in local government and business.
The inn was a rallying place for supporters of the Colonial cause, and it was
rumored that patriots made musket balls in the basement. On April 27, 1777
British troops fired on the tavern because of its clandestine activities, and a
small cannonball is still imbedded in the corner post of the house. The house
was also owned by Abijah Resseguie, who ran the inn for many years and
Cass Gilbert, a leading Neo-classical architect (designer of the Supreme
Court building in Washington, D.C.) who made the inn his summer home.

The Keeler Tavern probably began as a simple two room house built by
Benjamin Hoyt. When Keeler purchased the property in 1769, the house had
long since been expanded into a two-story Colonial frame residence with
gambrel roof, central chimney, and four rooms on each floor. One unique
feature of the house is an upstairs ballroom/bedroom with a hinged wall
that can be raised to make one large room out of two. The two-story addition
built in 1800 includes a new kitchen of contemporary design.

All furnishings are from the 18th and 19th centuries. Some of the pieces belonged to the Keeler family and descendants. These include portraits, tavern signs, clocks, and chairs. Other items were collected and belonged to Ridgefield families.

### Notable Collections on Exhibit

The collection includes kitchen equipment and woodenware of the 18th century, 18th and 19th-century china, costumes of the 19th and early 20th centuries (changing exhibit), and paintings of residents and local sites.

### Additional Information

An archival room is located in the garden house addition (1989) with many important records of the Keeler Tavern and Ridgefield. The Keeler Tavern Museum is on the National Register of Historic Places.

# Capt. Elisha Phelps House

800 Hopmeadow Street
Simsbury, CT 06070
(203) 658-2500

**Contact:** Simsbury Historical Society

**Open:** May-Oct., Sun-Fri.

**Admission:** Adults $5; seniors $4; children (5-18) $2.50; group rates available. Guided Tours. Annual event first week in Dec. (costumed docents); Canal Days in Jan. and Feb.; Heirloom Discovery Day in April.

**Suggested Time to View House:** 45 minutes; entire plantation 90 minutes

**Facilities on Premises:** Gift Shop

**Description of Grounds:** Tastefully landscaped in keeping with period plantation, maintained herb, rose, and parlor gardens

**Best Season to View House:** Summer and fall

**Number of Yearly Visitors:** 2000

**Style of Architecture:** Colonial

**Year House Built:** 1771

**On-Site Parking:** Yes  **Wheelchair Access:** No

## Description of House

The house was lived in by members of the Phelps family from 1771 until 1965 when an heir gave the house and property to the Simsbury Historical Society. Through the years, the Phelps were active in local and state goverment, serving as judges and legislators as well as prosperous farmers and breeders of prize livestock. The house at one time was owned by Noah Phelps, to whom credit is given for Ethan Allen's ultimate capture of the fort.

The Phelps House is a gambrel-roof Colonial clapboard structure. An ell was added in the 1870s. Several unusual ceilings distinguish the house: a ballroom with a barrel ceiling; and a tavern room with a canvas ceiling and witches crosses. The tavern mantle has an unusual window treatment of seven arched glass domed cupboards at the top.

The furnishings represent the period of 1820 to 1840, the years of the Farmington Canal when the house became a Tavern and Inn.

## Notable Collections on Exhibit

Exhibits include one devoted to Higley copper ,the first copper coin minted in America from copper mines located in what was then Simsbury.

## Additional Information

The Phelps House is part of Massacoh Plantation. Other buildings on the property include the 1740 Schoolhouse, a replica of the first meeting house in Simsbury (1683). As Simsbury was the site of the first safety fuse manufactured in this country, some of the machinery used in its manufacture is on exhibit. A unique tin peddlars cart is also on display.

# Hoyt-Barnum House

1508 High Ridge Road
Stamford, CT 06903
(203) 329-1183

**Contact:** Stamford Historical Society

**Open:** April-Columbus Day, Sat.-Sun., 12-4 p.m.; mid Oct.-mid April, by special appointment

**Admission:** Adults $2; children $1. Guided tours.

**Suggested Time to View House:** 45 minutes

**Best Season to View House:** Spring-fall

**Number of Yearly Visitors:** 2,500

**Year House Built:** 1699 basement; upper 1½ floors-mid to late 18th century

**Style of Architecture:** Saltbox

**Number of Rooms:** 3 plus attic and basement, basement not open to public

**On-Site Parking:** No  **Wheelchair Access:** No

## Description of House

In 1699, Samuel Hoyt, the town blacksmith, began building this home for his bride-to-be. Members of the Hoyt family owned and lived in the house for nearly a century until the Ferris family purchased it in the mid to late 1790s. They appear to have enlarged it substantially at that time, adding a second floor and attic. The house was lived in continuously until the early 1950s, when the historical society took it over as their headquarters. Genealogies on owners have been worked out by the society; the social context of the building is still being developed.

The house has been studied by Abbot Lowell Cummings and Daniel Hopping, restoration architects and scholars; a videotape of their thoughts about the structure is available to the public.

The Hoyt-Barnum House is furnished according to the 1738 inventory. They are, to a large degree, appropriate to the house in style, form and quantities.

## Notable Collections on Exhibit

The society houses its main collections at another facility five miles away from the house. Major collections include textiles, 17th to 18th-century furniture, a 3500 volume library, and a 3000 photograph collection of Stamford 1880 to 1990.

# *Judson House*

967 Academy Hill
Stratford, CT 06497
(203) 378-0630

**Contact:** Stratford Historical Society
**Open:** Wed., Sat.-Sun. 11 a.m.–4 p.m.
**Admission:** Adults $2; seniors $1.50;
students $1. Guided tours.
**Suggested Time to View House:** 1 hour
**Description of Grounds:** Large lawn

**Best Season to View House:** Mid April
to Oct.
**Year House Built:** 1750
**Style of Architecture:** Georgian
**Number of Rooms:** 8
**On-Site Parking:** No  **Wheelchair Access:** No

## Description of House

Captain David Judson built the house that we see today in 1750. The foundation of the house is said to be that of a stone house built in 1639 by Captain David Judson's great-grandfather, William Judson, one of the first settlers of Stratford. A prominent man in the area, David Judson was chosen captain of Stratford's local militia train band, a position second only to the minister in importance in the community. He also served as auditor of the Connecticut colony records and as deputy to the general assembly.

Judson House is an elegant house for the period in almost original condition. The structure has a fine entrance with a broken pediment and has the original "bullseye" glass. The house, with its large central chimney into which are built six fireplaces, and its post and beam two-story construction, represents a transition between the saltbox house and the Georgian style. The hardware on the door is original, and the Connecticut latch and strap hinges are typical in the area.

An unusual feature of this northern Colonial home is the slave quarters in the Judson House cellar. Here visitors will see an enormous fireplace, ten feet long and seven feet high, containing two bake ovens of beehive design, a large crane and complete 18th-century cooking equipment.

The house is furnished according to the period with furniture from Stratford homes, some of it Stratford-made.

## Notable Collections on Exhibit

The period furnishings feature many noteworthy Stratford artifacts such as a rare 18th-century press for hanging clothes, an 18th-century corner chair from the David Plant family, a 19th century cradle used by the descendants of Moses Wheeler, the town's ferryman, and one of the society's oldest artifacts, an oak chest manufactured in 1650.

# King House Museum

232 South Main Street
Suffield, CT 06078
(203)668-5256

**Contact:** Suffield Historical Society
**Open:** May-Sept., Wed. and Sat. 1–4 p.m.
**Admission:** Adults $1; students free.
  Guided tours.
**Suggested Time to View House:**
  Approximately 45 minutes.
**Facilities on Premises:** Rest room
**Number of Yearly Visitors:** 800
**Year House Built:** 1764
**Style of Architecture:** Georgian Colonial
**Number of Rooms:** 12
**On-Site Parking:** Yes
**Wheelchair Access:** No

## Description of House

Dr. Alexander King (1737-1802) built this attractive house in 1764 and lived here until 1793. He was educated at Yale (class of 1759) and practiced medicine in Suffield. In addition to his medical practice, he was a farmer and was active for many years in town and state government.

The King House is a typical and well-executed example of an 18th century Connecticut house with a central chimney. The one and a half story wooden structure has retained many original features including an unusual side porch. The rear of the porch is enclosed and is believed to have been Dr. King's office. The main entrance relieves the stark exterior lines with its fluted pilasters. The tudor roses and swelling of the entablature introduce motifs which are repeated in the interior, particularly the dining room.

The King House is furnished with 18th and early 19th-century pieces assembled by mid 20th-century owners for museum purposes. The Borning room wall is covered with drawings believed to be from late 18th-century masonic designs.

## Notable Collections on Exhibit

The furniture includes a number of excellent pieces made locally, including a 1807 Hepplewhite sideboard; an 1801 tall case clock; and a Hepplewhite card table (c. 1795). The historical exhibits feature an extensive collection of local tobacco and cigar memorabilia, a large display of early bottles and flasks, considerable Bennington pottery, embroidery samplers, and a collection of tenth-anniversary tinware from 1869.

# Hatheway House

55 South Main Street
Suffield, CT
(203) 668-0055

**Contact:** Antiquarian and Landmarks Society
**Open:** May 15-Oct. 15, Wed., Sat. and Sun. 1–4 p.m.; also Thur. and Fri. in July and Aug.
**Admission:** Adults $2; students $1. Guided tours, Holidayfest first weekend in Dec., and other special programs.
**Suggested Time to View House:** 45 minutes
**Description of Grounds:** Attractive grounds with formal flower beds and mid-19th-century farm buildings, also contains 5th largest tree in state

**Best Season to View House:** June-Sept.
**Number of Yearly Visitors:** 1,000
**Year House Built:** c. 1761, expanded in 1788 and 1794
**Style of Architecture:** Center chimney colonial with neoclassical addition
**Number of Rooms:** 12 (on tour)
**On-Site Parking:** Yes **Wheelchair Access:** No

## Description of House

The main block of the house was built by Shem Burbank, a farmer, for his bride. They raised a large family here until financial troubles forced them to sell their home to Oliver Phelps. Phelps was a self-made man who made a fortune after the Revolutionary War through land speculation. He was very involved with the settlement of upstate New York and the Western Reserve (Ohio). He over extended himself, however, and died insolvent. After his death, the property was purchased by Asahel Hatheway and remained in the Hatheway family for a century. The house was a private home until 1956.

Hatheway House was built as a typical center-chimney Colonial home in the 1760s. During a prosperous period, the second owner, Oliver Phelps, expanded upon the original structure by adding a wing. The north wing is considered the earliest example of the neoclassical style in the Connecticut

Valley. The interior is decorated with magnificent French wallpapers installed in 1795. The entire house is furnished to interpret the life styles of the first two owners. Another wing, added by the last private owners in 1930, serves as caretaker's quarters.

The house has the largest assemblage of 18th-century wallpaper *in situ* (three rooms and two hallways) in the country. The woodwork in one room is signed and dated by Thomas Hayden, Windsor, 1795. Asher Benjamin carved some column capitals, the earliest documented example of his work.

The museum rooms are furnished with period pieces appropriate to illustrating colonial family life, including some fine examples of country New England furniture.

A handsome summer house overlooks formal flower beds, maintained by the local garden club. These attractive grounds are set off from the street with an ornate fence designed by Phelps.

### Notable Collections on Exhibit

In addition to the remarkable wallpaper on display, the Hatheway House displays fine examples of 18th-century furniture including a pair of 1849 mirrors, New York shieldback chairs (c. 1800), a chest of drawers and writing table manufactured in Salem, Massachusetts, (c. 1800), and a canopy bed with original white-on-white bedspread.

### Additional Information

The Hatheway House is situated in a charming town, whose two mile long Main Street borders many 18th-century houses. A self guided walking tour brochure is available for interested visitors.

# Hotchkiss-Fyler House

192 Main Street
Torrington, CT 06790
(203) 482-8260

**Contact:** Torrington Historical Society, Inc.
**Open:** Mon.-Fri. 9 a.m.–4 p.m.; Sat.
10 a.m.–3 p.m.; closed bank holidays
**Admission:** Adults,$2; children under 12,
free. Guided tours, special programs
(winter lecture series, local history talks to
groups and schools).
**Suggested Time to View House:** 45 minutes

**Description of Grounds:** Gardens have not
yet been restored but the public is
welcome to walk through the grounds.
**Best Season to View House:** Spring
**Number of Yearly Visitors:** 5,000
**Year House Built:** 1900
**Style of Architecture:** Queen Anne-style
**Number of Rooms:** 17
**On-Site Parking:** Yes  **Wheelchair Access:** No

## Description of House

The Hotchkiss-Fyler House has remained virtually unchanged since its
the last occupants left in 1956. The house was commissioned by Orsamus R.
Fyler and his wife, Mary Vaill Fyler, both descendants of old New England
families. O.R. Fyler (1840-1909) was well known throughout Connecticut,
having served as postmaster of Torrington for several years in addition to
serving as a state representative, and a variety of other state-level offices.
He was also a veteran of the Civil War. His wife, Mary (1844-1935), was a
teacher before marrying Fyler in 1865. They has one child, Gertrude, who
married Edward Hotchkiss, later owner of the Hotchkiss Brother Co. (lumber mill) and a state legislator.

One of the first mansions to be built in Torrington, this seventeen room
Queen Anne style home was designed by architect William H. Allen of New
Haven and constructed by Orasmus Fyler's son-in-law's business,
Hotchkiss Brothers Co. The main hall reflects the opulence of the mansion's
interior with its mahogany panelling, coffered ceiling, and the gold-leafed
hand-stencilled wall in the Tree of Life pattern. The ambience is further
enhanced by parquet floors, and a variety of woods used throughout the

house (birdseye maple, quartersawn oak, ash, and red birch, etc.). The decorations of the reception room are particularly ornate and include a hand-painted ceiling, and walls covered with a soft-green Italian cotton damask. The walls of the library are also embellished with hand-painting in a foliate design.

The furnishings date from the late 19th century through 1956 when the last family member lived there. All furnishings were collected by the family and includes mainly reproductions of French-style furniture.

### Notable Collections on Exhibit
Included in the collection are approximately ten Oriental carpets, a large collection of art glass baskets, and a large variety of European porcelains such as Meissen, Dresden, Royal Vienna, and Royal Naples. There is also a large collection of Staffordshire pieces, lusterware, china, and crystal. Paintings in the adjoining museum are by Connecticut artists, Winfield Scott Clime and George Lawrence Nelson, as well as six portraits of the Hotchkiss family by Ammi Phillips.

### Additional Information
In addition to the house, the estate has two other buildings: the carriage house (1895) now used as a lecture/meeting area and the museum housed in a small house (c. 1890) which the family always rented out. This building was gutted in the 1970s and converted into an exhibit space for changing history exhibits. The society also maintains a separate history collection in addition to the Hotchkiss-Fyler collections.

# Samuel Parsons House

**180 South Main Street**
**Wallingford, CT 06492**
**(203) 294-1996**

**Contact:** Wallingford Historical Society
**Open:** Memorial Day-Labor Day weekend,
Sun. 2–4 p.m.
**Admission:** Free
**Suggested Time to View House:** 1–2 hours
**Description of Grounds:** lovely backyard
with kitchen herb garden
**Best Season to View House:** Summer
**Number of Yearly Visitors:** 100 plus
**Year House Built:** 1759
**Style of Architecture:** Gambrel
**Number of Rooms:** 8

**On-Site Parking:** No **Wheelchair Access:** No

## Description of House

The Parsons family lived in this simple wood-framed structure during the American Revolution and remained occupants until the end of the 18th century. In 1803, it was bought by Caleb Thompson, an artisan who built of wagons, carriages, and coffins in a shop located at the front end of the lot. One of his descendants, Fannie Ives Schember, deeded the family home to the historical society as a result of her interest in preserving the town's history.

Located on the original main street of Wallingford among other fine homes, the 18th-century gambrel-roofed Parsons House retains much of its early construction with the exception of a small kitchen ell added in 1855, and other structural changes. There are six fireplaces built around the two large chimneys at each end of the house. Many of the furnishings on display are from the same period as the house, though not from the original owners.

## Notable Collections on Exhibit

Highlights of the collection on display include an 18th-century highboy, paintings by past and present Wallingford artists, silver and pewter made by local craftsmen; early maps of Wallingford; a large collection of period clothing and iron cooking utensils made by early town blacksmiths.

## Additional Information

On the grounds to the house, visitors may also view a kitchen herb garden maintained by the local garden club, the Old Town Hall bell, and school bells that tolled for generations of Wallingford children.

# Gunn Historical Museum

Route 47 and Wykeham Road
Washington Green, CT 06793
(203) 868-7756

**Contact:** Gunn Historical Museum
**Open:** Thur.-Sat. noon–4 p.m.
**Admission:** Free
**Suggested Time to View House:** 45 minutes
**Description of Grounds:** Flower beds along front walk, a little herb garden to the side, a wide sweep of lawn with flowering shrubs and trees

**Best Season to View House:** Spring, summer, fall
**Number of Yearly Visitors:** 1,500
**Year House Built:** 1781
**Style of Architecture:** Greek Revival
**Number of Rooms:** 9 on view
**On-Site Parking:** Yes **Wheelchair Access:** No

## Description of House

Although named after Frederick W. Gunn, the founder of the Gunnery School did not actually live here. He was, however, a prominent resident of Washington Green who established an informal library association in the 1860s. The house took his name when it was bequeathed to the Gunn Memorial Library in 1964. One former resident of the house, Simon H. Mitchell (1809-1879), was described as a "private banker" with investments in local industries as well as being a member of the state militia. At the outbreak of the Civil War, Mitchell was drill master in the manual of arms for local volunteers. Frederick Galpin, who bought the house from Mitchell, owned a sawmill and was secretary of the Grange, founded in 1875.

Built in 1791, the house's original appearance is not clearly known, but it is one of the oldest structures on on Washington Green. Today the building has a clapboard exterior with a Greek Revival doorway. The house stands at the heart of the Washington Historical District, a wide circle of early houses that surround the 1801 Greek Revival Congregational church on the green.

There is an eclectic collection of furnishings donated by local people and typical of varying styles ranging from provincial interpretations of Colonial designs to late Empire and Renaissance Revival. The rooms include an 1820s bedroom centered around tester bed and chest of drawers with acanthus carvings; a Victorian bedroom with Renaissance Revival furnishings; an Empire dining room, and an 1890s bathroom.

## Notable Collections on Exhibit

The Gunn Historical Museum is noted for the rich assortment of its collections representing every aspect of life in this town in the early days, plus a fairly comprehensive file on people, places and events. The costume collection is unique for a museum of this size; it contains a thousand items beginning with a Revolutionary War jacket and continues on through shoes, stockings, gloves, hats, underclothes, nightgowns, and children clothes. The collection of women's dresses—375 examples from the 1820s to 1920s—are displayed in rooms throughout the building. Among paintings held by museum are portraits by Richard Jennys of Judge Daniel Nathaniel Brinsmade and wife Abigail Ferrand Brinsmade (1794); portraits by George Wright of Dr. Remus Fowler and wife, Mary Fowler (1845); portraits by Aaron Dean Fletcher of Clarina Averill Ferris and her daughter Adeline Ferris Goodsell (1845); a schoolmaster's desk with butterfly leg from the late 1700s; a Hoadley grandfather's clock, early 1800s; an 1870 chair made from Texas longhorn horns, once owned by P.T. Barnum; a woven hair wreath presented to Mr. and Mrs. Stephen Hollister on their Golden Wedding anniversary (1870); and a side room with toys, dolls, dollhouses, and a thimble collection. In addition, three rooms on the first floor are used for new exhibits mounted several times a year.

# Noah Webster House

227 South Main Street
West Hartford, CT 06107
(203)521-5362

**Contact:** Historical Society of West Hartford, Inc.

**Open:** Oct. 1-June 14, 1–4 p.m. daily except Wed.; June 15-Sept. 30; 10 a.m.–4 p.m. daily except Wed., Sat. and Sun. 1–4 p.m.

**Admission:** Senior citizens $1; adults $3; children (6-15) $2; children under 6 free. Guided tours with costumed docent; changing gallery exhibits; 15 minute introductory video on the life of Noah Webster

**Suggested Time to View House:** 1 hour

**Facilities on Premises:** Gift shop.

**Description of Grounds:** Colonial garden

**Best Season to View House:** Spring and summer

**Number of Yearly Visitors:** 3,000-5,000

**Year House Built:** 1748

**Number of Rooms:** Original house– 4 rooms with additions

**Style of Architecture:** Colonial Saltbox

**On-Site Parking:** Yes  **Wheelchair Access:** Yes

## Description of House

This simple saltbox home could almost be called the birthplace of the American language as Noah Webster was born here. This man of many words left home at the age to sixteen to attend Yale University. All Americans owe a debt to Webster as the author of the blue backed speller, first published in 1783. And while he may not be associated with the great authors of American literature, his masterwork, a 70,000 word dictionary (1828) completed alone and by hand, has secured a place on every American bookshelf.

The house is noteworthy, not only because of its famous resident, but because it is a well-preserved example of a typical farmhouse with central-chimney construction. The cavernous fireplace dominated the kitchen and provided both heat and light for the Webster family. The lean-to kitchen, which gives the house its familiar saltbox appearance, was added at the end of the 18th century along with a buttery, gallery, and a reception room.

The furnishings of the house are from the inventories of families who lived during the same period. Today, the house appears much as it would have in 1774.

## Notable Collections on Exhibit

In addition to the 18th-century furniture, the most unique objects on exhibit include Noah Webster's clock and desk, as well as a massive loom.

# Bradley Wheeler House

25 Avery Place
Westport, CT 06880
(203) 222-1424

**Contact:** Westport Historical Society

**Open:** Tues., Thur. and Sat. 11 a.m.–2 p.m.

**Admission:** Free, donations accepted. Guided tours, Jennings Trail (special appointment), cooking demonstrations on a Victorian stove

**Suggested Time to View House:** 30 minutes

**Facilities on Premises:** Gift shop

**Description of Grounds:** The house is located near the main part of town and the town hall.

**Best Season to View House:** Spring-fall

**Number of Yearly Visitors:** 5,000

**Year House Built:** 1795

**Style of Architecture:** Saltbox and remodeled into Italianate

**Number of Rooms:** 7

**On-Site Parking:** No  **Wheelchair Access:** No

## Description of House

The house has long been associated with several of Westport's most prominent citizens: Ebinizer Coley, a local merchant, who built the house for his son, Michael, and Farmin Patchem, Morris Bradley and Charles B. Wheeler, local businessmen who lived in the house during the 19th century. Ebinizer Coley was a landowner in Wetson,where he ran a grist mill and owned slaves. By 1795, he and his three sons ran a business in Westport. Around 1860 the Morris Bradley family moved to Westport. In 1868, he and Fredrick Morehouse purchased three stores in the center of the village. One store "Bradley and Wheeler Grocers" was run by his son, Abram, and son-in-law, Charles Wheeler. In the 1870 census, Morris Bradley's real estate was valued at $90,000.

The Bradley-Wheeler House was built in 1795 as a typical five-bay Colonial-style house with a central chimney. It was remodeled during the second half of the 19th century into an Italianate Villa, probably under Bradley's ownership. The house has been altered little since this remodeling and represents the evolution of taste and changing styles and methods of residential construction in Westport. The furnishings have been collected and are appropriate to period.

## Notable Collections on Exhibit

Many fine furnishings are on display including a marble top hall table, Parian ware, gilt Pier mirror, a black mantle clock, Eastlake wall toilet case, and a Rococco love seat.

# *Buttolph-Williams House*

249 Broad Street
Wethersfield, CT
(203) 529-0460

**Contact:** Antiquarian and Landmarks Society
**Open:** May 15-Oct. 15, Tues.-Sun. 1–4 p.m.
**Admission:** Adults $2; students $1.  Guided tours, lantern light tour in Oct., special programs.
**Suggested Time to View House:** 30 minutes

**Description of Grounds:** House is set on grassy lot.
**Number of Yearly Visitors:** 1,400
**Year House Built:** c. 1700
**Style of Architecture:** Pilgrim Century
**Number of Rooms:** 4
**On-Site Parking:** No  **Wheelchair Access:** No

## Description of House

Located in one the state's oldest towns, the picturesque Buttolph-Williams House provided the setting for the children's literary classic, *The Witch of Blackbird Pond*. The house was probably built by members of the Williams family, a prosperous local family.

This simple frame house has a hewn overhang, small casement windows, and a huge center chimney stack which gives it a medieval character. The interior is furnished to represent the life style of a family at the turn of the 18th century. All of the furnishings were collected for exhibit in the house museum.

## Notable Collections on Exhibit

There is an excellent collection of late 17th-century furniture and a large number of tree pieces on display.

# Silas Deane, Joseph Webb & Isaac Stevens Museum

211 Main Street
Wethersfield, CT 06109
(203) 529-0612

**Contact:** Webb-Deane-Stevens Museum
**Open:** May 1-Oct. 31, Tues.-Sun.
10 a.m.–4 p.m.; Nov. 1-April 30, Fri.-Sun.
10 a.m.–4 p.m.
**Admission:** Adults $5; seniors $4; students
(8-12) $2.50; children $1; under age 5 free.
Guided tours, special programs
**Suggested Time to View House:** 90 minutes
**Facilities on Premises:** gift/book shop

**Description of Grounds:** Plantings of shrubs,
trees, perennials, annuals and herbs. Trees
of particular note for size and age.
**Best Season to View House:** Mid summer
**Number of Yearly Visitors:** 6,000 plus
**Year House Built:** Deane 1766, Webb 1752,
Stevens 1781
**Style of Architecture:** Georgian
**On-Site Parking:** Yes **Wheelchair Access:** No

## Description of House

The Webb-Deane-Stevens Museum is actually three 18th-century houses which stand side by side in historic Wethersfield. The Webb House was built in 1752 by Joseph Webb, a successful shopkeeper and West Indies merchant. He was later imprisoned for debt after losing money by selling supplies to the colonial forces at a time of extreme inflation. His widow married Silas Deane, who would later become a controversial figure in American Revolution. He built a new house in 1766 along side the original home. Due to a dispute over expenses while in France on behalf of his government, he was declared a traitor and died in 1789, but was later exonerated by Congress in 1842. The third house which comprises the museum, the Stevens House, was built by Isaac Stevens, a saddlemaker, between 1788 and 1789.

All three houses comprising the Webb-Deane Stevens Museum are fine examples of Georgian architecture of the Connecticut Valley. The original one-room structure of the Webb House was raised to become the second floor. Underneath the gambrel roof is an enormous one and a half story attic. The Webb House also contains a bedroom where George Washington slept in 1781. The room still has the special red flock wallpaper which was hung in honor of his visit.

The structural restorations and rehabilitations of the interiors of the three houses have been done with great attention to authenticity. Even the interior and exterior paint has been restored to the original colors. Two of the houses, the Webb and Deane Houses, are registered National Historic Landmarks.

The furnishings are of the same period as the houses and while many are from the original residents, others have been collected.

## Notable Collections on Exhibit

There are many noteworthy examples of early American furniture on display in the three houses such as a Chippendale cherry side chair and mahogany secretary, a carved Rhode Island magogany tea table, a New England maple gateleg table, a mahogany side chair (c. 1780), and a locally made black-painted Windsor chair. There are also many other interesting artifacts on display including the account books of Joseph Webb Jr. and Issac Stevens, a quilted calamanco coverlet (1788), kitchen equipment (includes early wooden and pewter bowls, pottery, homespun cloths, an 18th-century iron pot lifter and a brass and iron clock jack, and many other items typical to homes of this period.

## Additional Information

The Stevens House has medicinal and culinary gardens open to the public which contain plants only known to have grown in Connecticut before 1800. All three houses are administered by the Connecticut chapter of the National Society of Colonial Dames.

Visitors to historic Wethersfield should not miss the opportunity to tour the *Captain James Francis House* located nearby at 120 Hartford Avenue. This Federal house, built by Captain James Francis in 1793, features decorative wood paneling (installed by Francis), an Eastlake bedroom set, a high chest and cradle, period textiles, and other furnishings from the 18th and 19th centuries. Contact the Wethersfield Historical Society at (203) 529-7656 for more information.

# *Sloan-Raymond-Fitch House*

249 Danbury Road
Wilton, CT 06897
(203)762-7257

**Contact:** Wilton Historical Society
**Open:** Tues.-Thurs. 10–4 p.m.; Sun. for special programs
**Admission:** Senior citizens $1; Adults $2; children under 12 free accompanied by a parent and groups by appointment. Tours and special programs.
**Suggested Time to View House:** 1 hour

**Facilities on Premises:** Gift shop
**Number of Yearly Visitors:** 1,000
**Year House Built:** 1757
**Style of Architecture:** Classic Colonial
**Number of Rooms:** 6 period rooms
**On-Site Parking:** No  **Wheelchair Access:** No

### Description of House

The Sloan-Raymond-Fitch House is an 18th-century Colonial farmhouse with a design structured around a classic central chimney. The kitchen features a large fireplace with a rear bake oven. A corner cabinet displays genuine 18th-century ceramics. The Federal dining room and bedroom are furnished with authentic furniture, and decorative and functional furnishings of the period. The period rooms show a time continuum illustrating the changes in style from 1750 to 1840.

### Notable Collections on Exhibit

Exhibits at the house include a costume collection, a Ralph Earl painting and 18th and 19th-century ceramics including Norwalk redware. A toy room exhibits late 19th and early 20th-century dolls, toys, and dollhouses.

# 1640 Lt. Walter Fyler House

96 Palisado Avenue
Windsor, CT 06095
(203) 688-3813

**Contact:** The Windsor Historical Society, Inc.
**Open:** April 1-Nov. 30, Tues.-Sat.
10 a.m.–4 p.m.; during winter months,
by appointment
**Admission:** Adults $2; seniors $1.50;
members, students and children free.
Guided tour of house and museum; use of
our genealogical and historical research
library.
**Suggested Time to View House:**
60–90 minutes

**Facilities on Premises:** Gift shop
**Description of Grounds:** Small herb and
flower garden, in season
**Best Season to View House:** May-Oct.
**Number of Yearly Visitors:** 1,500 plus
**Year House Built:** 1640
**Style of Architecture:** Gambrel roof, colonial
**Number of Rooms:** 9
**On-Site Parking:** Yes  **Wheelchair Access:** Yes

## Description of House

The original owners and builders of the house were Lt. Walter Fyler and
his wife who arrived in Windsor in 1635 after spending five years in
Dorchester, Massachusetts. They came to America in 1630 from Plymouth,
England, on the ship "Mary and John". The Fylers retained ownership of
the house until 1763. The Allyn, Howard, Stiles and Denslow families
occupied the house until 1925 when it was purchased by The Windsor
Historical Society.

Constructed in 1640, the house is one of the state's oldest frame houses.
The Fyler House has many features typical of this early period: a gambrel
roof, random-width pine flooring, vertical panel room separators, and a
cellar fireplace and baking oven. The house also contained an early general
store and restoration of Windsor's first post office.

The keeping room is furnished with late 17th and early 18th-century period originals. The parlor is furnished with early 19th-century pieces while the remainder of the house has mix of 18th and 19th-century period originals. A few pieces are from the original residents.

### Notable Collections on Exhibit

The Fyler house displays original antique period furniture and decorative arts from the 17th, 18th and 19th centuries. This includes furniture, pewter, fireplace tools, clock, samplers, mourning pictures, primitive portraits, china and glassware.

### Additional Information

The 1640 Lt. Walter Fyler House is the only surviving 17th-century building that once stood within a "Pallizado" or stockade fort, hurriedly erected in 1637 when the settlers were threatened with an Indian attack. The house is on the south side of the original commons, which still maintains its original size as laid out by Windsor's founders.

# 1765 Dr. Hezekiah Chaffee House

108 Palisado Avenue
Windsor, CT 06095
(203) 688-3813

**Contact:** The Windsor Historical
Society, Inc.
**Open:** April 1-Nov. 30, Tues.-Sat.
10 a.m.–4 p.m.; during winter months,
by appointment
**Admission:** Adults $1; members and
children free. Guided tour of house and
museum; use of our genealogical and
historical research library and exhibits.
**Suggested Time to View House:** 1–2 hours
**Facilities on Premises:** Gift shop
**Description of Grounds:** Small herb and
flower garden, in season
**Best Season to View House:** May-Oct.
**Number of Yearly Visitors:** 1,500 plus
**Year House Built:** 1765
**Number of Rooms:** 7 first floor rooms
(2nd and 3rd floors not open to public)

**Style of Architecture:** Georgian colonial
**Wheelchair Access:** Yes

## Description of House

Dr, Chaffee carried on a medical practice here until his death in 1819.
His son, John Chaffee, who lived in the house after his father's death, was
a partner in the great importing and exporting firm of Hooker and Chaffee,
which served businesses all over southern New England. The property
remained in the family line until sold to the Loomis Institute, a preparatory
school for boys. At this time (1926) the Chaffee School for Girls was begun.
After forty-four years as a site for the school, it returned to private ownership in 1972. The Chaffee house was taken over by the Windsor Historical
Society in 1992.

This is one of the few surviving, gambrel roof structures in Connecticut.
This distinguished brick house was constructed by Dr. Chaffee in 1765.
Many of its original features can still be seen including original paneling,
random-width flooring, and fireplace. A one story ell on the south side of
the house which served as Dr. Chaffee's office remains intact. The furnishings are appropriate to the period 1765 to 1850.

## Notable Collections on Exhibit

Original antique period furniture and decorative arts from the late 18th
to mid 19th century are on permanent display. This includes pewter,
fireplace tools, clock, china and glassware.

# Glebe House Museum

Hollow Road P.O. Box 245
Woodbury, CT 06798
(203) 263-2855

**Contact:** Glebe House Museum and
Gertrude Jekyll Gardens

**Open:** April-Nov., Wed.-Sun. 1–4 p.m.

**Admission:** Adults $3, children under 12
free. Guided tours, special programs.

**Suggested Time to View House:** 30 minutes

**Facilities on Premises:** Gift shop, book store

**Description of Grounds:** Gertrude Jekyll
Gardens

**Best Season to View House:** Summer

**Number of Yearly Visitors:** 4000 plus

**Year House Built:** 1750

**Style of Architecture:** Gambrel Saltbox

**Number of Rooms:** 8

**On-Site Parking:** Yes **Wheelchair Access:** No

## Description of House

Like many Colonial houses, Glebe House has witnessed many momentous events. It was home to Reverend John Rutgers Marshall, his wife, Sarah, and nine children from 1771 through the Revolutionary War. As followers of the Anglican religion, they often suffered oppression because it was assumed that they were loyal to England. After America achieved independence, a group of Episcopalians met secretly at Glebe House and made an important decision to take part in the building of a new nation while upholding their religious heritage. The house was also home to Gideon Botsford, a silversmith, and his large family.

The Glebe House was restored in 1923 under the direction of William Henry Kent, pioneer of early American decorative arts at the Metropolitan Museum of Art in New York. When it opened its doors in 1925, Glebe House was one of the earliest historic house museums in the nation.

## Additional Information

This simple but elegant farmhouse is noteworthy for having the only extant American garden designed by the famed English garden designer Gertrude Jekyll. She is widely considered the greatest gardener of the 20th century and an important influence on modern garden design.

# Hurd House

**Main Street South and Hollow Road**
**Woodbury, CT 06798**
**(203) 263-2696**

**Contact:** Old Woodbury Historical
Society Inc.

**Open:** June-Oct., Sun. 2–4 p.m.; also open
History Day, Woodbury Festival Days
and other special times

**Admission:** Free. Guided tours.

**Suggested Time to View House:** 20 minutes

**Best Season to View House:** Summer
and fall

**Number of Yearly Visitors:** 500

**Year House Built:** 1680

**Style of Architecture:** Saltbox (modified)

**Number of Rooms:** 4

**On-Site Parking:** Yes  **Wheelchair Access:** No

## Description of House

Hurd House is actually two houses combined with one having been home to the town miller, John Hurd. Constructed in 1680, the small, original house is the oldest structure at its original site in Litchfield County. The south half of the house was joined with the earlier house about 1718, and may have belonged to one of the sons of the original miller.

The Hurd House in its present form consists of two houses combined to form a single house of two rooms on the first floor and two rooms on the second. When the two houses were joined, the original framing was retained. The summer beams of both houses were framed into a central chimney. The corner posts of the two houses remain and are about a foot apart. The clapboards cover the gap between the corner posts. Sometime between 1718 and 1779, a lean-to was added to the back, giving the house the saltbox appearance it retained until the lean-to's removal early this century. At some period prior to 1822, an ell was added to the southeast corner of the house. The furnishings have been collected and all are appropriate to period of the Hurd family's occupancy.

## Additional Information

The society also maintains a 19th-century district schoolhouse and an archives building for the town of Woodbury.

# Bowen House, Roseland Cottage

Route 169
Woodstock, CT 06281
(203) 928-4074

**Contact:** Soc. for the Preservation of New England Antiquities

**Open:** Memorial Day weekend-Labor Day weekend, Wed.-Sun.; Mid Sept.-Mid Oct., Fri.-Sun.

**Admission:** $4. Tours at 12 p.m., 1 p.m., 2 p.m., 3 p.m., 4 p.m. Special events include a Fourth of July party, concerts, an arts and crafts fair and a Victorian wedding show.

**Description of Grounds:** The complex includes a boxwood parterre garden with original plantings, an icehouse, a garden house, and a carriage barn with [more]

**Year House Built:** 1846

**Style of Architecture:** Gothic Revival

## Description of House

The house provided a seasonal escape from a more formal city existence for Henry Chandler Bowen and his family. Bowen, a Woodstock native, made his fortune in New York and became an active abolitionist, Congregationalist, and Republican.

Roseland Cottage depicts the summer life of a prosperous family in mid 19th-century America. The house reflects the principles of writer and designer Andrew Jackson Downing. In his widely poplular books, Downing stressed practicality along with the picturesque and offered detailed instructions on room function, sanitation, and landscaping. The house remains virtually unchanged with its original Gothic furniture and embossed Lincrusta Walton wallcoverings. Visitors will also be charmed by the cottage's bright pink exterior.

# Maine

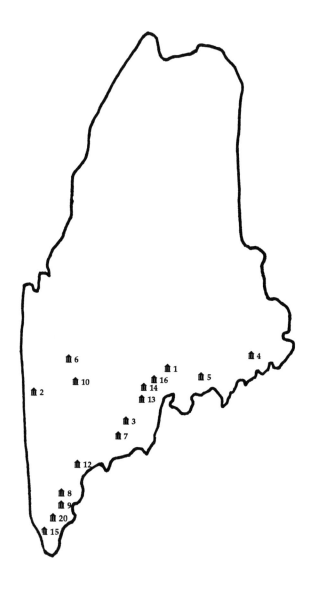

1. **Bangor**
   *Thomas A. Hill House*

2. **Bethel**
   *Dr. Moses Mason House*

3. **Brunswick**
   *Joshua L. Chamberlain House*
   *Skolfield-Whittier House*

4. **Columbia**
   *Thomas Ruggles House*

5. **Ellsworth**
   *The Black House*

6. **Farmington**
   *Nordica Homestead*

7. **Freeport**
   *Harrington House*
   *Pettengill Farm*

8. **Kennebunk**
   *The Taylor-Barry House*

9. **Kennebunkport**
   *Nott House -White Columns*

10. **Livermore Falls**
    *Washburn Mansion*

11. **Poland Springs**
    *The Shaker Museum*

12. **Portland**
    *Wadsworth-Longfellow House*
    *Tate House*
    *The Victoria Mansion*

13. **Rockland**
    *Farnsworth Homestead*

14. **Searsport**
    *Fowler-True-Ross House*

15. **South Berwick**
    *Sarah Orne Jewitt House*
    *Hamilton House*

16. **South Hampden**
    *Kinsley House*

17. **Standish**
    *Marrett House*

18. **Wells**
    *Historic Meetinghouse Museum*

19. **Wiscasset**
    *Nickels-Sortwell House*

20. **York Harbor**
    *Sayward-Wheeler House*

# Thomas A. Hill House

159 Union Street
Bangor, ME 04401
(207) 942-5766

**Contact:** Bangor Historical Society

**Open:** March-mid Dec., Tues.-Fri.
12–4 p.m.; July-Sept., Sun. 12–4 p.m.;
closed on holidays

**Admission:** Adults $2; children $.50.
Guided tours, bus tours, lectures on
local history topics.

**Suggested Time to View House:** 1 hour

**Facilities on Premises:** Small gift shop

**Best Season to View House:** Summer

**Number of Yearly Visitors:** 1750

**Year House Built:** 1836

**Number of Rooms:** 11

**Style of Architecture:** Greek Revival

**On-Site Parking:** No  **Wheelchair Access:** No

## Description of House

The original owner, Thomas A. Hill, was a prominent attorney and businessman. The house was later owned by mayor Samuel Dale who entertained such distinguished guests as Ulysses S. Grant. Mayor Dale committed suicide in the house over an embezzlement scandal. The house was later owned by a doctor and then became headquarters of the G.A.R., a veterans group. Hill House became the home of the Bangor Historical Society during the 1970s.

Designed by Richard Upjohn, the Thomas Hill House has a brick exterior, with a three-sided portico with Ionic columns. The downstairs interior has been restored to its original form and features an elegant double parlor with an unusual hand-carved room divider with Corinthian columns and an arabesque frieze. The upstairs formerly had four bedrooms which were gutted during the period of G.A.R. ownership and now displays changing exhibits.

The furnishings are Victorian era, collected from other Bangor homes or made in the area. The only items which remain from the original residents are the light fixtures, pier mirrors, and fireplaces.

## Notable Collections on Exhibit

The house displays a unique collection of portraits of local people, mostly by local artists, some locally made furniture, and a variety of locally produced and owned decorative objects.

# Dr. Moses Mason House

15 Broad Street, P.O. Box 12
Bethel, ME 04217-0012
(207) 824-2908

**Contact:** Bethel Historical House

**Open:** July-Aug., Tues.-Sun. 1–4 p.m.; rest of the year, Mon.-Fri. 10 a.m–4 p.m.; also by appointment

**Admission:** Adults $2; children (6-12) $1; groups by donation. Guided tours, special events, exhibits, lectures and films.

**Suggested Time to View House:** 30 minutes

**Description of Grounds:** Period gardens, and a Victorian summer house on grounds

**Best Season to View House:** Spring-fall

**Number of Yearly Visitors:** 2,500 plus

**Year House Built:** 1813

**Number of Rooms:** 8

**Style of Architecture:** Federal

**On-Site Parking:** Yes

## Description of House

Dr. Moses Mason, a physician and businessman was one of Bethel's most prominent citizens. Born in Dublin, New Hampshire in 1789, the son of a soldier of the American Revolution and the fifth of eleven children, he began his career in medicine in 1813. He soon became interested in politics and worked as postmaster in Bethel, before serving two terms as Congressman from Maine. His wife, Agnes Straw Mason, was a leader in the temperance movement in Oxford county.

The house is an elegant white clapboard dwelling standing two stories with a graceful central entrance complete with fanlight and sidewindows. The stairway hall which divides upstairs and downstairs is the most intriguing feature of the house. The walls are decorated with murals depicting distant seascapes and engaging landscapes with lush foliage. They were painted by an itinerant artist, perhaps the famed Rufus Porter or his nephew Jonathan Poor, but certainly someone working in the Porter style.

Many of the furnishings on display belonged to the Masons, others are appropriate to the period.

## Notable Collections on Exhibit

Two of the prized items in the collection are autograph books kept by the Masons containing the signatures of Presidents John Quincy Adams, Andrew Jackson, and Martin Van Buren, among others. Also on display are portraits of Dr. and Mrs. Mason by Chester Harding, a well-known 19th-century painter. Other landscapes and portraits are by James Welch and unknown folk artists.

# *Joshua L. Chamberlain House*

**Contact:** Pejepscot Historical Society
**Open:** Memorial Day-Labor Day, Tues.-Sat.
1–4 p.m. and by appointment
**Admission:** Adults $3; children $1.
Guided tours, gallery talks.
**Suggested Time to View House:** 1 hour
**Facilities on Premises:** Gift shop, book store

**Best Season to View House:** Summer
**Number of Yearly Visitors:** 3,000
**Year House Built:** 1825
**Style of Architecture:** Federal with Victorian
additions
**Number of Rooms:** 6
**On-Site Parking:** Yes  **Wheelchair Access:** No

## *Description of House*

Joshua Chamberlain's accomplishments in his nation's service as well as for the state of Maine are legendary. He was a Civil War hero, gaining recognition through commanding the 20th regiment at Gettysburg as well as fighting heroically at Little Round Top. When he returnedto civilian life, he served four terms as governor of Maine and later became president of Bowdoin College.

The Chamberlain House is an unusual architectural hybrid as the original Federal structure was raised eleven feet and a new first story was built below in a Victorian style. The house is partially furnished with the Chamberlain family's artifacts and memorabilia. Visitors to Brunswick are advised to also stop by and visit the society's other historic property, the Skolfield-Whittier House.

# Skolfield-Whittier House

**159 Park Row**
**Brunswick, ME 04011**
**(207) 729-5606**

**Contact:** Pejepscot Historical Society

**Open:** Tues.-Fri 10 a.m.–3 p.m.;
Sat. 1–4 p.m.; and by appointment

**Admission:** Adults $4; children (6-12) $2.
Guided tours, lectures, gallery talks.

**Suggested Time to View House:** 1 hour

**Facilities on Premises:** Gift shop, book store

**Best Season to View House:** Summer

**Number of Yearly Visitors:** 3,000

**Year House Built:** 1856

**Style of Architecture:** Italianate

**Number of Rooms:** 17

**On-Site Parking:** Yes

**Wheelchair Access:** No

## Description of House

George Skofield, a master shipbuilder, built this Italianate house in 1858. Other noteworthy residents include Dr. Frank Whittier who was known as the father of modern ballistics, in addition to being a noted pathologist. The last resident, widow Eugenie Whittier, lived here until 1925 when she closed up the seventeen room house. Her daughter, Alice Whittier, Maine's first woman pediatrician, also lived here.

Stepping across the threshold of the Skolfield-Whittier House is like walking into a time capsule because all of the furnishings and artifacts have been magnificently preserved. After the house had been closed for more than fifty years, curators opened it in 1982 to discover many treasures in their original condition. Everything was still intact, from receipts for the house's construction to spices in the kitchen. The parlor, with its two marble fireplaces, had not changed since the 1880s and was filled with chintz, velvet, painted screens and Elizabethan revival furniture.

The other furnishings reflect the extent of the travels of the original family. This eclectic group includes 19th-century British furnishings, Japanese lamps, a pair of Belgian chandeliers and a porcelain ornamental French clock with matching vases.

## Notable Collections on Exhibit

The Skolfield-Whittier House has an extraordinary collection of Victorian and early 20th-century artifacts including six well-stocked pantries filled with Wedgwood, Minton and Davenport china. There are also paintings by several minor British artists as well as fine collections of Castlane furniture.

# *Thomas Ruggles House*

**Contact:** Ruggles House Society
**Open:** June 1-Oct. 15, weekdays
   9:30 a.m.–4:30 p.m.; Sun. 11 a.m.– 4:30 p.m.
**Admission:** Donations accepted. Guided tours.
**Suggested Time to View House:**
   30 minutes–1 hour
**Description of Grounds:** Small lawn

**Best Season to View House:** Summer
**Number of Yearly Visitors:** 2,500
**Year House Built:** 1818
**Style of Architecture:** Federal
**Number of Rooms:** 6
**On-Site Parking:** Yes **Wheelchair Access:** No

## Description of House

The Ruggles House was built for Judge Thomas Ruggles, a wealthy lumber dealer, store owner, postmaster, prominent citizen, captain of the militia, and Justice of the Court of Sessions. Judge Ruggles left the house to his son Frederick, who raised his family here. Eventually, descendants of the family started the Ruggles House Society to preserve the house.

Standing practically the same as when it was built a century and a half ago, the Ruggles House is reminiscent of exotic elegance. One distinctive feature of the house is the elaborate wood carving, completed with a penknife by an English woodcarver who toiled three years at the job. Another impressive feature is the flying staircase which rises from the center of the wide hall without lateral support to the landing and then divides into two half flights. Its unique structure continues to amaze both contemporary craftsmen and architects. The furnishings are of the same period as the house and belonged to the owners.

## Notable Collections on Exhibit

The house also exhibits a donated collection of Stiegel glass bottles.

# The Black House

81 West Main Street
Ellsworth, ME 04606
(207) 667-8671

**Contact:** Hancock County Trustees of
Public Reservation

**Open:** June 1-Oct. 1, Mon.-Sat.
10 a.m.–5 p.m.; last tour at 4:30 p.m.

**Admission:** Adults $5; children 12 and
under $2. Guided tours.

**Suggested Time to View House:**
45 minutes–1 hour

**Description of Grounds:** The property has
a restored formal garden, and carriage
and sleigh houses.

**Best Season to View House:** June-Oct.

**Year House Built:** 1824 to 1828

**Style of Architecture:** Modified Georgian

**Number of Rooms:** 12

**On-Site Parking:** Yes  **Wheelchair Access:** No

## Description of House

Shortly after the Revolutionary War, William Bingham, a banker in Philadelphia, bought a tract of land in Maine and employed General David Cobb to sell the land to settlers. Cobb was an influential man. He had served on Washington's staff for four years, and in this capacity had been present at the surrender of Cornwallis and afterward lived at Mount Vernon as a member of Washington's military family. He came to Maine in 1795. During the panic of 1792, Bingham sold half of his Maine holdings to Hope and Company of London. The firm appointed an English boy, John Black to be General Cobb's assistant. In 1802, Black married the General's daughter, Mary and they later moved to Ellsworth and built this impressive residence.

Black Mansion is constructed of red brick in a modified Georgian style, and is surrounded by sloping lawns. The bricks of the house are said to have come by sea from Philadelphia. Skilled workmen toiled for over three years to complete its construction. The elegant interior is enhanced by a beautiful circular staircase which leads to richly furnished bedrooms, complete with canopied beds and tapestries. Entering Black Mansion is like stepping into the past, as the house remains as it was at the time of its original occupancy by John Black and his family.

## Notable Collections on Exhibit

The house is furnished with many pieces of period furniture—Jacobean, Queen Anne, Chippendale, Sheraton and Hepplewhite. Among objects of historic value are a rare volume of Massachusetts colonial laws, a miniature of Washington which he presented to General Cobb after the Revolutionary War, and a Bible box dating back to the early 17th century. One of the most interesting of the many fine chairs in the house is a rare old Dutch chair with a high winged back and a hinged seat that can be lengthened into a couch or bed. This is one of two or three known in the United States. There is also a collection of Waterford crystal on exhibit.

# Nordica Homestead

R3, Box 3062
Farmington, ME 04938
(207) 778-2042

**Contact:** Nordica Memorial Association

**Open:** June 1-Labor Day, Tues.-Sat. 10 a.m.–12 p.m. and 1–5 p.m., Labor Day-Mid Oct. by appointment

**Admission:** Adults $2, children and students $1. Guided tours, Nordica Day held Aug. 17 annually; open house, free admission, refreshments and concert.

**Suggested Time to View House:** 30–45 minutes

**Facilities on Premises:** Gift shop

**Description of Grounds:** Five acres of maintained lawns and grounds with maple trees, apple trees and flowers

**Best Season to View House:** Summer and fall

**Number of Yearly Visitors:** 350–400

**Year House Built:** 1840

**Number of Rooms:** 5 open to public

**Style of Architecture:** New England Cape

**On-Site Parking:** Yes  **Wheelchair Access:** Yes

## Description of House

This house is the birthplace of the famous opera singer, Lillian Nordica. She gained international recognition for the exceptional range and power of her voice and sang at the Paris Grand Opera House in 1882, and the Metropolitan Opera House in the 1890s. She was the first American woman invited to sing at the Bayreuth Festival. She died of pneumonia while on a concert tour in 1914.

This modest homestead house preserves the simple atmosphere of the famed opera singer's early beginnings. The low ceilings and sprigged wallpaper are typical of farmhouses of the area, but the collections and furnishings of the famed resident inside represent a life spent travelling far beyond the borders of Maine. The furnishings include a heavily, carved chair from Diamond Jim Brady, and an elaborate teakwood console, a gift from the Emperor of China.

## Notable Collections on Exhibit

The house contains the extensive collection of memorabilia of Lillian Nordica's personal and professional life. This exhibit includes elaborate concert gowns fashioned by Worth of Paris, and the mysterious insignia of Aida's festal dress. Marguerite's pale blue puffs and swinging chatelaine stand in a corner as lovely as when they appeared in the Kermesse crowd. Nordica's stage jewelry is on exhibit, glittering as if fresh from the property department. The display also includes her entire collection of opera scores, with personal notations, and choice china and glass used in her various homes.

# Harrington House

45 Main Street
Freeport, ME 04032
207-865-3170

**Contact:** Freeport Historical Society

**Open:** Mon.-Sat. 10 a.m–6 p.m.,
Sun. 12–5 p.m.

**Admission:** Free. Self guided tours,
changing exhibits of local-regional
significance, research library.

**Suggested Time to View House:** 30 minutes

**Facilities on Premises:** Gift shop

**Description of Grounds:** Open year round

**Best Season to View House:** May-Oct.

**Number of Yearly Visitors:** 3,100

**Year House Built:** 1830

**Style of Architecture:** Transitional Greek
Revival

**Number of Rooms:** 9

**On-Site Parking:** Yes  **Wheelchair Access:** No

## Description of House

Harrington House was built by general store merchant Enoch Harrington in 1830. He and his wife, Eliza Harrington, lived here until 1900
when the house was sold to the Patterson family. The Pattersons rented the
second floor rooms to shoe factory workers during the early 1900s.

This modest two-and-a-half story house is made of locally manufactured brick with the front door located on the gable end facing the side
garden. Several interior changes were made in the late 19th century including the installation of a tin ceiling in the kitchen and narrow board flooring
in the north parlor. The house also features original wallpaper and a set
kettle in the kitchen. The last original barn on Main Street in Freeport is on
the property.

Most of the period furnishings are in storage but can be seen on request.
The Harrington House Gallery Store sells many reproductions of 18th and
19th-century furniture and other artifacts.

## Notable Collections on Exhibit

An exhibit space changes every few months and includes photographs,
decorative arts and memorabilia from the collection of the Freeport Historical Society. The extensive photograph collection is catalogued and available
to researchers.

# *Pettengill Farm*

Pettengill Road
Freeport, ME 04032
(207) 865-3170

**Contact:** Freeport Historical Society
**Open:** Open year round, shown by
  appoinment only
**Suggested Time to View House:** 30 minutes
**Description of Grounds:** The house is half
  mile in on a dirt road which is not
  accessible by vehicle.

**Best Season to View House:** May-Oct.
**Number of Yearly Visitors:** 200
**Year House Built:** c.1800
**Style of Architecture:** Saltbox
**Number of Rooms:** 7
**On-Site Parking:** Yes  **Wheelchair Access:** No

## Description of House

The Pettengills purchased this picturesque property in 1876. At that time the lands included a saltmarsh, fields, woods and a saltbox-style house. Produce grown on the farm was the family's main source of income. Two children, Mildred and Frank, worked and lived on the farm until 1956.

There have been very few changes made to this simple homestead since it was first settled in the late 19th century as a salt water farm. There are three working fireplaces on the first floor, and the house was never modernized with electricity or indoor plumbing. There are some unique etchings of 19th-century sailing vessels in the plaster on the second floor.

There are period furnishings in the collection which can be viewed or studied by notifying the Freeport Historical Socity.

# The Taylor-Barry House

24 Summer Street, P.O Box 177
Kennebunk, ME 04043
(207) 985-4802

**Contact:** The Brick Store Museum
**Open:** June-Sept., Tues.-Fri. 1–4 p.m.; and by
appointment
**Admission:** $2. Guided tours.
**Suggested Time to View House:**
20–30 minutes

**Facilities on Premises:** Gift shop
**Number of Yearly Visitors:** 1,000
**Year House Built:** 1803
**Style of Architecture:** Federal
**Number of Rooms:** 4 open to the public
**On-Site Parking:** Yes  **Wheelchair Access:** No

## Description of House

The house was built for William Taylor in 1803 by housewright (designer-builder) Thomas Eaton. He followed the pattern books of Boston architect Asher Benjamin. Eaton is also known to have designed the steeple of the Unitarian Church, the front section of the William Lord Mansion next door, and other noteworthy houses in Maine. In 1818, William Taylor auctioned the house and it was purchased by Charles Williams whose wife was a member of the Lord family. The last inhabitant was Edith Cleaves Barry, great granddaughter of William Lord, and the founder of the Brick Store Museum.

The Taylor-Barry House is a five bayed Federal structure with a hipped roof and twin interior chimneys. The original windows were replaced in the 1860s with larger six over six sashes. The house retains its original hallway stenciling by Moses Eaton which was discovered when wallpaper was removed in the 1940s. The gabled entry portico was built in 1872 and was an addition designed by architect William Barry. An addition connecting the barn and the house was built in the early 1870s. All of the furniture, with the exception of three period pieces, belonged to the Barry family.

## Additional Information

The Taylor Barry House is part of a splendid architectural walking tour of Kennebunk's National Register Historic District. Contact the Brick Store Museum at (207) 985-4802 for more information.

# Nott House–White Columns

Main Street
(at the head of Spring Street)
Kennebunkport, ME 04046
(207) 967-2513

**Contact:** Kennebunkport Historical Society

**Open:** Mid June-mid Oct., Wed.-Fri.
1–4 p.m.

**Admission:** Adults $3; children $1; Friday
tea and tour of the house, $5 per person.
Guided tours.

**Suggested Time to View House:**
30–45 minutes

**Description of Grounds:** Simple
foundation plantings with a back lawn
stretching to a mill Pond.

**Best Season to View House:** May-Oct.

**Number of Yearly Visitors:** 500

**Year House Built:** 1853

**Style of Architecture:** Greek Revival

**On-Site Parking:** No

**Wheelchair Access:** No

## Description of House

White Columns was built by Eliphalet Perkins III. His son, Charles Edwin Perkins, became the owner in 1853, the year he married Celia Parker-Nott. The Perkinses were descended from one of Kennebunkport's founding families, and were the third generation to run the shipping business of "E. Perkins and Son" from the present Bookport building in Dock Square. During his lifetime, Charles Perkins was reputed to be Kennebunkport's wealthiest man. Celia Nott, was the oldest daughter of the Reverend Handel Nott, who was a minister of the Village Baptist Church from 1848 to 1860.

The matchboarded and clapboarded house, with its monumental Doric colonnade and bold triangular pediment, has been a landmark in the town since 1853. It is one of the most impressive houses in a village of extraordinary homes. This rare period house will give visitors insight into the colorful history of this seacoast town, as well as a new appreciation of the Victorian era.

The furnishings of White Columns reflect superbly the decorative taste of Victorians, who believed more was better. The house is only one of a handful in Maine to retain original wallpapers, carpets and furnishings.

## Notable Collections on Exhibit

The parlor, with its original wallpaper, brilliant carpet, chandelier, black iron mantlepiece—all of which were installed by Charles and Celia, is an exceptional period room. Another notable room is the parlor chamber with its massive black walnut bedroom set. Moreover, included among the furnishings of the house are many fine pieces from an earlier period, which belonged to Charles's parents.

# Washburn Mansion

RFD-2, Box 3395
Livermore Falls, ME 04254
(207) 897-2236

**Contact:** Washburn-Norlands Foundation

**Open:** July-Aug., Mon.-Sun. 10 a.m.–4 p.m. Please make advance reservations for groups.

**Admission:** Adults $4.50; students (K-HS) $2. Guided tours, 1870 presentations, and special programs.

**Suggested Time to View House:** 2–3 hours

**Facilities on Premises:** Gift shop, book store, and library

**Description of Grounds:** One hundred acres are accessible for carriage rides, winter sleigh rides, hay rides, wilderness skiing and year-round hiking.

**Best Season to View House:** Year round

**Number of Yearly Visitors:** 30,000

**Year House Built:** 1867

**Style of Architecture:** Italianate

**Number of Rooms:** 10

**On-Site Parking:** Yes  **Wheelchair Access:** Yes

## Description of House

The Washburn family was one of America's great political dynasties. All seven Washburn brothers played instrumental roles in the governing of the country. Israel Jr. served ten years in Congress, became Governor of Maine and was a prime organizer of the Republican party. Algernon was a prominent financier. Eliher Benjamin served eighteen years in Congress, was Secretary of State and a close personal friend of Lincoln and Grant. Cadwallader spent ten years in Congress, was governor of Wisconsin and a General in the Civil War. Charles was a foreign minister to Paraguay for eight years and inventor of a typewriter. Samuel Benjamin was a Navy captain during the Civil War. William served as both Congressman and Senator, and was a successful businessman.

This exceptional Victorian country home contains large, square high ceilinged rooms, balustrades, a central reception hall, and large kitchen. The Washburn House also has unusually ornate ceilings which are undergoing restoration. The widow's walk and wrap-around veranda enhance the beauty of the exterior. Further, the 440 acre site displays an eight room farmer's cottage for the "hired help" which is attached by way of a hallway from the Washburn kitchen. This, in turn, is connected to numerous sheds and a huge cavern of a barn. Presently it is run as an 1870 period historic farm with oxen, horses, cows, pigs, sheep and poultry.

The furnishings in the Washburn house are all personal belongings from the various members of the family. The collection on display consists of furniture, dishes, bric a brac, decorative objects, photographs and paintings.

## Notable Collections on Exhibit

Exhibits include a portrait collection by Healy, Skeele and others; an etching collection by Cadwallader Lincoln Washburn, son of William Drew; and an outstanding Washburn archival collection in the library.

## Additional Information

The house and land and the two adjoining properties comprise a National Historic District.

# The Shaker Museum

RR #1 Box 640
Poland Spring, ME 04274
(207) 926-4597

**Contact:** The United Society of Shakers

**Open:** Memorial Day-Columbus Day, Mon.-Sat. 10 a.m.–4:30 p.m.

**Admission:** Adults $3; children $1.50; group rates available. Introductory and extended tours; audiovisual presentations (fee prearranged), concerts, workshops, and demontrations.

**Suggested Time to View House:** 75 minutes

**Facilities on Premises:** Gift shop and book store

**Number of Yearly Visitors:** 8,000

**Year House Built:** Meetinghouse in 1794, Ministry Shop in 1839

**Style of Architecture:** Dutch gambrel-Meetinghouse, and Greek Revival-Ministry Shop

**Number of Rooms:** 12

**On-Site Parking:** Yes **Wheelchair Access:** No

## Description of House

The Sabbathday Lake Shaker community was established in 1783 and formally organized in 1794. Sabbathday Lake today is one of the few remaining active communities with eight Shakers in residence.

Considered the best surviving example of an intact meetinghouse, the 1794 Shaker Meetinghouse has two-and-a-half stories with clapboard siding and a gambrel roof. The meeting room for worship is on the first floor. The upper floors are former Ministry's apartments with original paint on the wall and trim. The 1839 Ministry shop is a two-and-a-half story clapboarded building with an ell. It was renovated in the mid-1870s. Two bedrooms and workrooms are on the first and second floors. The back ell has two rooms that are temporary exhibit rooms. The furnishings represent the full span of the Shaker material culture from the 18th century into this century.

## Notable Collections on Exhibit

The permanent exhibits include displays of furniture and artifacts which represent the major periods of Shaker design; Primitive (c.1780-1820), Classic (c.1820-1860), Victorian (c.1860-1910) and represent all the major Shaker settlements. The temporary exhibits feature many themes including the work of the individual Shaker craftsmen, comestibles, textiles, and visual arts.

# Wadsworth-Longfellow House

485 Congress Street
Portland, ME 04101
(207) 774-1807

**Contact:** Maine Historical Society

**Open:** June-mid Oct., Tues.-Sat.
10 a.m.–4 p.m.

**Admission:** Adults $3; children under 12 $1.
Self-guided tours with staff present to
answer questions, Dec. holiday program.

**Suggested Time to View House:** 1 hour

**Facilities on Premises:** Gift shop, book store,
Maine Historical Society Library

**Description of Grounds:** The garden in the
back of house creates a surprising "oasis"
in the middle of downtown Portland.

**Style of Architecture:** Georgian, with some
Federal additions and remodeling

**Best Season to View House:** Summer

**Number of Yearly Visitors:** 6,500

**Year House Built:** 1785-86

**Number of Rooms:** 8 open to public

**On-Site Parking:** No  **Wheelchair Access:** No

## Description of House

The famed 19th century poet Henry Wadworth Longfellow spent his childhood in this house. His grandfather, General Peleg Wadsworth (1748-1829), built the house after fighting in the American Revolution. General Wadworth also served six terms in the U.S. Congress. One of his daughters, Zilpah (1778-1851) married Stephen Longfellow (1776-1849), a lawyer who also served one term in Congress. One of the poet's sisters, Anne Longfellow Pierce, lived in the house almost her entire life. She left the house to the Maine Historical Society when she died in 1901.

The Wadsworth-Longfellow House is the last vestige of 18th century Portland to be found on Congress Street, Portland's main artery. It was the first private residence in the city to be built entirely of brick. This three story, hip-roofed structure was originally two stories with a gable roof. In 1814, the house caught fire and the roof was destroyed. A third story was added when the house was restored. The house apparently never had gas lines although they were available in the area in the 1950s, or running water as the house was the last on the Portland peninsula to have an outdoor privy.

All furnishings are from the three generations of the family who lived here from 1785 to 1901 the year that it opened as an historic house museum.

## Notable Collections on Exhibit

The collection spans much of the 19th century with a few family pieces from the 18th century. Most of the furniture is early to mid-19th century, often of local manufacture. A needlework collection includes samplers based on the work of artists Charles Bird King and Eastman Johnson, among others, and crocheted tablecloths made by the family. Visitors will also be intrigued by a writing-arm Windsor chair.

# Tate House

**Contact:** National Society of Colonial Dames in Maine

**Open:** July 1-Labor Day; Tues.-Sat. 10 a.m.–4 p.m. and Sun. 1–4 p.m.; Sept.-Oct.; Fri.-Sat. 10a.m.–4 p.m. and Sun. 1–4p.m.

**Admission:** Adults $3; children (under 12) $1. Guided tours by appointment and audiovisual presentations.

**Suggested Time to View House:** 45 minutes

**Description of Grounds:** The grounds contain 18th-century plantings and a raised bed herb garden overlooking the Stroudwater River.

**Best Season to View House:** June-Aug.

**Number of Yearly Visitors:** 3,000

**Year House Built:** 1755

**Number of Rooms:** 8

**Style of Architecture:** Georgian

**On-Site Parking:** Yes  **Wheelchair Access:** No

## Description of House

George Tate came to America in 1751, after a successful career as the captain of a mast ship in the Baltics. He was a father of four sons, two of whom supported England during the American Revolution. His fourth son became a Senator in Russia and was also the First Admiral of the Russian Navy under Tsar Alexander First.

The Tate House is a large and elegant dwelling built in 1755, to mark Captain George Tate's success and status in the community. This Georgian style home is one of two houses in Maine with an unusual indented clerestory gambrel and a large central chimney, which creates the impression of a full third floor. Further, it is the only remaining residence of an English mast agent in the US. While the furnishings did not belong to the Tates, they bring into focus the lives of the family, and the social and economic issues of colonial Maine.

## Notable Collections on Exhibit

The collection is based on local archeology, inventories and history; it reflects home life in the province of Maine of a wealthy merchant. Also on display is an exceptional collection of chairs, pottery, porcelain, textiles, prints, silver, and ironware.

# The Victoria Mansion

109 Danforth Street
Portland, ME 04101
(207) 772-4841

**Contact:** Victoria Society of Maine

**Open:** June-early Oct., Tues.-Sat.
10 a.m.–4 p.m.; Sun. 1–4 p.m. Closed
July 4 and Labor Day

**Admission:** Adults $4; ages 6-18 $1.50;
under 6 free. Senior citizen discounts
available. Guided tours.

**Suggested Time to View House:**
45 minutes minimum

**Facilities on Premises:** Gift shop,
book store

**Description of Grounds:** Urban site

**Best Season to View House:** Summer
and fall

**Number of Yearly Visitors:** 12,000

**Year House Built:** 1858 to 1860

**Style of Architecture:** Italianate Villa

**Number of Rooms:** 14 plus vast halls

**On-Site Parking:** No

**Wheelchair Access:** No

## Description of House

This magnificent villa in the heart of downtown Portland was built in the 1850's for Ruggles Sylvester Morse (1816-93), a successful hotel entrepeneur.

The Victoria House, also known as the Morse-Libby House, is one of the country's finest examples of Italianate Villa. Designed by New Haven architect Henry Austin, the house is constructed of brownstone and features a tall, square tower. The opulent Victorian interior displays colorful frescoes, richly carved woodwork, and brilliant stained and etched glass. This remarkable house has been described as "an encyclopedia of mid-19th-century decoration, domestic life and determined elegance."

The interior finish and all furnishings were designed or commissioned by Gustav Herter, founder of Herter Bros.

## Notable Collections on Exhibit

All of the furniture, paintings, fabrics, sculpture, and lighting devices owned by the Morses are on display and provide insight into the lifestyle of a wealthy Victorian.

## Additional Information

The Victorian Mansion was a designated a National Historic Landmark in 1971.

# Farnsworth Homestead

19 Elm Street
Rockland, ME 04841
(207) 596-6457

**Contact:** Farnsworth Art Museum

**Open:** June 1-Sept. 30, Mon.-Sat.
10 a.m.–4:30 p.m. and Sun. 1–4 p.m.

**Activities:** Annual Victorian lawn party in August

**Suggested Time to View House:**
30 minutes–1 hour

**Facilities on Premises:** Museum

**Description of Grounds:** Recreated Victorian gardens with seating and tables.

**Best Season to View House:** Summer

**Number of Yearly Visitors:** 4,000

**Year House Built:** 1850

**Style of Architecture:** Greek Revival, Victorian interior

**Number of Rooms:** 12

**On-Site Parking:** Yes  **Wheelchair Access:** No

## Description of House

Mr. William Farnsworth was a prosperous Rockland businessman. He began his business with a general store in the 1840s. He soon became involved in the limestone industry, a staple of the local economy. He also held a number of real estate holdings throughout the city. In addition, Farnsworth was a founder and early president of the Rockland Water Company. William and his wife Mary had six children. Their daughter, Lucy lived in the home until her death in 1935. She left a sizable estate, the majority to be used to establish the William A. Farnsworth Library and Art Museum as a memorial to her father.

This Greek Revival home was built on a much larger scale than most of the neighborhood homes. It is two full stories, with twelve rooms and a spacious attic. A large carriage house was attached to the main house via a breezeway, a common feature in New England extended architecture. In the front of the house on the first floor is a parlor and a sitting room, both have elaborate fireplaces with faux marble facades reverse-painted on glass panels. Furnishings are original to the period and belonged to the Farnsworth family.

The kitchen contains an 1848 Walker's Range #7, a great improvement over the open hearths that were still widely used at the time. Another distinctive feature can be seen in the hand-grained woodwork in the kitchen and dining room. Two bedrooms in the house have marble sinks with hot and cold water taps.

# Fowler-True-Ross House

Church Street
Searsport, ME 04974
207-548-2529

**Contact:** Penobscot Marine Museum
**Open:** May 30-Oct.15, Mon.-Sat.
9:30 a.m.–5 p.m., Sun. 1–5 p.m.
**Admission:** Adults $4; seniors $3.50,
children (7-15) $1.50., under 6 free.
Guided tours.
**Suggested Time to View House:** 30 minutes
**Facilities on Premises:** Museum store

**Best Season to View House:** Summer and
fall
**Number of Yearly Visitors:** 15,000
**Year House Built:** 1820
**Style of Architecture:** Federal
**Number of Rooms:** 8
**On-Site Parking:** Yes **Wheelchair Access:** Yes

## Description of House

The seafaring legacy of Searsport is well served by the Fowler-Ross-True House. In the late 19th century, Searsport was recognized for shipbuilding and as the hailing port of numerous foreign trade vessels. This small home was originally constructed by Captain Miles Fowler who willed it to his son Captain Rufus Fowler. In 1873, he passed it to brother Cyrus Trye, and in 1905 to nephew Andrew McGilvery Ross, a ship captain. The daughter, Rebecca, inherited the house in 1932.

The Fowler House and adjoing barn typify the "post and beam" construction of the early 19th century. This small, clapboard house is actually part of a historic district known as the Penobscot Marine Museum. The district has several other historic houses, including the Captain Merithew House (c. 1860) and an historic town hall.

The furnishings are collected and appropriate to the period 1800 to 1910. A Samuel Mose desk is among the notable items found here.

## Notable Collections on Exhibit

The exhibit traces the story of the Dow and Eaton families of Searsport and their seafaring legacy. Mementoes of their seagoing days can be seen in the unique collection of China trade porcelains, Chinese port ship portraits, and Chinese laquerware.

# Hamilton House

Vaughan's Lane
South Berwick, ME 03908
(603) 436-3205

**Contact:** Soc. for the Preservation for New England Antiquities

**Open:** June-mid Oct., Tues., Thurs., Sat.-Sun. 12–5 p.m.

**Admission:** $4. Guided tours on the hour.

**Suggested Time to View House:** 1 hour

**Description of Grounds:** Formal gardens

**Year House Built:**c. 1785

**Style of Architecture:** Georgian

**On-Site Parking:** Yes

## Description of House

After railroads made the region accessible in the late 19th century, coastal Maine became a fashionable destination for wealthy summer people. Many of the newcomers bought and restored the fine old houses built during the prosperous years following the Revolution. In 1898, Mrs. Emily Tyson and her stepdaughter, Elise, purchased the Hamilton House, built on a magnificent site overlooking the Salmon Falls River, and flung themselves into a lifelong project to restore it to its former splendor.

The Tysons were influenced by literary imagery, including the writings of their friend and neighbor Sarah Orne Jewett, in their decoration and restoration efforts. They decorated the house with a mixture of elegant antiques, painted murals, wallpaper, and simple country furnishings to create their own romantic interpretation of America's colonial past.

## Additional Information

The extensive grounds include a formal garden. Paths provide access to a nearby state park. Summer events include Sunday concerts in the garden.

Summertime visitors to South Berwick should also take the opportunity to visit the historic Counting House located on the corner of Main and Liberty Streets. This Greek Revival building, originally the business office for a local cotton mill, contains a ballroom on the second floor which has been restored to its original splendor. The first floor houses a small museum and library which displays a collection of papers, photographs, and artifacts of local historical significance. The Counting House is open Saturdays in July and August from 1–4 p.m.

# *Sarah Orne Jewett House*

5 Portland Street
South Berwick, ME 03908
(603) 436-3205

**Contact:** Soc. for the Preservation for
New England Antiquities

**Open:** June-mid Oct., Tues.,Thurs.,
Sat.-Sun. 12–5 p.m.

**Admission:** $4. Guided tours on the hour,
annual birthday celebration on
September 3rd.

**Suggested Time to View House:** 1 hour

**Facilities:** Bookstore

**Year House Built:** 1774

**Style of Architecture:** Georgian

**On-Site Parking:** Yes

## Description of House

Writer Sarah Orne Jewett spent most of her life in this stately Georgian residence, owned by her family since 1819. The view from her desk in the second-floor hall surveys the town's major intersection and provided her with material for her books, such as *The Country of the Pointed Firs*, which describe the character of the Maine countryside and seacoast with accuracy and affection.

In decorating the house for their own use, Jewett and her sister expressed both a pride in their family's past and their own independent, sophisticated tastes. The result is an eclectic mix of 18th-century architecture, antiques, and old wallpapers with furnishings showing the influence of the Arts and Crafts movement.

## Additional Information

Jewett was also interested in preserving the Hamilton House, also located in South Berwick, which she used as the setting for her historical novel *The Tory Lover*. Every year the Friends of Sarah Orne Jewett host a birthday celebration at the house and maintain a selection of books by and about the author for sale at the house.

# Kinsley House

83 Main Road
South Hampden, ME 04444
(207) 862-2027

**Contact:** The Hampden Historical Society
**Open:** Tue. 10 a.m.–4 p.m.; or by appointment
**Admission:** Adults $1; children (12-18) $.50; under 12, free. Guided tours (by appointment), gourmet dinners, guest speakers, and private parties.
**Suggested Time to View House:** 1 hour

**Facilities on Premises:** Complete working blackshop
**Best Season to View House:** Summer
**Number of Yearly Visitors:** 500
**Year House Built:** 1794
**Style of Architecture:** Federal-Colonial
**Number of Rooms:** 9
**On-Site Parking:** Yes  **Wheelchair Access:** Yes

## Description of House

Martin Kinsley lived in the house from 1800 to 1835. After graduating from Harvard in 1778, he served as a postmaster, judge, representative to the Massachusetts legislature and a United States Senator. As a Senator, Kinsley was a member of the Missouri Compromise in 1820. The house also holds the unusual historical distinction of having been advanced upon by British troops during the Battle of Hampden in 1814.

Visitors to the Kinsley House will immediately notice a wealth of extraordinary 18th-century details. Visitors are welcomed through a fan light front door leading to the interior. Once inside the house, the pine board floors, stenciled walls, and Christian doors demonstrate the attention given to particulars in colonial America. The furnishings are collected and appropriate for the period.

## Notable Collections on Exhibit

There is an unusual variety of collections on display. One notable example is a complete recreation of Hannibal Hamlin's law office including an exact replica of his desk, an original bookcase and law books. A complete bedroom from the 1800s with a nanny's bench is on exhibit. The dining room displays fawn chairs from Hannibal Hamlin's office in Washington D.C.; a floor to ceiling hutch c. 1864, a bookcase, a parlor organ. In addition, the house exhibits memorabilia from the S.S. Belfast, a steamship which transported residents by river between Hampden and Boston.

# Marrett House

Route 25
Standish, ME 04084
(207) 642-3032

**Contact:** Soc. for the Preservation of
New England Antiquities
**Open:** May 15-Sept. 1, Tues, Thurs., Sat.
and Sun 12–5 p.m.; tours on the hour
**Admission:** $4. Perennial and Herb sale.
**Description of Grounds:** The extensive
herb and perennial garden, which they
laid out in the 1920s and 1930s, has been
restored.
**Year House Built:** 1789

## Description of House

In 1796, young Daniel Marrett, a recent Harvard graduate, moved to Standish to become the town parson. The grand house reflected his status as the community's leading citizen. The house remained in the family for three generations.

This grand colonial house has been enlarged and updated over the years by residents but left many furnishings and interior arrangements as relics of the past. The southwest parlor remains as it was in 1847.

Many of the furnishings are of the same period as the house and belonged to the Marrett family.

## Additional Information

In 1889, the family celebrated the house's centennial by refurbishing several of the rooms with reproduction heirloom wallpapers and bedhangings and organizing a large family reunion to honor the Marrett legacy. Today, the visitor can see the layering of eras and tastes that occurs when a family resides in a house for three generations.

# Historic Meetinghouse Museum

P.O. Box 801
Wells, ME 04090
(207) 646-4775

**Contact:** Historical Society of Wells & Ogunuit, Inc.
**Open:** Winter, Thur. 1–4p.m.; May 15–Oct. 15, Wed., Thur., Sat. 9 a.m.–1 p.m.
**Admission:** $2 donation suggested. Guided tours.
**Suggested Time to View House:** 30–60 minutes

**Facilities on Premises:** Historical and Genealogical Research Library and gift shop
**Number of Yearly Visitors:** 200 plus
**Year House Built:** 1862
**Style of Architecture:** Mix of Romanesque and Gothic
**Number of Rooms:** 6
**On-Site Parking:** Yes  **Wheelchair Access:** No

## Description of House

The Historic First Church of Wells was built over a century ago while the country was being torn apart by the Civil War. While not a dwelling, the museum's period rooms provide wonderful insight into life in 19th-century Maine. The church now houses a local history museum with rooms devoted to early residents of Wells and the local shipbuilding industry. One room is devoted to Edmund Littlefield, the first permanent settler, known as the "Father of Wells." Through his family's efforts the first saw and grist mills were operational on the town's rivers. The availability of these mills was an important factor in enticing additional settlers to this frontier community.

The former first Congregational Church is an intact wooden frame building with a three stage tower and a mix of Romanesque and Gothic detailing. The present church stands on or near the site occupied three earlier structures, the first of which is thought to have been erected in 1664. Although the exterior of the church is rather modest in its configuration and not unlike other Maine churches, the interior detailing is unusual and well worth a visit.

## Notable Collections on Exhibit

The meeting house also displays the Barbara Kimball Collection (art of stenciling) and early Wells photography of Leroy Nason. In addition, artifacts, artwork and handicraft portray an earlier era when horse and buggies brought people to these doors.

# Nickels-Sortwell House

Corner of Main and
Federal St., Route 1
Wiscasset, ME 04578
(207) 882- 6218

**Contact:** Soc. for the Preservation of
New England Antiquities
**Open:** June 1-Sept. 30, Wed.-Sun. 12–5 p.m.;
tours on the hour
**Admission:** $4. Guided tours.

**Description of Grounds:** The grounds,
landscaped in 1926 with period gardens
and an elaborate classical fence, are being
restored.
**Year House Built:** 1807

## Description of House

The house was built by Captain William Nickels, a ship owner and
trader. Soon after the house was built, however, the Embargo Act of 1807,
followed by the War of 1812, crippled the shipping industry, and many
coastal families lost their fortunes. Around 1930, the house was transformed
into a hotel. Towards the end of the century, when the Maine coast had
become fashionable as a summer resort, Alvin Sortwell purchase the building as a summer residence. He and his daughter refurbished it in the
Colonial Revival manner.

The Nickels-Sortwell Houses's elegant facade dominates the main street
of Wiscasset. Its architecture recalls a period when ship-building and the
maritime trade brought prosperity and sophisticated tastes to this riverside
community. Like the society's other properties, the house is filled with fine
examples of period furniture.

# Sayward-Wheeler House

79 Barrell Lane
York Harbor, ME 03911
(603) 436-3205

**Contact:** Soc. for the Preservation of
New England Antiquities
**Open:** June 1-Oct. 15, Wed.-Sun. 12–5 p.m.
Tours on the hour.

**Admission:** $4. Guided tours.
**Description of Grounds:** Waterfront
**Year House Built:** 1718

## Description of House

The Sayward-Wheeler House was home to Jonathan Sayward, a local merchant and civic leader. Sayward participated in the attack on the French fortress at Louisburg, Nova Scotia, in 1745, served as representativve to the Massachusetts General Court, and despite outspoken Tory views,retained the respect of his neighbors during the Revolution. His descendants made very few changes to the house after his death, in part, this was due to the family's reverence for the founding partriarch.

This beautiful colonial house overlooks what once was a thriving water-front. Jonathan Sayward remodeled and furnished the house in the 1760s according to his own conservative taste. After his death, his heirs and descendants made very few changes to the house. As early as the 1860s, Saywards descendants opened the house to visitors to show how their ancestors had lived in colonial days. By the early 20th century, the house was refurbished for use as a summer residence, with fresh wall-papers and white-painted woodwork, but the original furnishings and family portraits remain in place. Today, the house still projects the sturdy, independent character of provincial New England in the mid 18th century. The furnishing are original and belonged to the Sayward family.

# Massachusetts

## 1. Amesbury
*Mary Baker Eddy Historic House*
*John Greenleaf Whittier Home*

## 2. Amherst
*Amherst History Museum and*
*18th-Century Garden*

## 3. Andover
*Amos Blanchard House and*
*Barn Museum*

## 4. Ashley Falls
*The Col. John Ashley House*

## 5. Belchertown
*Stone House*

6. **Beverly**
   *John Cabot House*

7. **Boston**
   *Harrison Gray Otis House*
   *Nichols House*
   *Old State House*
   *The Paul Revere House*
   *The Pierce-Hichborn House*

8. **Braintree**
   *General Sylvanus Thayer*
   *Birthplace*

9. **Brookline**
   *John F. Kennedy National*
   *Historic Site*
   *Longyear Family Mansion*

10. **Cambridge**
    *Hooper-Lee-Nichols House*

11. **Centerville**
    *Mary Lincoln House*

12. **Chatham**
    *Atwood House*

13. **Concord**
    *Alcott/Orchard House*

14. **Cummington**
    *William Cullen Bryant*
    *Homestead*

15. **Danvers**
    *Glen Magna*
    *Jeremiah Page House*
    *Rebecca Nurse Homestead*

16. **Deerfield**
    *Ashley House*
    *Historic Deerfield*
    *Indian House*
    *Wells-Thorne House*

17. **Dorchester**
    *William Clapp House*

18. **Falmouth**
    *Conant House Museum*
    *The Julia Wood House*

19. **Gloucester**
    *Beauport-Sleeper-McCann House*

20. **Hadley**
    *Porter-Phelps-Huntington*
    *Historic House Museum*

21. **Lexington**
    *Hancock-Clarke House*

22. **Lincoln**
    *Codman House-The Grange*
    *Gropius House*

23. **Manchester-by-the-Sea**
    *Trask House*

24. **Marblehead**
    *Jeremiah Lee Mansion*

25. **Nantucket**
    *Hadwen House*
    *Jethro Coffin House*
    *Macy-Christian House*

26. **New Bedford**
    *Rotch-Jones-Duff House and*
    *Garden Museum*

27. **Newbury**
    *Coffin House*
    *Spencer-Pierce-Little Farm*

28. **Newburyport**
    *Cushing House*

29. **North Oxford**
    *Clara Barton Birthplace Museum*

30. **Pittsfield**
    *1830 Brick Dwelling*
    *Arrowhead*

### 31. Plymouth
*Harlow Old Fort House*
*Hedge House*
*Plimoth Plantation*
*Spooner House*

### 32. Quincy
*Adams National Historic Site*
*Quincy Homestead*

### 33. Salem
*Derby House*
*Narbonne House*

### 34. Sandwich
*Hoxie House*

### 35. Saugus
*Iron Works House*

### 36. Sheffield
*Dan Raymond House*

### 37. Stockbridge
*Merwin House-Tranquility*
*The Mission House*
*The Naumkeag Museum*
*  and Gardens*

### 38. Stoughton
*Mary Baker Eddy Historic House*

### 39. Sturbridge
*Old Sturbridge Village*

### 40. Topsfield
*Parson Capon House*

### 41. Waltham
*Gore Place*
*Lyman Estate, Vale House*

### 42. Wayland
*Grout-Heard House*

### 43. Wellesley Hills
*Dadmun-McNamara House*

### 44. Wenham
*Claflin-Richards House*

### 45. West Springfield
*The Phillips House*
*The Potter Mansion*

### 46. Yarmouth Port
*Winslow Crocker House*

# Mary Baker Eddy Historic House

277 Main Street
Amesbury, MA 01913
(617) 388-1361

**Contact:** Longyear Museum and Historical Society
**Open:** May-Oct., Tues.-Sun. 1–4 p.m.
**Admission:** $1.50.  Guided tours.
**Suggested Time to View House:** 30 minutes

**Facilities on Premises:** Gift area
**Description of Grounds:** Yard
**Year House Built:**
**On-Site Parking:** Yes **Wheelchair Access:** No

## Description of House

This is the home of Sarah Bagley. Mary Baker Eddy lived here several times during the period of 1868 to 1870. It was here that Mary Baker Eddy, who discovered Christian Science in 1866, began her first teaching manual, *The Science of Man*.

The furnishings are from the Bagley family, from whom Mary Baker Eddy had rented rooms.

## Additional Information

Visitors interested in Mary Baker Eddy's life are encouraged to visit some, or all, of the Longyear Museum's other properties in Swampscott, Stoughton, and Brookline. Contact the Longyear Museum for more information.

# John Greenleaf Whittier Home

**86 Friend Street**
**Amesbury, MA 01903**
**(508) 388-1337**

**Contact:** Whittier Home Association

**Open:** May 1-Oct. 31, Tues.-Sat.
10 a.m.–4 p.m.

**Admission:** Adults $3; children $1.
Guided tours, audiovisual presentations,
and special programs for groups.

**Suggested Time to View House:**
30 minutes–1 hour

**Facilities on Premises:** Books and gifts
relating to the Whittier home

**Description of Grounds:** There is a lovely
garden in the rear of the house and a
summer kitchen.

**Best Season to View House:**
Spring-summer

**Number of Yearly Visitors:** 400

**Year House Built:** 1826

**Number of Rooms:** 6 rooms open to the
public

**Style of Architecture:** Victorian

**On-Site Parking:** Yes  **Wheelchair Access:** No

## Description of House

The house is owned and maintained by the Whittier Home Association,
a society of Amesbury women who, in 1918, purchased the house and its
contents from Mr. Whittier's heirs. The house is a memorial to the Quaker
poet and abolitionist John Greenleaf Whittier, who, during his long life
covering most of the 19th century, made outstanding contributions to the
life and literature of his country. As a young man Whittier was an editor of
several anti-slavery newspapers and wrote poems and articles against
slavery. After the Civil War and after his family died, he became nostalgic
and began to write poetry about his boyhood. He was prominent in literary
circles in Boston and was a friend of Longfellow, Emerson, Lucy Larcom,
and Oliver Wendell Holmes.

The John Greenleaf Whittier Home was built in 1826. This beautiful
Victorian house is painted white and has dark green blinds. Although there
have been many additions, the rooms and the furnishings of the main house
remain nearly the same as when the family occupied them.

## Notable Collections on Exhibit

There are beautiful portraits of Whittier, his brother and mother done
by the itinerant artist Gallatin Holt. There are also several Rogers groups
sculptures and painted miniatures.

## Additional Information

In the Garden Room, John Greenleaf Whittier wrote all the poetry, prose,
and editorial work of over forty years, including "Snow Bound" and the
"Eternal Goodness."

# Amherst History Museum and 18th-Century Garden

**67 Amity Street
Amherst, MA 01002
(413) 256-0678**

**Contact:** Amherst Historical Society

**Open:** Mid May-mid Oct., Wed.-Sat.
2–4 p.m.

**Admission:** Adults $2; children (under 12) free; $25 for groups of ten and over. Guided tours.

**Suggested Time to View House:** 30 minutes

**Facilities on Premises:** Gift shop

**Best Season to View House:** Spring-fall

**Number of Yearly Visitors:** 450

**Year House Built:** 1740

**Style of Architecture:** Connecticut Valley Colonial

**Number of Rooms:** 6

**On-Site Parking:** Yes **Wheelchair Access:** Yes

## Description of House

The house belonged to Nehemiah and Hannah Strong, originally Northampton farmers. Following generations of the Strong family helped build Amherst College, went to Yale, became doctors, lawyers and were represented in the state legislature.

The Amherst History Museum at the Strong House was built in the mid-18th century. The home was contructed as a saltbox around a huge central chimney with two rooms on the main floor and two upstairs. The timber frame construction was assembled by local villagers using handmade nails. Hand-hewn corner timbers and ceiling beams can still be seen. The clapboard walls were insulated with straw and mud. Stylistic changes have been made over time and changing tastes in architecture of interior design are evident.

With the exception of the 18th-century bedroom, virtually all of the furniture and arifacts on display in the house date from the 19th century. The floral decorative motifs in the rugs and vases, the heavy velvet covered furniture, and the oil lamps—originally whale oil and later kerosene—are all prime examples of the Victorian style.

## Notable Collections on Exhibit

The house exhibits oil portraits of Amherst residents of the 18th and 19th centuries, decorative arts, 18th and 19th-century furniture, English and China trade tableware, a loom room, a military room, and tool shed.

# *Amos Blanchard House and Barn Museum*

97 Main Street
Andover, MA 01810
(508) 475-2236

**Contact:** Andover Historical Society

**Open:** Mon.-Fri. 9 a.m.–5 p.m.; Wed. evenings until 8:30 p.m.

**Admission:** Adults $2; students $1. Guided tours (1–3 p.m. only), lectures, workshops, slide tape shows, field trips, concerts.

**Suggested Time to View House:** 1 hour

**Facilities on Premises:** Research library

**Description of Grounds:** Side yard used for lunch-time programs

**Best Season to View House:** May-Sept.

**Number of Yearly Visitors:** 5,000

**Year House Built:** 1819 (barn); 1820 (house)

**Number of Rooms:** 5

**Style of Architecture:** Federal

**On-Site Parking:** No **Wheelchair Access:** No

## Description of House

The house was built for Amos Blanchard, the first clerk at the Andover National Bank, and he lived here until his death in 1847. Later occupants include deacon Edward Taylor and Dr. Selah Merrill who served for many years as the United States consul in Jerusalem.

This Federal-style home is filled with early American and imported furnishings and artifacts. Trained guides introduce visitors to the life and times of a middle class Andover businessman and his family. Their lives are discussed in the context of America's early 19th-century transition from an agricultural to an industrial economy and new developments in household management, education, religion and politics.

## Notable Collections on Exhibit

Temporary exhibitions in the society's two gallery spaces feature significant themes in the life of Andover and its people. In all, the museum's collection total over 12,000 objects, most with local histories of ownership or manufacture. Visitors with a particular interest in furniture portraits, ceramics, glass, metalware or textiles are invited to make an appointment to examine the society's extensive study collections. The largest and most noteworthy is the fine collection of women's and children's costumes from the late 18th century to the present.

## Additional Information

The adjoining barn museum contains an extensive collection of 19th-century agricultural and animal husbandry equipment, woodworking tools and even a human-drawn fire pump.

# The Col. John Ashley House

Cooper Hill Road, Box 128
Ashley Falls, MA 01222
(413) 229-8600

**Contact:** The Trustees of Reservations

**Open:** Memorial Day-Columbus Day, Wed.-Sun. and holidays 1–5 p.m.

**Admission:** Adults $3.50; children (6-12) $1; groups of 15 plus $3. Guided house tours.

**Suggested Time to View House:** 45 minutes to 1 hour

**Description of Grounds:** The house is located on a 227 acres reservation with Bartholomew's Cobble abbuting the Ashley House. There are excellent walking trails bordering the Housatonic River.

**Best Season to View House:** Spring and summer

**Number of Yearly Visitors:** 1300

**Year House Built:** 1735

**Number of Rooms:** 9

**Style of Architecture:** Colonial

**On-Site Parking:** Yes **Wheelchair Access:** No

## Description of House

The oldest dwelling in Berkshire County, this mansion is rich in colonial history. The house was built by the early patriot and farmer John Ashley for his Dutch bride, Hannah Hogeboom, of Claverack New York. In the five years between his graduation from Yale and his marriage, John had surveyed land in Sheffield and had read sufficient law to be admitted to the bar of Hampshire County. As his father's agent in profitable business ventures, he was active in the sawmill, gristmill and iron foundry on the Iron Works River in the village that came to be called Ashley Falls. Col. John Ashley would become a leading citizen of Sheffield.

The Ashley House is famous for being the site of the "Sheffield Declaration", a petition against British tyranny, written in 1773. Another celebrated legal decision also took place here, the Mum Bett affair in which a slave won her freedom. In addition to its historic significance, this beautiful colonial house is worth a visit just to see its exquisite paneling. A few pieces of furniture remain from the Ashley family, but most of the collection was collected at a later time.

Ashley Mansion is located in an area of Berkshire county which has not changed in 200 years, visitors can truly appreciate the house in its natural environment.

## Notable Collections on Exhibit

There is an excellent collection of redware pieces and early industrial tools on exhibit.

# *Stone House*

P.O. Box 1211
Belchertown, MA 01007
(413) 323-6573

**Contact:** Belchertown Historical Association
**Open:** May-Oct., Wed.-Sat. 2–5 p.m.; special
    tours by appointment
**Admission:** Adults $3; children $.50.
    Guided tours.

| | |
|---|---|
| **Suggested Time to View House:** 1 hour | **Best Season to View House:** Spring-fall |
| **Number of Yearly Visitors:** 500 | **Year House Built:** 1827 |
| **Style of Architecture:** Federal | **Number of Rooms:** 10 |
| **On-Site Parking:** Yes | **Wheelchair Access:** No |

## Description of House

The Stone House was built in 1827 by Jonathan Dwight as a wedding present for his daughter, Julia Diantha. Until it was acquired by the Belchertown Historical Association in 1921, it remained in related branches of the Dwight family for nearly a century.

The Stone House Museum is a complex of three buildings consisting of a gracious early 19th-century home, a stone barn, and a printshop where Belchertown's newspaper, *The Sentinel*, was first published. The Federal-style building is constructed entirely of stone, a most unusual Connecticut Valley medium. The house is furnished with furniture donated by local residents in the period of 1827 to 1860.

## Notable Collections on Exhibit

The Stone House has one of the largest museum collections of Rogers Group sculptures in New England. These Plaster-of-Paris works typified rural American life, the work of John Rogers, active during the years 1859 to 1889. On display upstairs are fine laces, elaborate hats and gowns that conjure up the images of fashionable ladies preparing for an evening of card-playing or dancing. In the upstairs children's room, visitors can see dolls of all shapes and sizes, along with Mary Sanford's 1863 doll house, mechanical and stuffed toys, games and other items that amused the younger folk. On display throughout the museum is a large and varied collection of Staffordshire china, glass and pottery—items typical of those used by families in the 1800s.

# John Cabot House

117 Cabot Street
Beverly, MA 01915
(508) 922-1186

**Contact:** Beverly Historical Society and Museum

**Open:** Wed.-Sat., 10 a.m.–4 p.m.

**Admission:** Adults $2; children $1; seniors $1.50. Guided tours, exhibits.

**Suggested Time to View House:** 45 minutes

**Facilities on Premises:** Book store/research library

**Number of Yearly Visitors:** 2,000

**Year House Built:** 1781

**Style of Architecture:** Federal

**Number of Rooms:** 7

**On-Site Parking:** No

**Wheelchair Access:** Yes

## Description of House

One of the finest mansions of the Revolution era, the three story brick home was built for the wealthy merchant John Cabot, and was later the site of the tenth oldest bank in America.

Beverly's protected harbor was the most active privateering port in the early years of the Revolution; John Cabot and his brothers made a large fortune through attacking and capturing enemy vessels. By the end of the Revolution they would be identified as "by far the most wealthy in New England." Their maritime funds were invested in real estate, transportation, and new industries. Cabot and others also hold the distinction of forming the first cotton mill in America in 1787-88—an important beginning to the industrialization of their new country.

## Notable Collections on Exhibit

Beside period rooms, the Cabot House now features maritime, military and children's exhibits as well as major changing exhibits. In addition, the Edward Burley Room is an important center for marine, genealogical, and local history research. The society's extensive textile collection is also available for specialized study.

## Additional Information

There are two other houses on the site: the Balch House, one of the oldest wood-framed houses in the U.S., and the Hale House, home of Beverly's first minister active in witchcraft trials.

# Old State House

**206 Washington Street**
**Boston, MA 02109**
**(617) 720-1713**

**Contact:** The Bostonian Society
**Open:** Call to verify hours
**Admission:** Adults $1.25; students $.75;
children (6-16) $.50. Tours, programs
throughout the year.
**Number of Yearly Visitors:** 90,000 plus
**Year House Built:** 1713
**Style of Architecture:** Georgian
**Number of Rooms:** 10 open to the public
**On-Site Parking:** No
**Wheelchair Access:** Yes

### Description of House

Although not a residential dwelling, the Old State House holds a special place as a birthplace for ideas crucial to our nation's history. The Old State House was the setting for many stirring speeches and debates by dedicated patriots against the abuses of the Crown. Possibly the most significant was James Otis's speech against the Writs of Assistance in 1761, which inspired events that would eventually lead to independence. The Boston Massacre, the first blood shed in the cause of colonial resistance, occurred on the street just below the balcony on March 5, 1770, when a handful of British soldiers fired into the taunting crowd on King Street. On July 18, 1770, the Declaration of Independence was first read to the jubilant citizens of Massachusetts from the historic balcony.

In the 18th century the first floor of the Old State House served as a merchant's exchange. The basement was rented by John Hancock and others as a warehouse space. Representatives Hall, at the west end of the building, was the meeting place of the Massachusetts assembly, one of the most independent of the colonial legislatures.

### Notable Collections on Exhibit

The Bostonian Society maintains an important museum of Boston history within the Old State House. On view are paintings, prints, folk art, ship models, revolutionary War materials, and domestic artifacts which trace the political, economic, social and cultural life of the city from the early 17th century to the turn of the 20th century.

### Additional Information

The society's library is an important research facility for Boston history. Its resources encompass more than 6,000 volumes, over 1,000 maps and architectural plans, and a selection of rare manuscripts and broadsides dating from Colonial times. The Society's extensive collection of Boston views comprises over 10,000 photographs, prints, drawings and watercolors. The library is at 15 State Street, adjacent to the Old State House.

# Nichols House

55 Mount Vernon Street
Boston, MA 02108
(617) 227-6973

**Contact:** Nichols House Museum, Inc.

**Open:** June 1-Aug. 31, Tues.-Sat., 1–5 p.m.;
Sept. 1-Nov. 30, Mon., Wed. and Sat.
1–5 p.m.; Dec. 1-Feb. 28, Sat. 1–5 p.m.;
Mar. 1-May. 31; Mon., Wed., Sat. 1–p.m.

**Admission:** Adults $3; $25 minimum for
group visits scheduled off hours.
Guided tours; programs reserved as
membership priviliges.

**Suggested Time to View House:** 35 minutes

**Description of Grounds:** Small front yard
open to Mt. Vernon Street

**Best Season to View House:** Spring

**Number of Yearly Visitors:** 2,500

**Year House Built:** 1804

**Style of Architecture:** Federal

**Number of Rooms:** 17, 7 open to public

**On-Site Parking:** No **Wheelchair Access:** No

## Description of House

The original builder and owner of the house was U.S. Senator Jonathan Mason. A later owner, Arthur Nichols, was a practicing physican noted for his promotion of English bell ringing; his wife, Elizabeth, had artistic relatives and connections. Rose Standish Nichols, the last of the family to occupy the house, established the museum in a legacy. She was a noted landscape architect and lifelong pacifist who travelled extensively throughout the world and was widely known for her interest in international politics.

This impressive four-story town house was constructed in 1804, when Yankee fortunes were being amassed through mercantile trading. The original Federal design is attributed to Charles Bulfinch, the eminent architect who also designed the Massachusetts State House. Evolving architectural styles are reflected in doorframes remodeled to incorporate Greek Revival on one side, leaving the original Federal style intact on the other side. One of the main features of the house is an elegant spiral staircase in the entrance. There is a wrought iron gate at the head of the exquisite garden leading to the entrance of the house. The furnishings are authentic to the Nichols family, owner-occupants from 1885 to 1960, and are eclectic (17th to 20th century, European, American, and Oriental). This is the only Beacon Hill Boston Brahmin house open to the public.

## Notable Collections on Exhibit

The collection includes possessions accumulated over several generations including ancestral portraits, Flemish tapestries, Oriental rugs, European and Asian art, and works by America's foremost sculptor of the 19th century, Augustus Saint Gaudens.

# The Paul Revere House

19 North Square
Boston, MA 02113
(617) 523-2338

**Contact:** The Paul Revere Memorial
Association

**Open:** Nov. 1-April 14, 9:30 a.m.–4:15 p.m.;
April 15-Oct. 31, 9:30 a.m.–5:15 p.m.;
closed Mon. Jan.-March

**Admission:** Adults $2; seniors $1.50;
college students $1.50; children (5-17)
$.75. Self-guided tours, slide programs,
lectures.

**Suggested Time to View House:** 30 minutes

**Facilities on Premises:** Sales booth

**Description of Grounds:** Garden
courtyard area

**Best Season to View House:** Year-round

**Number of Yearly Visitors:** 200,000

**Year House Built:** c. 1680

**Style of Architecture:** Traditional English
post-and-beam

**Number of Rooms:** 4 rooms open to the
public

**On-Site Parking:** No

**Wheelchair Access:** Yes

## Description of House

Although named after its most famous occupant, the first owner of this modest house was actually Robert Howard, a wealthy merchant who purchased the building in 1681. Following his death in 1717, Howard's daughter inherited the house, after which the Knox family, mostly craftsmen and mariners, occupied the structure until it was sold to artisan Paul Revere in 1770. Revere sold the property in 1800, after which it became an apartment house and shop building under a series of absentee owners. In 1902, the building was purchased by a Revere descendant. The house was restored and opened as a museum in 1907-08.

The Paul Revere House is a two and a half story post and beam wooden house fronting on North Square in Boston's North End. The facade shows a second floor overhanging with pendant drops, leaded casement windows and colonial style clapboarding painted grey-green.

The Paul Revere House has very high ceilings and unusually large front rooms for a house of this type. Perhaps the most unique feature is a 2nd floor overhang at the side of the back ell portion of the building. This back overhang is so unusual that it has led to speculation that the ell was a surviving portion of an earlier structure. The house is a fine example of English building style in America and is is the only known 17th-century structure in downtown Boston.

The furnishings are mainly collected and appropriate to the period, with some exceptions. The hall is furnished to the period of the first owner, Robert Howard (c. 1680 to 1717). The remaining rooms reflect Paul Revere's lifetime (18th to early 19th century). Six pieces of furniture have a history of ownership by Revere: a bow front dresser, a sewing table, one wing chair and three Windsor chairs.

## Notable Collections on Exhibit

There are many Revere artifacts on display on display: a mezzotint of Revere from 1800, his saddlebags, eyeglasses and case, walking stick, pistols, document box, scales and weights, silver gauge and hammer, penknife and several Revere documents. Portions of the legendary Revere silver collection is also exhibited including silverware, creamers and sugar tongs. There are also two paintings showing the house, one by Rupert Sadler (1845) and the other by Sylvester P. Hodgdon (1869), along with a sketch by Hodgdon (c. 1880). A fascinating display of early maps of the northeast coast of North America by Bleau (1635) and John Speed (1676) can also be seen in the house.

# The Pierce-Hichborn House

19 North Square
Boston, MA 02113
(617) 523-2338

**Contact:** The Paul Revere Memorial Association

**Open:** Nov. 1-April 14, 9:30 a.m.–4:15 p.m.; April 15-Oct. 31, 9:30 a.m.–5:15 p.m.; closed Mon. Jan.-March

**Admission:** Adults $2; seniors $1.50; college students $1.50; children (5-17) $.75. Guided tours, summer program series on Sat., holiday program first full weekend of Dec., period theatricals on Sun. in late Aug.

**Suggested Time to View House:** 30 minutes

**Facilities on Premises:** Sales booth

**Description of Grounds:** Garden courtyard area

**Best Season to View House:** Year-round

**Number of Yearly Visitors:** 200,000

**Year House Built:** 1711

**Style of Architecture:** English Renaissance

**Number of Rooms:** 4 (open to the public)

**On-Site Parking:** No

**Wheelchair Access:** Yes

## Description of House

The Pierce-Hichborn House was first owned by Moses Pierce, a Boston glazier (window-maker). In the late 1740s, William Shippard, mariner, aquired the house. In 1781, Nathaniel Hichborn, boatbuilder and first cousin of Paul Revere, bought the house where he lived with his wife and family until his death in 1797. Various Hichborn relatives and descendants of Nathaniel owned the house until the 1860s, by which time it had become a rooming house with first floor shops like most of its neighbors. Tenants occupied the house until 1949-50, when it was restored and opened as a museum.

The Pierce-Hichborn House is one of the earliest remaining brick structures in Boston. The three story structure with attached two story ell (added c. 1805) is a fine example of American vernacular architecture in the English Renaissance style. The exterior decoration is restrained, consisting of shallow segmented arches over the doors and windows, brick belt courses between floors, large window openings, and a low, hipped roof essentially invisible from the street. Perhaps the most interesting feature of the house is its unusual shape at the street end, dictated by a house lot that intersects the street at nearly a 45 degree angle.

One of the most noteworthy features of the house is the main staircase with its turned balusters, shadow-molding, and acorn-drop decorations. The fireplaces in all four period rooms show evidence of original decorative painting, as does the ceiling of the second floor east chamber. Perhaps the most interesting feature of the house is the dragon-beam in the third floor east chamber, used to support the roof at the junction of the elongated south wall and the street wall.

The furnishings are collected and appropriate to the periods of the different owners. The first floor contains 17th and early 18th-century furniture representing the period of Moses Pierce's ownership. The Hichborn's occupancy is shown in the late 18th-century to early 19th-century pieces on the second floor.

### Notable Collections on Exhibit

The Pierce-Hichborn furniture collection contains many outstanding pieces including a late 17th-century painted pine blanket chest with decorative false graining, a cherry high chest, a maple William and Mary high chest with herringbone inlay, an English oak carved press cupboard of the late 17th century, a banjo clock with reverse glass painting of Boston's New State House, a mahogony drop leaf tea table, a field bed with early red paint, an early 18th-century ladder back arm chair with red paint, and a rush seat covered by a piece of linen.

# Harrison Gray Otis House

141 Cambridge Street
Boston, MA 02114
(617) 227-3956

**Contact:** Soc. for the Preservation for New England Antiquities

**Open:** Tues.-Fri. 12–5 p.m.; Sat. 10 a.m.–5 p.m.

**Admission:** Adults $4; seniors $2.50; children under 12 $1.50; SPNEA members free. Guided tours, call to schedule appointment for use of archives.

**Suggested Time to View House:** 1 hour

**Facilities on Premises:** Archives

**Number of Yearly Visitors:** 10,000

**Year House Built:** 1796

**Style of Architecture:** Federal

## Description of House

The Otis House exemplifies the elegant life led by Boston's governing class in the years immediately following the Revolution. Otis made a fortune developing nearby Beacon Hill, and later served as a representative in Congress, and later was mayor of Boston. He and his wife, Sally, were noted for their frequent entertaining.

Located at the foot of Beacon Hill, this was the first of three houses designed for the Otises by their friend Charles Bullfinch, the architect of the Massachusetts State House. The house's design reflects the proportions and delicate detail of the Federal style which Bullfinch introduced to Boston. The interior provides insight into social, business and family life, as well as behind-the-scenes functioning of the household. The restoration of the Otis House, with its brilliantly colored wallpapers and high-style furnishings of the Federal era, is based on meticulous historical and scientific research.

## Additional Information

The Otis House also houses the headquarters of the SPNEA and their archives of historic photographs and other primary materials relating to daily life in New England.

# General Sylvanus Thayer Birthplace

786 Washington Street
Braintree, MA 02184
(617) 848-1640

**Contact:** Braintree Historical Society
**Open:** Mid-April-mid Oct., Sat. and Sun.
1:30–4 p.m.; other times by appointment
**Admission:** Adults $1.50; children $.50.
**Suggested Time to View House:** 1–2 hours
**Facilities on Premises:** Gift shop
**Description of Grounds:** The Braintree
Garden Club maintains the period herb
gardens.
**Best Season to View House:** May-Sept.

**Number of Yearly Visitors:** 600
**Year House Built:** 1720; addition 1750;
restoration 1960
**Style of Architecture:** Early frame, Federal,
cape, saltbox
**Number of Rooms:** 5
**On-Site Parking:** Yes
**Wheelchair Access:** No

## Description of House

The original four room house was built in 1720 by Nathaniel Thayer, the great-great-grandfather of Sylvanus Thayer. Sylvanus, who would later achieve fame as a military educator, was born in 1785 in one of the upper chambers. After attending Dartmouth College and West Point, he distinguished himself in the War of 1812. Thayer later went to Europe to study military education and returned to the U.S. Military Academy where he completely organized the school, designing a new curriculum in the fields of mathematics, engineering and military strategy. For his work there, he became known as the "Father of West Point." In 1965, he was elected to the Hall of Fame for Great Americans for his work in engineering education.

Several additions have been added to the original structure over the years. In 1760, the lean-to was added and the central chimney was altered to make the large fireplace in the kitchen. Double huge windows replaced the original front leaded windows. In restoring the birthplace, the original sheathing and paneling were uncovered. The original wallpaper was found in several rooms, and all four original fireplaces were found intact behind modern boarding. The house today is very much as it was in 1785.

In furnishing the house, care has been taken to use only examples in use prior to 1785. Each piece found in the house is suitable for a well-to-do-New England farmer and landholder. These include a rare candle stand with wind screen, an oval Queen Anne table, a Charles II standing mirror, and a harmonium, circa 1640, which belonged to Peregrine White (the baby born on the Mayflower voyage to Plymouth). The house is listed on the National Register of Historic Places.

### Notable Collections on Exhibit

The basement of the house contains three rooms devoted to different aspects of history: the Braintree room, the military room, and the colonial living room.

# *John F. Kennedy National Historic Site*

**83 Beals Street**
**Brookline, MA 02146**
**(617) 566-7937**

**Contact:** National Park Service

**Open:** Year round, 10 a.m.–4:30 p.m.; closed Christmas, Thanksgiving, and New Year's Day

**Admission:** Adults $1; seniors and children (under 16) free. 20–25 minute guided tour, audiovisual presentations and educational programs; neighborhood walks in the summer.

**Suggested Time to View House:** 30 minutes

**Facilities on Premises:** Gift shop and book store

**Description of Grounds:** A small backyard

**Number of Yearly Visitors:** 16,000

**Year House Built:** 1908 to 1909

**Style of Architecture:** Colonial Vernacular

**Number of Rooms:** 7

**On-Site Parking:** No **Wheelchair Access:** No

## Description of House

John Fitzgerald Kennedy, thirty-fifth President of the United States, was born and spent his infancy in this house. In 1914, Joseph P. Kennedy purchased the Beals Street house in anticipation of his marriage to Rose Fitzgerald. They moved into it on returning from their wedding trip. Four of their nine children were born while they lived here: Joseph, at Hull Massachusetts, in 1915, John in 1917, Rosemary in 1918, and Kathleen in 1920. In 1921, when John was four years old, the family moved, having sold the house to the wife of Edward E. Moore, a closefriend and business associate. Since then the house has had various owners. The house was repurchased by the family in 1966; Rose Kennedy supervised the restoration and refurnishing of the house to its appearance in 1917.

Approximately half of the furnishings are original to the house, the rest are modern pieces, part of the Kennedy collection not original to the house and reproductions of antiques. Kennedy family personal belongings include photographs, china, and crystal.

## Additional Information

The neighborhood walking tour allows visitors to see other sites important to JFK's early years, including the Edward Devotown School, the first public school attended by the future president, the Dexter School, and St. Aidan's Catholic Church where the entire family was baptized.

# Longyear Family Mansion

120 Seaver Street
Brookline, MA 02146
(617) 277-8943

**Contact:** Longyear Museum and Historical Society

**Open:** Tues.-Sat. 10 a.m.–4:15 p.m.; Sun 1–4:15 p.m., closed month of Feb., Mondays, andd legal holidays

**Admission:** Adults $3; students and seniors $2; members free; guest of members $1.50. Special rates for AAA members. Guided tours, concerts, special programs related to subject matter, research library, publishes *Quarterly News*.

**Suggested Time to View House:** 45–60 minutes

**Facilities on Premises:** Gift shop

**Description of Grounds:** There are 8 acres of lovely grounds and gardens open to the public during museum hours.

**Best Season to View House:** April-Oct.

**Year House Built:** Originally built in 1890; then dismantled and rebuilt with some design changes from 1903 to 1906.

**Style of Architecture:** Richardson Romanesque style stone mansion

**Number of Rooms:** 88

**On-Site Parking:** Yes

**Wheelchair Access:** Yes

## Description of House

The stately mansion has an unusual history behind its beautiful facade. Originally built by John Munro Longyear, the house was enjoyed by the Longyear family from 1892 until 1902 on its promontory location above the waters of Lake Superior. However, when a new railroad line obstructed the scenic view, and Longyear was unable to find a buyer for the house he loved so dearly. Longyear consulted with architects and the builder and decided to move it to a suitable location. Various locatons were considered and Fisher Hill, Brookline, was the unanimous choice of the family. Most of the stone in the house came from two different strata of rock; one is deep brown and the other is a lighter shade with a spattered appearance known as "raindrop sandstone." Other noteworthy features include a high stained glass dome of octagonal shape above the center hall, the ornamental balustrades, the marble fireplace, and cherry woodwork in the sitting-room. There are some period furnishings that are original to the house including an Aubusson French rug and many pieces of rare furniture.

## Notable Collections on Exhibit

There are many examples of portraiture, mainly early 20th-century oils; some home furnishings collected on world travels by the Longyears but not specifically highlighted; books and manuscript material (1821-1910); textiles and personal effects from the Bagley family of Amesbury (found in their home when it was acquired by Mrs. Longyear in the 1920s). However, the main collections are related to the life and work of religious and historical figure Mary Baker Eddy (1821-1910). She was a friend of the Longyears and a border in the home in 1868 and 1870.

## Additional Information

The museum owns and maintains five other historic houses in Amesbury, Swampscott and Stoughton, Massachusetts and in Concord, North Groton and Rumney, New Hamphsire. These are all former residences of Mary Baker Eddy. (The house in Concord is not yet open to the public).

# Hooper-Lee-Nichols House

159 Brattle Street
Cambridge, MA 02138
(617) 547-4252

**Contact:** Cambridge Historical Society

**Open:** Tues. and Thur. or by appointment

**Admission:** Adults $2; seniors and children under 16 $1. Tours, winter lecture series, and school groups.

**Suggested Time to View House:** 30–40 minutes

**Description of Grounds:** Award-winning gardens maintained by the Cambridge Garden Club.

**Best Season to View House:** Spring/early summer

**Number of Yearly Visitors:** 200 plus

**Year House Built:** 1685 (original structure)

**Style of Architecture:** Federalized Georgian

**Number of Rooms:** 16 plus

**On-Site Parking:** No **Wheelchair Access:** Yes

## Description of House

The house was initially built by physician Richard Hooper and added to by his son Henry in 1716. A later occupant, Cornelius Waldo, added the third floor and the Georgian interiors when he acquired the house in 1733. Tory Judge Joseph Lee purchased the house in 1758 and used it as a "county seat" until being forced to flee the colonies on the eve of the revolution. Lee's heirs lived in the house until 1850 when George Nichols purchased the property and added the Federal balustrade. Nichols also added the distinctive French wallpapers, "Straits of Bosphorus" and "Bay of Naples," to the interior. In the early 20th century, Nichols's heirs hired colonial revival architect Joseph Chandler to build the rear addition.

One of Cambridge's famous "Tory Row" structures, the Hooper-Lee-Nichols House is the oldest dwelling on Brattle Street. The original structure was a small medieval farmhouse with steeply pitched roof and a massive chimney. It grew considerably over the years as later occupants remodeled and built additional floors and an east wing.

The house is one of the few places in New England where one can still see a rough cast wall. This 18th-century plaster technique, meant to look like stone, still baffles restoration experts. In addition, there is a colonial revival library known as the "The Chandler Room".

The current furnishing plan represents the house as it looked in the early years of the 19th century. The materials collected are Cambridge-related.

## Additional Information

Of interest to architects is the fact that the home was owned and lived in by William Emerson, dean of architecture at the Massachusetts Institute of Technology, from 1923 to 1957.

# Mary Lincoln House

513 Main Street
Centerville, MA 02632
(508) 775-0331

**Contact:** Centerville Historical Society and Museum

**Open:** mid June-Sept., Wed..-Sun. 1:30–4:30 p.m.

**Admission:** Adults $2.50; children under 12 $.50; group rates available. Guided tours with a video presentation on the history of Centerville, educational programs, lecture series, and membership events.

**Suggested Time to View House:** 1 hour

**Facilities on Premises:** Small area for selling souvenir items

**Number of Yearly Visitors:** 900

**Year House Built:** 1840

**Style of Architecture:** Cape Cod Clapboard

**Number of Rooms:** 14 in museum, 6 in Mary Lincoln House

**On-Site Parking:** No

**Wheelchair Access:** No

## Description of House

Mary Lincoln lived in this simple clapboard house her entire life (1868-1955) and, while it has no major architectural significance, the dwelling holds a treasure trove of New England history. Mary's father Clark moved to Centerville in 1840 and owned both a tin shop and a plumbing business. The Centerville Historical Society acquired the house upon Mary Lincoln's death. In her honor, the house is maintained as a Victorian house with a museum for visitors.

From the outside the house appears to be a small, typical, Victorian Cape Cod clapboard. Inside, however, the museum boasts fourteen exhibit rooms. In 1962, the Harriet Crosby Phinney Wing was added to house the extensive costume and gown collection. In 1971, the Charles Lincoln Ayling Wing was added to house the collection that Charles Ayling had collected and then donated to the Centerville Historical Society. Mr. Ayling was a prominent Centerville citizen, who dedicated a large portion of his time to acquiring items related to the history, art, and culture of Cape Cod.

Some of the furnishings are original to the residents, while others were collected. The collection in the rest of the museum spans the late 19th century and early 20th century period of Cape Cod history. Of note is a period furnished 19th-century parlor, bedroom and child's room and a completely furnished Colonial Revival kitchen.

### Notable Collections on Exhibit

The comprehensive and unusual exhibits include a 300 piece collection of quilts and costumes dating from 1650 to 1950, a large number of of European and American perfume bottles dating from 1760 to 1920, an unusual series of miniature bird carvings by Anthony Elmer Crowell (1862-1950), and a unique collection of sandwich glass. There are also paintings by Dodge MacKnight (1861-1950), marina artifacts and ship models, Civil War artifacts, children dolls and toys.

### Additional Information

The Mary Lincoln House is included in the National Register of Historic Places as part of the Centerville Historic District.

# Atwood House

347 Stage Harbor Road
Chatham, MA 02633
(508) 945-2493

**Contact:** Chatham Historical Society
**Open:** Mid June-Sept. 26, Wed.-Sat. 2–5 p.m.
**Admission:** Adults $3; under 12 free.
  Guided tours, special programs.
**Suggested Time to View House:**
  60–90 minutes

**Best Season to View House:** Summer
**Number of Yearly Visitors:** 1,200-1,500
**Year House Built:** 1752
**Style of Architecture:** Gambrel
**Number of Rooms:** 7
**On-Site Parking:** Yes

## Description of House

The house has been in the Atwood family for nearly a century—from 1752 to 1926 when it was sold to the Chatham Historical Society. From 1825 to 1850 it held a store and a school room on the second floor.

The Atwood House is one of Chatam's oldest homes. Nearby trees provided the planks and the timbers, the latter having been hewn into shape with adzes and fashioned with mortise and tenon joints firmly held with oak pins. The floor planking is typically of uneven width. The gambrel roof, which provides a full second story, is not that of the usual type of Cape Cod house. The main entrance has pilasters terminating in unusual spearhead tops. A large central brick chimney with a very wide base provides a beehive oven and fireplaces for three rooms downstairs and one upstairs. The furnishings are collected and appropriate to period.

## Notable Collections on Exhibit

The nationally known Stallknecht murals are on display in the barn. Alice Stallknecht Wight (1880-1973) completed the murals between 1941 and 1943. They depict Christ preaching from a dory behind Chatham Light, a church supper, and various people in their daily tasks. Over 150 Chatham residents are depicted, some still living and all identified. In addition, the Durand wing exhibits seashells and Sandwich glass, and the New Gallery has an unusual exhibit of portraits of Cape Cod sea captains.

# Alcott/Orchard House

399 Lexington Road
Concord, MA 01742
(508) 369-4118

**Contact:** Louisa May Alcott Memorial
Association
**Activities:** Guided tours, special programs,
living history
**Suggested Time to View House:**
30–40 minutes
**Facilities on Premises:** Gift shop, book store
**Best Season to View House:** Spring
**Number of Yearly Visitors:** 30,000
**Year House Built:** 1690
**Number of Rooms:** 9 for visitors
**On-Site Parking:** No **Wheelchair Access:** No

## Description of House

One of the oldest houses in Concord, the Orchard House was home to one of America's best-loved authors, Louisa May Alcott. Alcott lived here in the house built by her father with the rest of her highly talented family. Her father, Bronson Alcott, was a Transcendentalist, philisopher, educater, and writer who was associated with Emerson, Thoreau and Hawthorne. Her mother, Abigail, was an outspoken advocate of women's rights and her sister, May, was an artist of considerable talent. Her sister, Amy, was an accomplished amateur actress who participated in the Concord Dramatic Union. The Orchard House provided the setting for Alcott's best known work, *Little Women*.

The house has been lovingly restored to its original condition by the Friends of the Alcotts. Many of the furnishings belonged to the Alcotts while others have been collected and are appropriate to the period.

## Notable Collections on Exhibit

The house features an important collection of Alcott memorabilia and also displays paintings by May Alcott.

## Additional Information

VIsitors to Concord are also encouraged to visit the homes of some its other famous residents, Ralph Waldo Emerson (located on the Cambridge Turnpike) and the Old Manse, home of Emerson and Hawthorne (located next to the North Bridge).

# William Cullen Bryant Homestead

**Bryant Road
RR1 Box 132
Cummington, MA 01026
(413) 634-2244**

**Contact:** The Trustees of Reservations
**Open:** Last weekend in June through Columbus Day, Fri.-Sun. 1–5 p.m.
**Admission:** Adults $4; children (6-12) $2.50; groups $3.50. Annual craft fair third weekend in July.
**Suggested Time to View House:** 1 hour
**Facilities on Premises:** Shop is being planned

**Description of Grounds:** 160 acres grounds are free—includes Rivolet Trail where Bryant strolled
**Best Season to View House:** Autumn
**Number of Yearly Visitors:** 3,000
**Year House Built:** 1785; reconstructed in 1865
**Style of Architecture:** Victorian
**Number of Rooms:** 23
**On-Site Parking:** Yes **Wheelchair Access:** No

## Description of House

This was the boyhood home of William Cullen Bryant (1794—1878) who achieved fame as a poet and as the influential editor of the *New York Evening Post*. He was New York City's leading citizen of the day and was the force behind the creation of Central Park. He spent many summers in his later years at the house now known as the Bryant Homestead.

This beautiful farmhouse is divided into four sections. The main is Colonial gambrel-raised and converted into Victorian. Other sections include a library, kitchen/servants' quarters, and woodshed/servants' quarters. In 1875, Bryant raised the house and had a new first floor built beneath.

The furnishings on display belonged to Bryant and his family and are from the 1840s through the 1870s. The furnishings in the parlor, for example, are of Louis XV Victorian and Empire style.

## Notable Collections on Exhibit

There is an eclectic mix of Victorian era furniture and collectibles—many from Bryant's overseas travels. Many of Bryant's mementoes are located throughout the house.

# Glen Magna

Ingersoll Street
Danvers, MA 01923
(508) 774-9165

**Contact:** Danvers Historical Society

**Open:** Tues. and Thur. 10 a.m.–4 p.m.

**Admission:** Adults $3; children under 12 free. Rented for weddings and parties on weekends.

**Suggested Time to View House:** 1 hour

**Description of Grounds:** Magnificent restored gardens with reproduced gazebo, Derby summer house

**Best Season to View House:** Spring-fall

**Number of Yearly Visitors:** 1,500

**Year House Built:** 1690, addition in 1814, rebuilt in 1894

**Style of Architecture:** Colonial Revival

**Number of Rooms:** 12

**On-Site Parking:** Yes **Wheelchair Access:** Yes

## Description of House

The property, which later came to be known as Glen Magna Farms, was owned by the Peabody and Endicott families for 144 years. Joseph Peabody, a wealthy Salem merchant, acquired the farm with dwelling house and other buildings in 1814 and used it as a haven for his family and goods during the War of 1812. Though the danger of war passed soon after Peabody bought the estate, he retained it as a country place. William Crowninshield Endicott, Jr., Joseph Peabody's great-grandson named the estate "Glen Magna Farms" believing that to be the name of the Endicott ancestral home in England.

Several generations of Peabody descendants enlarged and improved the farm until it became a country estate for elegant summer living. In the 1890s the house was reconstructed in the Colonial Revival style, farm buildings were moved away from the house and the surrounding grounds changed and improved. The Endicott family created an award winning landscape, the plans for which were drawn by the firm of Olmsted, Olmsted & Eliot. A Federal summer house, originally built in 1793 by architect Samuel McIntyre, was moved to Glen Magna in 1904. The Danvers Historical Society acquired eleven acres of the property in 1963 and is working to preserve and restore the buildings and gardens.

The furnishings are collected and appropriate to the period. Visitors can also see original French wallpaper depicting the "Love Story of Psyche."

# Jeremiah Page House

**Contact:** Danvers Historical Society

**Open:** Tues. and Thur., 10 a.m.–4 p.m.

**Admission:** Adults $3; children
under 12 free

**Suggested Time to View House:** 1 hour

**Number of Yearly Visitors:** 1,500

**Number of Rooms:** 10

**Style of Architecture:** Georgian-
Gambrel roof

**Best Season to View House:** Spring-fall

**Year House Built:** 1754

**On-Site Parking:** Yes **Wheelchair Access:** Yes

## Description of House

Page House has been home to three generations of the Page family since its construction in 1754. Jeremiah Page, the original owner, was a brickmaker who moved to Danvers in 1743. After marriage to Sarah Andrews in 1950, he built this gambrel roof structure and reared nine children. Jeremiah also used to rent out one parlor of the house as an office. One noteworthy tenant was the last British governor of Massachusetts before the Revolution, Thomas Gage. Jeremiah's son John, also a brickmaker, was the next occupant of the house. He and his family of ten children added to the existing structure.

The last member of the Page family to live here, John's youngest daughter Anne Lemist Page, was active in the kindergarten movement of the late 19th century. She taught classes in the house as well as at the local school.

Originally located on Ipswich Street in Danvers, Page House was moved by the Danvers Historical Society to its present location when it faced destruction in 1913. Today the house exhibits over 160 years of family and town history representing a unique portrait of life in colonial America.

# Rebecca Nurse Homestead

**149 Pine Street
Danvers, MA 01923
(508) 774-8799**

**Contact:** Danvers Alarm List Company

**Open:** June 15-Oct. 15, Tues.-Sat.
1–4:30 p.m.; Sun. 2–4:30 p.m.; or by
appointment

**Admission:** Adults $3.50; children (under
17) $1.50. Annual field day and muster
held in June.

**Description of Grounds:** 27 acres of
fields, pasture, and woods with
outbuildings

**Suggested Time to View House:** 1 hour

**Year House Built:** c. 1648

**Style of Architecture:** Saltbox

**On-Site Parking:** Yes

## Description of House

An old dirt road leads to the old saltbox-style Nurse Homestead situated on a small knoll in what was once known as Salem Village. Rebecca Nurse lived here with her husband, Francis, and their eight children. The house is best known today for the tragic events which befell Rebecca at the advanced age of seventy-one. In the winter of 1691, three girls in Salem Village began having horrid fits and the local doctor concluded that they were the victims of witchcraft. At the urging of their elders, the girls named three witches, the elderly and frail Rebecca Nurse, and two other women. Despite the support of forty members of the community who defended her character, Nurse was arrested and taken from her beloved homestead. Although she was originally found innocent, the decision was later reversed and she was finally hanged on July 19, 1692. Her children later secretly moved their mother's body to her homestead and buried the corpse in an unmarked grave.

Rebecca Nurse's simple lifestyle is well-represented in the homestead. Three restored rooms contain period furnishings together with the outbuildings, including a reproduction of a 1672 Meeting House, and exhibits tell the story of her remarkable life.

In 1885, the Nurse family erected a memorial to Rebecca in the family graveyard. The monument included a poetic sentiment written by poet John Greenleaf Whittier. Later, another marker dedicated to her forty neighbors and supporters was erected close by.

# Historic Deerfield

The Street, P.O. Box 321
Deerfield, MA 01342
(413) 774-5581

**Contact:** Historic Deerfield, Inc.

**Open:** Daily 9:30 a.m.–4:30 p.m.; closed Thanksgiving, Dec. 24-25

**Admission:** Adults $10; children $5; tickets valid for 2 consecutive days. Guided tours, open hearth cooking demonstrations, tavern games, workshops, lectures, etc.

**Suggested Time to View House:** 30 minutes per house

**Facilities on Premises:** Museum store (incl. books); food service

**Description of Grounds:** Mile-long street, suitable for walking

**Best Season to View House:** All year

**Number of Yearly Visitors:** 32,218

**Year House Built:** c. 1720 to 1872

**Style of Architecture:** New England vernacular

**Number of Rooms:** 97

**On-Site Parking:** Yes

**Wheelchair Access:** Yes

## Description of House

This 300 year old village has been beautifully preserved in a manner befitting its historic past. Today, visitors are able to walk a tree-lined street and view twelve historic homes from the period of 1720 to 1850 which represent a fascinating world devoted not only to Deerfield but to Connecticut Valley culture and early American arts.

The community was first settled in 1669 as a tiny frontier outpost. Two attacks, the Bloody Brook massacre of 1675 and the Deerfield massacre of 1704, nearly destroyed the settlement. From the ashes, rose the prosperous 18th-century houses that tell the story of the town's dramatic past.

The Allen House, a saltbox with feather-edge paneling built soon after the 1704 attack, was the home of Historic Deerfield's founders, Mr. and Mrs. Henry Flynt. The house exhibits their personal collection of American decorative arts.

The Stebbins House, a brick structure built in 1799, was home to the wealthiest landowner in the county. His particular taste in decoration can be seen in the the French scenic wallpaper by Joseph Dufour, the freehand wall-painting which may have been executed by itinerant artist Jared Jessup, and several portraits by Erastus Salisbury Field, a local artist.

Located on the town common, the 18th century Frary House was restored from ruinous condition in 1890. The 1795 addition known as the Barnard Tavern was a meeting place for groups and individuals in Deerfield. Cooking and spinning equipment is on display here, items which reflect the day-to-day living experience of local residents.

The Wright House, an 1824 Federal brick dwelling, exhibits the George Alfred Cluett collection of American furniture and clocks. Cluett was a discriminating collector of furniture of the Chippendale and Federal periods. In addition, the Wright House displays more than 1,500 pieces of Chinese export porcelain including two hong-decorated punch bowls, a variety of western forms unusual in Chinese porcelain.

The Dwight House is one of four houses in Historic Deerfield which is not original to the village. When it was threatened with demolition in 1950, this merchant's home was dismantled and moved from nearby Springfield. It now houses a comparative display of Boston and Connecticut Valley furniture including a mahogony blockfront bureau table made in Boston in 1770 and two extraordinary case pieces by the flamboyant cabinetmaker Cotton White of Hatfield.

### Notable Collections on Exhibit

The houses and museums of Historic Deerfield exhibit a significant number of well-preserved furnishings and decorative arts including more than 1,500 pieces of New England furniture, 1,800 pieces of early American silver, English ceramics, American and English pewter, and many American paintings and prints.

### Additional Information

There are several museums located in Historic Deerfield including Memorial Hall, one of America's oldest museums devoted to New England antiquities and the Helen Geier Flynt Textile Museum with more than 4,000 pieces of American, English, and European needlework, textiles and costumes.

# Ashley House

**Contact:** Historic Deerfield, Inc.

**Open:** Daily 9:30 a.m.–4:30 p.m.; closed Thanksgiving, Dec. 24-25

**Admission:** Adults $10; children, $5; tickets valid for entire Historic Deerfield tour. Guided tours.

**Suggested Time to View House:** 30 minutes

**Description of Grounds:** Small yard

**Best Season to View House:** All year

**Number of Yearly Visitors:** 32,218

**Year House Built:** c. 1730

**Style of Architecture:** New England vernacular

**Number of Rooms:** 10

**On-Site Parking:** Yes

**Wheelchair Access:** Yes

## Description of House

Located on The Street in Historic Deerfield, the Ashley House is a good example of Deerfield's mid-18th-century building boom. Constructed around 1730, it became the home of the Tory minister Jonathan Ashley, Deerfield's second minister, in 1733. Reverend Ashley prospered both from his own agricultural activities and from the expansion of the town's economy.

Ashley made substantial alterations to his house that included a grand doorway, a central staircase, fine paneling, and an imposing gambrel roof. Inside the house, visitors see the lifestyle of one of the Connecticut Valley "River Gods", the political-military-mercantile-ministerial elite that governed the towns of western Massachusetts until the American Revolution.

## Notable Collections on Exhibit

A number of Ashley's furnishings and possessions are on display including cherry and mahogany furniture, prints which showed his allegiance to England, imported English and Chinese ceramics, and a variety of textiles.

# Wells-Thorn House

The Street, P.O. Box 321
Deerfield, MA 01342
(413) 774-5581

**Contact:** Historic Deerfield, Inc.

**Open:** Daily 9:30 a.m.–4:30 p.m.; closed Thanksgiving, Dec. 24-25

**Admission:** Adults $10; children, $5; tickets valid for entire Historic Deerfield tour. Guided tours.

**Suggested Time to View House:** 30 minutes

**Description of Grounds:** Small yard

**Best Season to View House:** All year

**Number of Yearly Visitors:** 32,218

**Year House Built:** c. 1725

**Style of Architecture:** New England vernacular

**Number of Rooms:** 10

**On-Site Parking:** Yes

**Wheelchair Access:** Yes

## Description of House

The Wells-Thorn House gives visitors to Historic Deerfield a good introduction to the changes in lifestyle in a small New England village from the early 1700s to the sophisticated Federal period.

Wells-Thorne is actually two houses, the earlier, built around 1720 has been restored to its former appearance, served as an ell to the two and a half story house built in 1751 with cornice details from contemporary pattern books and painted light blue in the style of the period.

The house has been restored and furnished to illustrate the development of the agricultural economy, domestic life, and tasted in the Connecticut Valley from 1725 to 1850. The house's sparsely furnished early kitchen shows that life's necessities could be met with a few pots and pans, in fact there is not even a table a chairs for the early settlers comfort. 1735 parlor suggests the consumer choices made when agricultural prosperity began to yield a small surplus. This multi-purpose room contains a rope bed with corn husk mattress and an elegant case of drawers signed by Simeon Pomeroy of Northampton, Massachusetts. Later rooms in the Wells-Thorn House introduce wallpaper, window curtains, sets of chairs, and floor coverings. Finally, in the 1850s attic visitors can see the cast-offs of several generations.

## Notable Collections on Exhibit

In addition to the already mentioned furnishings, the house has on display a gilded Sheraton mirror, a side chair from the Hitchcock factory, needlepoint pictures, and imported brass candlesticks.

# Indian House

The Street, P.O Box 344
Deerfield, MA 01342
(413) 772-0845

**Contact:** Indian House Memorial, Inc.

**Open:** May-Oct., Mon.-Fri. 12:30–4:30 p.m.,
Sat.-Sun. 11 a.m.–4:30 p.m.

**Admission:** Adults $2; students $1.50;
children $1. Guided tours.

**Suggested Time to View House:**
20–30 minutes

**Facilities on Premises:** Gift shop

**Description of Grounds:** Flower gardens.
Limited on-site parking and handicap
access on first floor only.

**Best Season to View House:** Summer
and fall

**Number of Yearly Visitors:** 1,100

**Year House Built:** 1929 replicate of a home
built in 1699

**Style of Architecture:** Saltbox

**Number of Rooms:** 7

## Description of House

The replicate was built in 1929 by William Gass—a local carpenter who
had worked on the reconstruction of many Deerfield homes. (No family has
ever lived in the copy.) The original house was built in 1699 by Ensign John
Sheldon. John passed the house on to his son, Ebenezer, who sold it to Jon
Hoit in 1744. Ebenezer's daughter, Mercy, married Hoit's son, David, who
inherited the house. Ebenezer and the Hoits ran a tavern out of one of the
front parlors. The house became a museum in 1930.

The Indian House is an early reproduction of a standard saltbox with
an overhang across the front. The house has a central chimney with three
fireplaces and two bake ovens. The furnishings are mostly collected and
appropriate to the period.

The door of the original house survived, complete with gashes made by
the French and Indians in 1704. The door is now on display at The Pocum-
tuck Valley Memorial Hall Museum in Deerfield as a symbol of the early
pioneer spirit.

# William Clapp House

195 Boston Street
Dorchester, MA
(617) 265-7802

**Contact:** Dorchester Historical Society
**Open:** Hours vary, please call to verify
**Admission:** Free, donation accepted.Guided tours, monthly guets lectures, special events, Christmas and Spring open house.
**Suggested Time to View House:** 1 hour
**Facilities on Premises:** Gift shop

**Best Season to View House:** All seasons
**Year House Built:** 1806
**Style of Architecture:** Country Neo-classical Mansion
**Number of Rooms:** 7
**On-Site Parking:** Yes
**Wheelchair Access:** No

## Description of House

In 1945, the Dorchester Historical Society acquired the William Clapp House, the home of a member Frank L. Clapp, great-grandson of William Clapp. Built in 1806, the house is a fine example of a country neo-classical mansion. Mr. Clapp remained in the house as a caretaker of the forty acre estate until his death in 1953.

In addition to William Clapp House, the estate contains the smaller Lemuel Clapp House (c. 1710; 1765), a carriage house and a barn.

## Notable Collections on Exhibit

As the headquarters for the historical society, the house contains the main research collection of the Robinson-Lehane library devoted to cataloging and interpreting Dorchester history and architecture. Also displayed, is a unique collection of Dorchester pottery and Baker chocolate items.

## Additional Information

The society also administers the Blake House, built in 1648, and located in nearby Richardson Park. Activities of the Dorchester Historical and Antiquarian Society took place in this house from 1895 until its move to the William Clapp House in 1945.

# The Julia Wood House

55-65 Palmer Avenue
Village Green
Falmouth, MA
(508) 548-4857

**Contact:** The Falmouth Historical Society
**Open:** June 15-Sept. 15, Mon.-Fri., 2–5 p.m.
**Admission:** Adults $2; children $.50.
  Guided tours.
**Suggested Time to View House:** 1 hour
**Description of Grounds:** A typical colonial
  garden adjoins the house and is
  maintained by the Falmouth Garden
  Club.
**Best Season to View House:** May-Sept.
**Year House Built:** 1790
**Style of Architecture:** Colonial
**On-Site Parking:** Yes
**Wheelchair Access:** No

## Description of House

Home to the Falmouth Historical Society, the Julia Wood House was originally built in 1790 by Falmouth's famous early physician, Dr. Francis Wicks, who served as a medical corpsman during the American Revolution. This three-story house is unusual in that it has one of the town's few remaining "widow's walks".

## Notable Collections on Exhibit

The house exhibits a varied display of items related to the former occupants and Falmouth history. These include original 18th-century scenic wallpaper brought from Paris by a sea captain for his bride, period furniture portraits of notable Falmouth citizens, antique hooked rugs, an extensive hand-made quilt collection, toys and dolls of former days, and a restored kitchen with fireplace and early utensils. In addition, the adjoining Hallet Barn displays early tools and farm implements, a 19th-century sleigh, and the old town pump.

## Additional Information

In addition to its large archival holdings, the society maintains the Conant House Museum, sponsors guided walking tours and lectures of historical interest, and through the assistance of the Falmouth Garden Club makes available to the public an extensive memorial garden of shrubs, flowers, and herbs.

# Conant House Museum

**55-65 Palmer Avenue**
**Village Green**
**Falmouth, MA**
**(508) 548-4857**

**Contact:** The Falmouth Historical Society
**Open:** June 15-Sept. 15, Mon.-Fri. 2–5 p.m.
**Admission:** Adults $2; children $.50.
  Guided tours.
**Suggested Time to View House:** 1 hour
**Best Season to View House:** May-Sept.
**Year House Built:**
**Style of Architecture:** Colonial House
**On-Site Parking:** Yes
**Wheelchair Access:** No

## Description of House

This simple two-story structure houses a wealth of information on Falmouth's history and heritage. The exhibits display a wide variety of memorabilia related to Falmouth's tradition as a seafaring port. Visitors are able to see mourning samplers, mementoes of whaling days, a shell collection, and rare examples of "sailor's valentines." In addition there is a fascinating exhibit devoted to china, silver, and glass from the community. Another unusual military exhibit contains items ranging from the American Revolution to World War I. The Katherine Lee Bates Room contain's the society's collection of books and pictures pertaining to this little known author of *America the Beautiful,* and one of Falmouth's most famous citizens.

## Additional Information

The society maintains a comprehensive genealogical and historical research library in the Conant House, as well as an extensive picture collection. The society welcomes those doing research or tracing their family roots.

# Beauport-Sleeper-McCann House

**75 Eastern Point Blvd.
Gloucester, MA 01930
(508) 283-0800**

**Contact:** Soc. for the Preservation of
New England Antiquities
**Open:** Mid May-mid Sept., Mon.-Fri.
10 a.m.–4 p.m.; Mid Sept.-mid Oct.,
Mon.-Fri. 10 a.m.–4 p.m., Sat.-Sun.
1–4 p.m.

**Admission:** $5. Summer programs include
evening concerts and a sunset tour.
**Year House Built:** 1907 to 1934
**Style of Architecture:** Gothic

## Description of House

Beauport was the summer home of the collector and interior designer
Henry Davis Sleeper. Beauport served Sleeper as an escape, a backdrop for
summer parties, and as a showcase for his professional skills. The house was
frequently published in books and magazines, and its influence came to
shape the way we view America's past.

This fantasy house is built on the rocks overlooking the Gloucester
Harbor. Crowned by towers, dormers, and dovecotes, the structure encloses
a labyrinth of rooms decorated to evoke different historical or literary
themes. The settings—playful variations on subjects like the early American
kitchen, an English cottage, or the sea captains retreat—are arranged to
amuse and to stimulate the imagination.

## Notable Collections on Exhibit

Every nook and alcove holds a composition of curiosities, folk art, china,
or colored glass. Very often the colored glass is displayed against backlit
windows to increase the aesthetic impact.

# Porter-Phelps-Huntington Historic House Museum

130 River Drive
Hadley, MA 01035
(413) 584-4699

**Contact:** Porter-Phelps-Huntington Foundation, Inc.

**Open:** May 15–Oct. 15, Sat.-Wed. 1–4:30 p.m.

**Admission:** Adults $2.50, children 12 and under $1. Guided tours; Wednesday Folk Traditions concerts held June and July at 7 p.m.; A Perfect Spot of Tea series with music and pastries served on Saturdays in July and Aug.

**Suggested Time to View House:** 1 hour

**Description of Grounds:** A 1780s colonial garden and a 1930s sunken garden are open to the public.

**Best Season to View House:** Spring, summer or fall

**Number of Yearly Visitors:** 3,700

**Year House Built:** 1752

**Style of Architecture:** Georgian Colonial

**Number of Rooms:** 12

**On-Site Parking:** Yes

**Wheelchair Access:** No

## Description of House

Built in 1752 by Moses Porter, The Porter-Phelps Huntington House was the first to be erected outside the Hadley stockade on a tract of land known as "forty acres and its skirts" (the house is sometimes known as Forty Acres). Porter was, unfortunately, killed in 1755 at Battle of Bloody Morning Scout. His wife, Elizabeth Pitkin, and their daughter, Betsy, carried on the work of the farm. In 1770, Betsy married Charles Phelps, a selectman and representative to the legislature, and together they enlarged and refined the house. The house has been occupied by six generations of the same family, and became a museum in 1955, when the last occupant, Dr. James L. Huntington, began a foundation and opened the house to the public.

The house is one of the earliest to use a central hall plan in the Connecticut River Valley and was considered unusual because of its rusticated siding (which today is covered with clapboards). The daughter Betsy's improvements included the construction of a new kitchen ell in 1771, and a production kitchen in 1797. The corn barn and carriage house were added in 1773 and 1795 respectively. The roof was gambreled and an Adamsesque portico was added in 1799. The interior remodelling spans a variety of styles from Colonial to Georgian to Federal.

## Notable Collections on Exhibit

All of the objects displayed in the house represent a family's accumulation over ten generations. The furniture is representative of 18th and 19th-century styles including a Chippendale-style bedstead; a Sheraton-style parlor set purchased in 1799; a set of eight fancy Sheraton side chairs; and regionally made case furniture. A clothing collection of over 500 items includes a significant dress from each decade of the 19th century.

## Additional Information

The family papers—diaries, correspondence, wills, and deeds—and a historic structure report on the house are available at the Amherst College Archives.

# Hancock-Clarke House

36 Hancock Street
Lexington, MA 02173
(617) 862-1703

**Contact:** Lexington Historical Society
**Open:** Mid April-Oct. 31, Mon.-Sat.
10 a.m.–5 p.m., Sun. 1–5 p.m.
**Admission:** Adults $2.50, children (6-16)
$.50. Guided tours on the intellectual
turmoil preceding the Revolution and
on the visit of John Hancock and Samuel
Adams.
**Suggested Time to View House:** 40 minutes
**Best Season to View House:** All seasons
**Year House Built:** 1690s
**Number of Rooms:** 7

**Number of Yearly Visitors:** 5,000
**Style of Architecture:** Colonial
**On-Site Parking:** Yes **Wheelchair Access:** No

## Description of House

The Hancock-Clarke House was the home of the Reverend John Hancock and the Reverend Jonas Clarke, two ministers who served the spiritual and secular needs of Lexington for 105 years. The Reverend Hancock's grandson, John, a frequent visitor to this house, was the first signer of the Declaration of Independence and the first governor of Massachusetts. Succeeding Hancock as minister in 1752, the Reverend Jonas Clarke, who reared twelve children in this parsonage, was an elequent supporter of the colonial cause. The Reverend Clarke's fervent sermons were a source of inspiration to the citizens of Lexington during the crisis with Britain.

On the evening of April 18, 1775, John Hancock and Samuel Adams, prominent leaders in the colonial cause, were guests of the Reverend Jonas Clarke in this parsonage. Fearing that they might be captured by the British, Dr. Joseph Warren of Boston sent William Dawes and Paul Revere to Lexington with the news of the advancing British troops. Arriving separately, they stopped to warn Hancock and Adams, then set off for Concord. Today Dawes is all but forgotten, but Paul Revere's midnight ride has been immortalized by Longfellow.

Reverend Mr. Hancock built a small parsonage on this site in 1698 and in 1738 his son Thomas, a wealthy Boston merchant, enlarged his parents home. A significant number of pieces from the Hancock and Clarke families are on display.

## Notable Collections on Exhibit

This house is of particular interest because it contains furnishings and portraits owned by the Hancock and Clarke families and an exhibit area including William Diamond's drum and Major Pitcairn's pistols—treasured relics of April 19, 1775.

## Additional Information

Visitors to Lexington may also visit two other historic sites: Buckman Tavern, the Minuteman Headquarters, and the Munroe Tavern, the British headquarters and field hospital.

# Codman House – The Grange

Codman Road
Lincoln, MA 01773
(617) 259-8843

**Contact:** Soc. for the Preservation of New England Antiquities

**Open:** June 1-Oct. 15, Wed.-Sun. 12–5 p.m.; tours on the hour

**Admission:** $4. Guided tours, Antique Vehicle Meet and Artisans' Fair.

**Description of Grounds:** The grounds feature a hidden Italian garden, c. 1900, with perennial beds, statuary, and a pool filled with waterlilies.

**Year House Built:** 1740

**Style of Architecture:** Georgian

## Description of House

This gentleman's country seat was a powerful force in the lives of five generations of the Codman family. For the last generation of Codmans to live here, the estate was a symbol of their distinguished past.

The Codman House overlooks a prospect of farm and pleasure grounds. In the 1790s, John Codman risked his son's inheritance and remodeled the original Georgian structure. After John's death, his son promptly sold the property, but a generation later, his son, Ogden Codman, bought it back and invested substantial resources in its renovation. Today, the interiors preserve the decorative schemes of every era, including those of noted interior designer, Ogden Codman, Jr.

The house is richly furnished with portraits, memorabilia, and art works collected in Europe, the house is an extraordinary record of a family narrative.

## Additional Information

The grounds feature a hidden Italian garden (c. 1900) with perennial beds, statuary, and a pool filled with waterlillies, as well as an English cottage garden (c. 1930).

# Gropius House

68 Baker Bridge Road
Lincoln, MA 01773
(617) 259-8843

**Contact:** Soc. for the Preservation of New England Antiquities
**Open:** June-mid Oct., Fri.-Sun. 12–5 p.m.; Nov.-May, Sat.-Sun. 12–5 p.m. (only on first full weekend of the month)

**Admission:** Adults $5; SPNEA members free. Guided tours on the hour.
**Suggested Time to View House:** 1 hour
**Number of Yearly Visitors:** 10,000
**Year House Built:** 1937-1938
**Style of Architecture:** Bauhaus

## Description of House

Walter Gropius, founder of the German design school known as the Bauhaus, was one of the most influential architects of the 20th century. He designed this house as his family home in 1937, when he came to teach at Harvard University's Graduate School of Design.

Modest in scale, the house was revolutionary in impact. It combined the traditional elements of New England architecture—wood, brick, and fieldstone—with innovative materials rarely used in domestic settings at that time—glass block, acoustical plaster, and chrome bannisters, along with the latest technology in fixtures. In keeping with Bauhaus philosophy, every aspect of the house was planned for maximum efficiency and simplicity of design. Because the restoration is based on personal recollections and extensive photographic documentation, with all the family possessions still in place, the house house has an immediacy seldom found in historic properties.

## Notable Collections on Exhibit

The house contains an important collection designed by Marcel Breuer and made for the Gropiuses in the Bauhaus workshops.

# Trask House

10 Union Street
Manchester-by-the-Sea, MA 01944
(508) 526-7230

**Contact:** Manchester Historical Society

**Open:** July and Aug., Wed.-Fri. 1–4 p.m.; Dec., Sat.-Sun. 10 a.m.–4 p.m. Any time by appointment.

**Admission:** Contributions accepted. Open meetings with a speaker on the first Wed. of Oct., Nov., and Feb.-June at 8 p.m. Visitors welcome. Decorated for Christmas in December.

**Suggested Length of Time to View House:** 30–40 minutes

**Description of Grounds:** A simple New England garden

**Best Season to View House:** Summer

**Number of Yearly Visitors:** 300

**Year House Built:** 1823 (with later additions)

**Style of Architecture:** New England Clapboard

**Number of Rooms:** 7 museum rooms plus office, library, and kitchen

**On-Site Parking:** No   **Handicap Access:** Yes

## Description of House

Trask House became the home of the able businesswoman Abigail Hooper in 1823. She was a woman ahead of her time in many ways. While in her twenties and unmarried, she ran her own store, selling ship supplies like hardtack and rum as well as calico and lace. During the summer of 1823 she began to modernize and enlarge an old building in the center of town. In November of the same year, she surprised everyone by marrying Captain Richard Trask, a widower with a child. Captain Trask was a merchant ship captain who sailed the American coast to Cuba, England, Russia, and other ports.

Trask House is a typical white clapboard home from the heyday of the New England shipping era. In the 1830s she improved the house with a modern curving stair and a third-floor addition from which her husband could see the ocean. This independent woman retained title to the house after her marriage. Trask House and its gardens remained in the possession of Abigail Hooper Trask and her descendants for 100 years and was conveyed to the Manchester Historical Society in 1924. The furniture on display includes many family heirlooms such as a feather-grained chest, and an American Hepplewhite sideboard (ca. 1790).

## Notable Collections on Exhibit

The Manchester-made furniture (some made in the early 1800s) constitutes a small but notable collection housed in the Trask House. The society owns a collection of photographs of houses built from the early days of the summer colony here through the shingle-style cottages of the late 1800s, and the elaborate summer homes of the the 1920s.

## Additional Information

The Manchester Historical Society has become a useful resource for scholars and students interested in local history and houses.

# Jeremiah Lee Mansion

161 Washington Street, P.O. Box 1048
Marblehead, MA 01945
(617) 631-1069

**Contact:** Marblehead Historical Society
**Open:** Mid May-mid Oct.. Mon.-Fri.
10 a.m.–4 p.m.; Sat.-Sun. 1–4 p.m.;
closed holidays
**Admission:** Adults $4; seniors $3; students
(10-16) $2; children under 10 free. The
house is shown by guided tours only.
Special programs include lecture series.
**Suggested Time to View House:** 45 minutes

**Description of Grounds:** The grounds are
historically accurate in terms of design
and plantings and include 18th-century
plantings, trees, and shrubs.
**Best Season to View House:** Spring-fall
**Number of Yearly Visitors:** Approx. 2500
**Year House Built:** 1768
**Style of Architecture:** Georgian
**Number of Rooms:** 14
**On-Site Parking:** No **Wheelchair Access:** No

## Description of House

Colonel Jeremiah Lee, wealthy shipowner and town official, built the mansion in 1768. A patriot devoted to the cause of liberty, Lee carried ammunition to the 1775 Lexington/Concord battle. While avoiding capture by the British, he suffered extreme exposure and died of fever later that year.

The Jeremiah Lee Mansion has been called one of the finest Georgian structures existing in America. A distinctive feature of the Lee Mansion's front facade is the noble porch with its classical columns and deeply carved pediment. The exterior finish of wood blocks is a characteristic of American Georgian design. In addition, the house is adorned with classical Palladian windows and cupola. The furnishings are of the same period as the house. The magnificent garden changes from season to season and year to year.

## Notable Collections on Exhibit

The charming simplicity of J.O.J. Frost, Marblehead's primitive artist, is expressed in an outstanding collection of his paintings and carvings. The kitchen contains a wealth of cooking implements, a rare mechanical spit, early pewter pieces and other utensils used in the 18th and 19th centuries.

# Hadwen House

96 Main St. and corner of Pleasant St.
(508) 228-1894

**Contact:** Nantucket Historical Association
**Open:** Please call for times
**Admission:** $2-$3. Lectures, special events; guided tours; and childrens programs.
**Suggested Time to View House:** 45 minutes
**Facilities on Premises:** Museum shop in town

**Description of Grounds:** The gardens behind the house by the Nantucket Garden Club reflet the style of the 1850s.
**Best Season to View House:** Spring-fall
**Year House Built:** 1845
**Style of Architecture:** Greek Revival

## Description of House
The house was built by William Hadwen, co-owner of a spermaceti works (now the Whaling Museum). This Greek Revival Mansion reflects the days of Nantucket's whaling prosperity,and many consider it the most beautiful house on Nantucket. The house features magnificent sliding doors, carved Italian marble fireplace surrounds, silver doorknobs and molded plaster cornices and ceiling rosettes. The house is appointed with furnishings in the Federal, Empire and later revival styles.

## Notable Collections on Exhibit
The house displays portraits, needlework and fine furniture to create a luxurious atmosphere.

# Jethro Coffin House

Sunset Hill, off West Chester St.

**Contact:** Nantucket Historical Association
**Open:** Please call for times
**Admission:** $2–$3. Lectures; special events; guided tours; and childrens' programs.

**Suggested Time to View House:** 45 minutes
**Best Season to View House:** Spring-fall
**Year House Built:** 1686

## Description of House
The house was built as a wedding gift for Jethro and Mary Coffin. This simple saltbox structure is known as Nantucket's oldest house. The building is typical of the late 17th-century house plan of the Massachusetts Bay Colony.

# Macy-Christian House

12 Liberty Street

**Contact:** Nantucket Historical Association
**Open:** Please call for times
**Admission:** $2–$3. Lectures; special events; guided tours; and childrens programs.

**Suggested Time to View House:** 45 minutes
**Best Season to View House:** Spring-fall
**Year House Built:** 1740
**Style of Architecture:** Colonial

## Description of House
This lean-to stayed in the Thomas Macy family until 1827 when it was sold to Philip Folger. Reverend George P. Christian and his wife purchased it in 1934 and created a classical Colonial Revival ambiance. Reopened in 1992, the Macy-Christian House reflects both the Colonial style of its original inhabitants, and the late 19th-century revival of its most recent owners. The furnishings reflect and are appropriate to changes in style of the house.

# Rotch-Jones-Duff House and Garden Museum

**396 County Street
New Bedford, MA 02740
(508) 997-1401**

**Open:** Tues.-Sat. 11 a.m.–4 p.m.; Sun. 1–4 p.m.; closed Mon., Easter, Memorial Day, Fourth of July, Thankgiving and Christmas

**Admission:** Members free; seniors and students $1.50; children (under 12) free. Guided tours, special programs, lecture series, concerts, poetry, Christmas event.

**Suggested Time to View House:** 45 minutes

**Facilities on Premises:** Museum store

**Description of Grounds:** 19th-century designed formal parterre garden, including pergola and framed by a wildflower walk

**Best Season to View House:** May-Sept.

**Number of Yearly Visitors:** 10,000

**Year House Built:** 1834

**Number of Rooms:** 20

**Style of Architecture:** Greek Revival

**On-Site Parking:** No  **Wheelchair Access:** No

## Description of House

William Rotch, Jr. (1834-1851) was a prominent whaling merchant, founder of Friends Academy, and one of the original founders and first president of the New Bedford Institution for Savings Bank. Another occupant, Edward Coffin Jones (1851-1935), was also a successful whaling merchant. The last resident, Mark M. Duff (1935-1980), was an industrialist, owner of the New Bedford Hotel, and president of the Merchants Bank.

One of the nation's first examples of Greek Revival houses, the museum was designed by the young Richard Upjohn and built in 1834. Is is the only surviving whaling era mansion on the east coast with its original garden intact. The museum has had very little alteration to its original contruction; the property occupies a full city block. Furnishings are from the three periods of occupancy, both from original residents and collected.

## Notable Collections on Exhibit

The collection includes 19th and early 20th-century furniture, American decorative arts, and costumes.

## Additional Information

The Garden Club of Buzzards Bay, a chapter of the Garden Club of America, occupies the museum greenhouse and maintains the Wildflower Walk, which was established with a grant from the G.C.A. Foundation Award.

# Coffin House

14 High Road, Route 1A
Newbury, MA 01951
(508) 463-2057

**Contact:** Soc. for the Preservation of New England Antiquities
**Open:** June 1-Oct. 15, Wed.-Sun. 12–5 p.m.; tours on the hour

**Admission:** $4. Guided tours.
**Year House Built:** 1654
**Style of Architecture:** Saltbox

## Description of House

The house was owned by the Coffin family for generations. The Coffin House chronicles the evolution of domestic life in rural New England over three centuries. The structure began as a simple dwelling built in the post-medieval style. Subsequently, as the family grew, partitions and a small addition were built, so the different generations could live together under one roof. In 1725, the house was more than doubled in size to provide living space for a married son and his family. Sixty years later, two Coffin brothers legally divided the structure into two separate dwellings, each with its own kitchen and living spaces.

With rooms from the 17th, 18th, and 19th centuries, the Coffin House depicts the impact of an expanding economy and new concepts, such as the notion of privacy, on architecture and modes of living. Here, visitors can trace changes in food preparation and storage, technological improvements in heating, and increasing levels of comfort thanks to the growing availability of material goods.

# Spencer-Pierce-Little Farm

Little's Lane
Newbury, MA 01951
(617) 227-3956

**Contact:** Soc. for the Preservation of New England Antiquities
**Open:** June 1-Sept. 30., Sat.-Sun. 12–5 p.m.

**Admission:** $4; SPNEA members free
**Year House Built:** 1675 to 1700
**Style of Architecture:** Georgian

### Description of House

From the moment it was built near the end of the 17th century, this manor house has been the subject of folklore and legend. The farm's imposing size and costly construction—stone and brick in a region where wood was the customary material for houses—made it exceptional.

During the 17th, 18th, and early 19th centuries, the property served as the country seat of wealthy merchants. In the mid 19th century, the house and land were acquired by the Little family, who farmed the land and were prominent members of the community.

With the rise of the Colonial Revival movement in the late 19th century, the ancient house began to attract the attention of antiquarians, who declare it a true relic of America's colonial past.

### Additional Information

Today the house is undergoing extensive structural conservation. Visitors may see architectural and archaeological evidence, learn about the daily lives of the people who lived and worked here, and walk around the extensive farmland which has been under continuous cultivation since 1635.

# Cushing House

**Contact:** Historical Society of Old Newbury

**Open:** May 1-Oct. 31, Tues.-Sat.
10 a.m.–4 p.m.; closed holidays

**Admission:** Adults $3; children (6-18) $1;
under 6 free. Guided tours.

**Suggested Time to View House:**
60–90 minutes

**Facilities on Premises:** Gift shop

**Description of Grounds:** 19th-century rose
garden and barn

**Best Season to View House:** Nice all year
but roses peak second week of June

**Number of Yearly Visitors:** 3,000

**Year House Built:** 1808

**Number of Rooms:** 16 on view

**Style of Architecture:** Federal

**On-Site Parking:** No **Wheelchair Access:** No

## Description of House

The house was occupied from 1818 until 1955 by the Cushing family whose members were wealthy merchants and shipbuilders. The house was built by Captain William Hunt who died on a voyage to the West Indies shortly after the house's construction. To settle debts his widow was forced to sell the property in pieces with the Cushings becoming sole owners in 1822. John N. Cushing, another sea captain, rose from cabin boy to wealthy merchant during his lifetime and provided the fortune that educated his sons at Harvard and opened the doors of wealth and political prominence to them. While Caleb served in Washington and abroad, brothers John and William carried on the family business. Margret Cushing, the last occupant, was born in 1855, remained in the family home and made minimal changes.

This is an elegant three-story brick house set on an urban lot with 19th-century landscaping. It is furnished with the collections of the Historical Society of Old Newbury which date from 1700 to 1935.

## Notable Collections on Exhibit

Cushing House has an excellent collection of New England furniture. There are many portraits of local citizens including some by well known artists. The collection also features examples of Newbury silver, including the Towle Silver Company, and a large collection of Newbury samplers and needlework. There is a fine clock collection with work by David Wook and Jonathan Balch.

## Additional Information

The Cushing House represents a period in Newburyport's history when foreign trade ship building dominated the local economy and created a market for finely furnished homes. It is located on the most fashionable street where for two miles one sees example after example of Federal architecture expressing the character of the age.

# Clara Barton Birthplace Museum

P.O. Box 356
68 Clara Barton Road
North Oxford, MA 01537
(508) 987-5375

**Contact:** Clara Barton Camp for Girls with Diabetes

**Open:** April-Oct., Tues.-Sun. 11 a.m.–5 p.m.; Nov.-March by appointment

**Admission:** Adults $2.50; Children 16 and under $1; under 5 free. Special rates for groups. Guided tours and periodic special programs.

**Suggested Time to View House:** 30 minutes

**Facilities on Premises:** Gift shop

**Description of Grounds:** The house rests on 210 acres of land which is also home to a barn, 15 cabins, a camp center, playing fields

**Best Season to View House:** All seasons

**Year House Built:** 1818 to 1820

**Style of Architecture:** Cape

**Number of Rooms:** 10

**On-Site Parking:** Yes **Wheelchair Access:** No

## Description of House

Clara Barton, founder of the American Red Cross, was born in this house on December 25, 1821 and lived here until her eighth year. Clara taught in the Oxford area and opened a free school in Bordentown, New Jersey. Later, while working in Washington D.C., she became involved in nursing and aiding Civil War soldiers. After the war and a trip to Europe she learned about the International Red Cross. Upon her return to the States, Clara began a ten year campaign to establish a chapter of the Red Cross in the United States. In 1881, finally successful, Clara became the first president and represented the United States at several International Red Cross Conferences throughout the world. Clara resigned from the Red Cross in 1904 and 1905 founded the National First Aid Society.

What is now the summer kitchen was originally a one-room structure that was bought and then added on to by Captain Stephen Barton in 1818. The woodwork throughout the house is for the most part original. The dining room was also used a a winter kitchen, Other rooms open for display are the parlor, the room in which Clara Barton was born, the Worcester Room, the Stephen E. Barton room, and the pantry. The upstairs rooms are not open to the public. The north ell was added sometime in the 1820s and is presently the location for the gift shop and camp store. The house was restored in 1920 and in 1986 with significant attention paid to architectural details that are appropriate to the 1820s.

All furnishings are appropriate to the period. Most of the objects belonged to the original residents, although some were collected after the museum's opening in 1921. The indoor well located in the kitchen was a unique innovation at the time the house was built.

### Notable Collections on Exhibit
Among the many items of interest, are Barton's field desk which she used during the Civil War and while directing relief operations for the Red Cross, a quilt signed by Civil War officers and surgeons who benefitted from Clara's work, as well as many personal items that belonged to Clara.

# 1830 Brick Dwelling

Junction of Routes 20 and 41
P.O. Box 89
Pittsfield, MA 01202
(413) 443-0188

**Contact:** Hancock Shaker Village
**Open:** May-Oct., daily 9:30 a.m.–5 p.m.;
April and Nov., 10 a.m.–3 p.m.
**Activities:** Orientation, history, architecture
talks; guided tours May to Oct.,
self-guided tours April and Nov.
**Facilities on Premises:** Museum Shop, cafe
**Description of Grounds:** 1200 acres of farm
land and forest; 109 additional restored
buildings; heirloom vegetable and herb
gardens

**Best Season to View House:** May-Oct.
**Number of Yearly Visitors:** 70,000
**Year House Built:** 1830 to 1831
**Style of Architecture:** Shaker Vernacular
**Number of Rooms:** Approximately 25
rooms on view
**On-Site Parking:** Yes **Wheelchair Access:** No

## Description of House

The Hancock Shaker community was founded in 1790 as the third of
eighteen Shaker villages in the country and was occupied until 1959. Approximately 300 Shakers lived at Hancock at its peak in the 1830s and 1840s.
The Shakers were a communal, religious group, the most successful of the
Utopian experiments undertaken in the United States. Believing in separation and equality of the sexes, the celibate brothers and sisters resided in the
same buildings, with men on one side and women on the other. Although
Shaker design and craftsmanship are their most enduring legacy, the
Shakers also excelled in their agricultural practices and developed successful herbal medicine and garden seed industries as well as technological
innovations.

The five-story brick dwelling was used for 130 years as a communal home for up to 100 members of the Hancock Shaker community. Many features of the building—the peg rails, borrowed light windows, and kitchen equipment (arch kettles, dumb waiters, ovens, etc.)—reflect Shaker innovation and interest in technology.

### Notable Collections on Exhibit

Hancock Shaker Village contains the largest collection of Shaker furniture and artifacts in an original Shaker site. Notable in the Brick Dwelling are rooms devoted to sewing and tailoring, a pharmacy and clocks, children's furniture, kitchen and a canning room with extensive institution sized cooking equipmnent and devices.

### Additional Information

Hancock Shaker Village also encompasses a 1790s Meetinghouse; schoolhouse; barns (including the 1826 Round Stone Barn); workshops where resident craftspeople produce reproductions of the Shaker furniture, baskets, oval boxes and textiles; a 1790s laundry/machine shop, with water-powered machinery; the Victorian trustees house; and other buildings. Shaker and other 19th-century farming methods are used in the gardens. Special events include Winter Week in February, Shearing Days in May, the Americana Artisans Show in the Round Stone Barn in July; the Antiques Show in August; and the Festival of Shaker Crafts, Industries and Agriculture in October.

# *Arrowhead*

**780 Holmes Rd
Pittsfield, MA 01201
(413) 442-1793**

**Contact:** Berkshire County Historical
Society
**Admission:** Adults $4; seniors $3.50;
children (6-12) $2.50; under 6 free.
Group rates upon request. Guided
tours, "Berkshire Legacy", videos,
museum shop.
**Suggested Time to View House:** 90 minutes
**Best Season to View House:** Summer and
autumn
**Number of Yearly Visitors:** 8000
**Year House Built:** 1780
**Style of Architecture:** Federal
**Number of Rooms:** 6 open to public
**On-Site Parking:** Yes

## *Description of House*

In 1850, Herman Melville moved his family from New York to Pittsfield, seeking reprieve from city life and a quiet place in which to write. He purchased this 18th-century farmhouse which he named Arrowhead and completed his most famous novel, Moby Dick. Melville lived, farmed, and wrote at Arrowhead for thirteen years and developed many close friendships with other Berkshire authors including Nathaniel Hawthorne, Oliver Wendell Holmes, and the Sedgewick family. Melville returned to New York in 1863 but the house remained with the family until the 1920s.

This Federal farmhouse has a twelve foot center chimney which formed the inspiration for Melville's story "I and My Chimney". The Melville study is completely restored but there is other restoration work still in progress. The original barn still stands and visitors can walk around the grounds and see Mount Greylock which Melville thought looked like a great whale.

## *Notable Collections on Exhibit*

In addition to the Melville study with its first editions and other memorabilia, Arrowhead houses a fine collection of 18th and 19th-century Berkshire County furniture.

# Plimoth Plantation

Warren Avenue
Plymouth, MA 02360
(508) 746-1622

**Contact:** Plimoth Plantation

**Open:** April-Nov., 9 a.m.–5 p.m., except from late June to Labor Day 9 a.m.–6:30 p.m.; closed Dec.-March

**Admission:** $8.50. Self-guided tours, 12 minute orientation, multi-image show, special programs.

**Suggested Time to View House:** 2 hours

**Best Season to View House:** Spring-fall

**Number of Yearly Visitors:** 450,000

**Year House Built:** All houses are reproductions from 1621

**Style of Architecture:** Post & beam, wattle & daub

**On-Site Parking:** Yes **Wheelchair Access:** No

## Description of House

While none of the structures in the plantation complex is original, this living history museum has gone to great lengths to authentically reproduce the look and feel of 17th-century Pilgrim life. The fifteen one-room homes represent the Pilgrim's first dwellings after their arrival on the Mayflower. Each house has a recreated history related to the original members of the 1627 village—everyone from Captain Miles Standish to Deacon Samuel Fuller. Colonists, portrayed by costumed museum staff, tell visitors what it is like to come to this foreign land and build a "new" England in 17th-century dialects. Buildings on the site include historic houses, a Dutch barn, the Old Common House where newly-arrived Pilgrims would live, and the Old Fort/Meeting House where colonists would worship or seek refuge in time of attack.

The houses are furnished with reproductions made by studying originals and then reproduced using the tools and methods of 17th-century artisans.

# *Harlow Old Fort House*

P.O. Box 1137
Plymouth, MA 02362
(508) 746-0012

**Contact:** Plymouth Antiquarian Society
**Open:** June, Sat.-Sun.; July 1-Sept. 6,
Tues.-Sun.; Sept. 9-Oct. 10, Wed., Thurs.,
Sat. 11 a.m.–5 p.m.
**Admission:** Adults $2.50; children $.50.
Guided tours, educational programs,
changing exhibitions.
**Suggested Time to View House:** 45 minutes
**Facilities on Premises:** Gift shop and
classroom

**Description of Grounds:** A lovely period
garden. Limited on-site parking.
**Best Season to View House:** Summer-fall
**Number of Yearly Visitors:** 7,500
**Year House Built:** 1677
**Style of Architecture:** Folk
**Number of Rooms:** 7
**Wheelchair Access:** No

## *Description of House*

The Harlow Old Fort House is a working museum which represents an
intimate glimpse into the daily life of 17th-century settlers. The house was
built and occupied by William Harlow, a cooper by trade. This small, charming
one-and-a-half story dwelling has a gambrel roof. The framework includes
timbers from an old fort on Burial Hill which was dismantled after the
Indian Wars. The building stands on its original site and is furnished with
artifacts of the period.

# Hedge House

P.O. Box 1137
Plymouth, MA 02362
(508) 746-9697

**Contact:** Plymouth Antiquarian Society
**Open:** June, Sat.-Sun.; July 1-Sept. 6,
Tues.-Sun.; Sept. 9-Oct. 10, Wed., Thurs.,
Sat. 11 a.m.–5 p.m.
**Admission:** Adults $2.50; children $.50.
Guided tours, educational programs,
changing exhibitions.
**Suggested Time to View House:** 45 minutes
**Facilities on Premises:** Gift shop, classroom

**Description of Grounds:** A lovely period
garden. Limited on-site parking.
**Best Season to View House:** Summer-Fall
**Number of Yearly Visitors:** 7,500
**Year House Built:** 1809
**Style of Architecture:** Federal
**Number of Rooms:** 16
**Wheelchair Access:** No

## Description of House

The Hedge House was home of Thomas Hedge, a Plymouth 19th-century merchant-shipowner. The Hedge family occupied this house for nearly one hundred years, they also owned Hedge's wharf at Plymouth Rock. Daniel Webster, famous orator and statesman, was a frequent guest to this attractive house.

This beautiful waterfront house was built in the Federal style, and has several octagonal-shaped rooms. The furnishings are of the same period as the house.

## Notable Collections on Exhibit

The house has an excellent collection of China trade porcelains, quilts, samplers, children's toys, dolls and costumes, and also features a fully equipped 19th-century kitchen.

# Spooner House

P.O. Box 1137
Plymouth, MA 02362
(508) 746-0012

**Contact:** Plymouth Antiquarian Society
**Open:** June, Sat.-Sun.; July 1-Sept. 6,
Tues.-Sun.; Sept. 9-Oct. 10, Wed., Thurs.,
Sat. 11 a.m.–5 p.m.
**Admission:** Adults $2.50; children $.50.
Guided tours, educational programs,
changing exhibitions.
**Suggested Time to View House:** 45 minutes
**Facilities on Premises:** Gift shop, classroom

**Description of Grounds:** A lovely period
garden. Limited on-site parking.
**Best Season to View House:** Summer-Fall
**Number of Yearly Visitors:** 7,500
**Year House Built:** 1749
**Style of Architecture:** Federal
**Number of Rooms:** 12
**Wheelchair Access:** No

## Description of House

The Spooner House was the home of the Spooner family for five generations. Family members included town officials, merchants, sea captains, and Bourne Spooner, founder of the Plymouth Cordage Company, once the largest rope maker in the world. The Spooner's owned the house until 1954.

The house and its original furnishings tell the story of the changes in taste, occupations and daily acitivities that have occurred in Plymouth from pre-Revolutionary days until its last private owner in 1954. All furnishings are original and belonged to the Spooner family.

## Additional Information

Visitors to Plymouth may also visit the society's other historic sites: the Harlow Old Fort House and the Hedge House.

# Quincy Homestead

34 Butler Rd
Quincy, MA 02769
(617) 472-5117

**Contact:** The National Society of Colonial Dames.

**Open:** May-Oct., Wed.-Sun. 12–5 p.m. (last tour starts at 4 p.m.)

**Admission:** Adults $2.50; children $.50. Guided tours.

**Suggested Time to View House:** 1 hour

**Facilities on Premises:** Gift Shop

**Description of Grounds:** 1¾ acres of Colonial-style landscaping with a brook running through it, and an herb garden maintained by the Herb Society of America

**Best Season to View House:** May-Oct.

**Number of Yearly Visitors:** 800

**Year House Built:** Two rooms 1685-86, remainder 1706 with Victorian additions

**Number of Rooms:** 19; 10 open to public

**Style of Architecture:** Colonial-Style Georgian Mansion

**On-Site Parking:** Yes **Wheelchair Access:** No

## Description of House

The Quincy Homestead, built on land granted in 1635, served as the home of four generations of the Edmund Family, including the beautiful Dorothy Quincy, wife of governor and patriot John Hancock. Abigail Adams, wife of our second president John Adams, was a Quincy descendent, and named her son, John Quincy Adam, our sixth President for her grandfather, John Quincy. Oliver Wendell Holmes's great-grandmother, Dorothy Quincy Jackson, was born in the Homestead.

This house is a fine example of a family residence that was improved and enlarged over a period of more than two hundred years. Similarily, the collected furnishings represent the changes in style which occurred in succeeding generations, creating a fascinating historic record of every-day living in a house dating three centuries.

The homestead features superb wallpaper designed and manufactured by Reveillon Freres of Paris and installed in the parlor in 1792. Another unusual aspect of the house is the secret hiding place believed to have been used during the underground railroad period.

## Notable Collections on Exhibit

John Hancock's sleigh is on display in an adjacent coach house. An original Franklin Stove—presented by Benjamin Franklin to his friend, Edmund Quincy IV—is also exhibited, as is a modest collection of Chinese export porcelain.

# Adams National Historic Site

135 Adams Street
Quincy, MA 02269
(617) 773-1177

**Contact:** National Park Service
**Open:** April 19-Nov. 10
**Admission:** Adults $2; over 62 and under 16 free. Guided tours, lectures, story hours.
**Suggested Time to View House:** 45–60 minutes
**Facilities on Premises:** Visitor center/book store
**Description of Grounds:** 14 acre estate with house, carriage house, library and orchards, meadow and 18th-century formal garden

**Best Season to View House:** May and June
**Number of Yearly Visitors:** 32,000
**Year House Built:** 1731
**Style of Architecture:** Birthplaces-saltbox, Old House-Colonial
**Number of Rooms:** 6 (Birthplaces), 20 (Old House)
**On-Site Parking:** No
**Wheelchair Access:** Yes

## Description of House

This famouse site was the birthplace of two United States presidents: John Adams, the second president, and John Quincy Adams, the sixth president. John Adams was born in 1735 in the small house at 133 Franklin Street. He gained much of his early interest in municipal affairs and farming from his father, Deacon John Adams. The adjacent house was bequeathed to John at his father's death. He brought his bride, Abigail Smith, to live in the house and it was here that she gave birth in 1767 to their second child, the future president, John Quincy Adams. Other noteworthy Adams family members who lived here were Charles Francis Adams, U.S. foreign minister to England, and the writers Henry and Brooks Adams.

The original section of the house was built in 1730 by Leonard Vassall, a wealthy planter from the West Indies who had come to Massachusetts only eight years before. The house consisted of only six rooms, two on each of the three floors. At that time the kitchen was an unattached building on the property. Above the kitchen wing, which had been added to the house before the Adams's purchase, more bedrooms were added. Eventually, four windows were punched through the solid brick west wall of the house, two in the paneled room and two in the president's bedroom above. This provided these two rooms a beautiful view of what was then the orchard. These were some of the last changes made by John and Abigail.

Four generations lived in the Old House and each generation contributed furnishings and artifacts. The clock stopped in the Old House at the time of Brooks Adams's death in 1927, and the house is shown as he left it. The furnishings in the birthplace are mainly reproductions and a few period pieces.

### Notable Collections on Exhibit
The Old House is fully furnished with original furniture. Exhibits feature Canton china, Chippendale tables, and portraits of all family members by Gilbert Stuart, Edward Savage, and Copley. The Stone Library has about 14,000 volumes, more than half belonged to John Quincy Adams, only a few hundred to John Adams, and the rest were added by the last two generations of the family.

# Derby House

174 Derby Street
Salem, MA 01970
(508)745-1470

**Contact:** Salem Maritime National Historic Site

**Open:** Daily 9 a.m.–4 p.m. Call in advance to reserve tours for groups of up to 8.

**Admission:** Free. AV programs on Salem's maritime history. Ranger guided programs on Salem's maritime trade and house tours.

**Suggested Time to View House:** 1 hour.

**Facilities on Premises:** 1840s store/visitor center with sales area.

**Best Season to View House:** April-Oct.

**Number of Yearly Visitors:** 600,000

**Year House Built:** 1762

**Style of Architecture:** Georgian style

**Number of Rooms:** 8

## Description of House

Captain Richard Derby built the house as a wedding gift to his son Elias from 1760 to 1762. Elias married Elizabeth Crowenshield in 1760. They lived in the house for twenty years and had seven children (three girls and four boys). The Derbys were involved in trade in the West Indies and owned several privateer ships during the Revolutionary War. Probably more privateers sailed from Derby Wharf than any other in the nation, and Derby was one of the few Salem merchants to emerge from the war in the black. After the war, Elias opened trade to the Far East and eventually became one of America's first millionaires. This imaginative and demanding shipowner died in 1799.

Derby House represents typical Georgian style architecture, and is the oldest brick house left standing in Salem. The house has eight furnished rooms, an unfurnished kitchen ell (1782) and four rooms in the attic.

The house exhibits collected 18th-century furnishings, china, and paintings; very few of the pieces belong to the family.

# Narbonne House

174 Derby Street
Salem, MA 01970
(508) 745-1470

**Contact:** Salem Maritime National Historic Site

**Open:** By scheduled tour only.

**Admission:** Free admission. AV programs on Salem's maritime history. Ranger guided programs on Salem's maritime trade and house tours.

**Suggested Time to View House:** 1 hour

**Facilities on Premises:** Visitor center with sales area

**Best Season to View House:** April-Oct.

**Number of Yearly Visitors:** 600,000

**Year House Built:** 1672

**Style of Architecture:** Georgian

**Number of Rooms:** 3

## Description of House

The house was home to several families from 1672 to 1960 whose occupations ranged from sailors to butchers to shopkeepers to firemen. Narbonne House is representative of the homes of middle class families living in Salem. The house is named after one of its former residents, Sarah Narbonne, who lived in the house for 100 years.

The Narbonne house is unfurnished but it contains an extensive exhibit of three centuries of architecture from the 17th century to the early 20th century. There is also an exhibit of archeological artifacts found on the site in the 1970s.

## Additional Information

There are many interesting buildings for visitors to see at the Salem Maritime National Historic Site. One of the most famous is the United States Custom House where author Nathanial Hawthorne worked from 1846 to 1849.

In addition to the structures on the maritime site, visitors to Salem are encouraged to see the nearby House of the Seven Gables (54 Turner Street), made famous by author Nathaniel Hawthorne, and the beautiful Pierce-Nichols House (80 Federal Street), home of shipping merchant Jerathmiel Pierce.

The Witch House (310 Essex Street) will provide visitors with a unique glimpse of Salem's notoriety as the home of the famous witchcraft trials of the 17th century.

# *Hoxie House*

18 Water Street
Sandwich, MA 02563
(508) 888-1173

**Contact:** Town of Sandwich
**Open:** June 15-Oct.
**Admission:** Adults $1.50;
  children (12-16) $1. Guided tours.
**Suggested Time to View House:** 45 minutes

**Number of Yearly Visitors:** 1,500-2,000
**Year House Built:** 1675
**Style of Architecture:** Saltbox
**Number of Rooms:** 3

## Description of House

High on a bluff overlooking beautiful Shawne Lake, in the center of historic Sandwich, in its original location, rests the Hoxie House. The house was built by John Smith in 1675 and lived in by his descendants until 1857. The building was purchased in 1860 by Captain Abraham Hoxie, a whaling captain, whose descendants lived in the house until 1952. Restored by the Town of Sandwich in 1959, the dwelling was opened as a museum in 1960.

The Hoxie House utilizes post and beam construction and was found to architecturally date to the 1680 to 1690 period. The house has been restored and furnished to the effect and is truly representative of early colonial construction. The oldest saltbox style house in the area, Hoxie House has remained essentially unchanged through the centuries.

## Notable Collections on Exhibit

In addition to the period furniture, there is a 17th-century loom on exhibit.

# Iron Works House

244 Central Street
Saugus, MA 01906
(617) 233-0050

**Contact:** Saugus Ironworks National
Historic Site

**Open:** April 1-Oct. 1, 9 a.m.–5 p.m.;
Nov. 1-April 1, 9 a.m.–4 p.m.; closed
Thanksgiving, Christmas and New
Year's Day

**Activities:** Guided tours and slide shows

**Suggested Time to View House:** 1 hour

**Facilities on Premises:** Visitors station

**Description of Grounds:** A scenic one-half
mile nature trail consisting of marsh and
woodland trails

**Number of Yearly Visitors:** 95,000

**Year House Built:** Mid to late 1600s

**Style of Architecture:** Late Medieval, early
Colonial

**Number of Rooms:** 6

**On-Site Parking:** Yes **Wheelchair Access:** Yes

## Description of House

Most likely the first occupant of this unusual dwelling was Samuel Appleton, who ran the farm on The Old Ironworks site in the early 1680s. On February 15, 1688 the house was sold to James Taylor, a Boston merchant. The structure passed through several hands including the Mansfield family in the early 1800s. Eventually Wallace Nutting purchased and restored the house in 1915.

The Iron Works House is the sole-surviving 17th-century structure at Saugus Iron Works. The brown clapboard house is a garrison with pendants hanging off the corners and pinnacle on top of the gabled roof. Initially thought to be the Ironmasters house, there has been conflicting evidence indicating the house may not have been built until ten to twelve years after the Ironworks went out of business in 1668. It was, however, the impetus that led later to the discovery of the Ironworks sites and restoration between 1948 and 1954.

The first floor parlor, the second floor parlor chamber, and the study are furnished with a combination of authentic and reproduction 17th-century furnishings. There is also a working blacksmith shop on site.

## Notable Collections on Exhibit

Two rooms contain exhibits. The first floor hall is devoted to 17th-century architecture, building hardware, and tools. The upstairs bedroom is devoted to Wallace Nutting and his restoration of the house, furniture, and photography, as well as hardware by blacksmiths Edward and Edward Leslie Guy.

# Dan Raymond House

Route Seven, P.O. Box 1733
Sheffield, MA 01257
(413) 229-2694

**Contact:** Sheffield Historical Society

**Open:** Fri. 1:30–4 p.m. ( closed Fri. after Thanksgiving and Christmas); also open by appointment

**Admission:** Free. Guided tours, audio-visual history of Sheffield shown during open house programs. Annual tours by elementary school children and 8th grade classes.

**Suggested Time to View House:** 30 minutes–1 hour

**Description of Grounds:** Carriage house, 1820 law office, brick workshop, family history center

**Best Season to View House:** June-July

**Number of Yearly Visitors:** 200 plus

**Year House Built:** 1774

**Style of Architecture:** Georgian

**Number of Rooms:** 8 open to public

**On-Site Parking:** Yes **Wheelchair Access:** No

## Description of House

The house was built by Dan Raymond, a wealthy Sheffield merchant. He was a Tory at the beginning of the Revolution but later served in various town capacities, including chairman of a committee to recruit soldiers for the Continental Army. From 1816 to 1828 the house was owned by Mark Dewey, who built a shoe shop next door, now owned by the historical society and used as a family history center. Stephen Miller, who owned the house from 1871 to 1880, operated a well-known hotel and built the brick building behind the house to grow vegetables for his hotel.

Located in the Sheffield Center National Register Historic district, this two-and-a-half-story home with center hall and end chimneys was originally made of homemade brick, Flemish bond pattern, and is now painted salmon color. The 1840 addition is wood frame. The facade nine % windows with marble lintels and watercourses around a center entry, which has a leading glass transom. Furnishings in the original part of house are appropriate to the period, though not from the original residents. An 1840 addition contains an appropriately furnished keeping room on the first floor and a Victorian room on the second floor.

This is an excellent example of a home owned by various well-to-do Sheffield families, several of whom were prominent in town affairs. The interpretation of the guided tours includes references to the contributions of the owners to the property and to village life.

## Notable Collections on Exhibit

The changing exhibits include clothing, accessories, early photographs, and archival materials. The two 1847 paintings by Nelson Cook are of the fourth minister, the Reverend James Bradford, and Mrs. Bradford. An oil painting of Charles Sabin (1796-1833) hangs in the south parlor.

# *Merwin House – Tranquility*

**14 Main Street**
**Stockbridge, MA 01262**
**(413) 298-4703**

**Contact:** Soc. for the Preservation of New England Antiquities
**Open:** June 1-Oct. 15, Tue., Thurs., Sat., Sun. 12–5 p.m.; tours on the hour
**Admission:** $4. Guided tours, English teas, and party with Victorian lawn games.

**Description of Grounds:** Beautiful gardens and lawn which spreads down to the Housatonic River.
**Year House Built:** 1825
**Style of Architecture:** Late Federal

## Description of House

At the end of the 19th century, railroads opened up the Berkshires, which soon became a summer destination for wealthy New Yorkers. The house was purchased by William and Elizabeth Doane as a summer home in 1875. It was then preserved by their daughter, Vipont Merwin.

This handsome brick structure dates from the late Federal period. Around 1900, the Doanes doubled it size by adding a shingle-style ell remodeled the interior of the main house.

They decorated the house in an eclectic manner with European and American furnishings, much of which was collected during their extensive travels.

Situated in the heart of the charming resort town of Stockbridge, the house reflects a leisurely summer existence, with afternoons spent strolling through the gardens and down the lawn to the Housatonic River.

# *The Mission House*

Main Street, Box 792
Stockbridge, MA 01262
(413) 298-3239

**Contact:** The Trustees of Reservations
**Open:** Memorial Day–Columbus Day,
Tues.–Sun., 11 a.m.–4 p.m. and Mon.
holidays. Closed Tues. after holidays.
**Admission:** Adults $4; children (6-12) $1;
groups $3.50. Guided Tours, self
interpreted Indian Museum.
**Suggested Time to View House:** 40 minutes
**Facilities on Premises:** Sales desk

**Description of Grounds**: Colonial gardens
currently under restoration
**Number of Yearly Visitors:** 2700
**Year House Built:** 1739
**Style of Architecture:** Colonial house with
Connecticut doorway
**Number of Rooms:** 5 plus attic
**On-Site Parking:** Yes **Wheelchair Access:** No

## *Description of House*

John Sergeant was a tutor at Yale when he was asked to become a missionary to the Mohicans and Housatonic Indians in Berkshire County. In 1734, he moved to the area. Five years later the town of Stockbridge was incorporated and the Indians took the name Stockbridge Indians. The house was built as a residence for him and his wife, Abigail Williams. John Sergeant died in 1749, and, while his wife moved away to Great Barrington, Erastus Sergeant remained at the Mission House with his wife and twelve children. The house remained with the Sergeant family until 1870.

Moved to its present location in 1928, the Mission House is a very good example of of an accurate restoration of an early colonial house. The walls were painted with tempera base mixed with egg yolks, brick dust or paris green for yellow, red and green colors. The original paneling was also saved.

In addition to completely restoring the house, Miss Mabel Choate was also able to reassemble most of the original Sergeant furnishings which had been auctioned in 1908. There are many 17th and 18th-century pieces in impecable condition.

# The Naumkeag Museum and Gardens

Prospect Hill Road, Box 792
Stockbridge, MA 01262
(413) 298-3239

**Contact:** The Trustees of Reservations

**Open**: Memorial Day-Labor Day, 10 a.m.–4:15 p.m.; Labor Day-Columbus Day. Sat., Sun., and holidays only

**Admission:** Adults $6 (house and garden); $4 (garden only); children $1.50; groups $5. Guided house tour, self interpreted gardens.

**Suggested Time to View House:** 45 minutes-house, 30 minutes-garden

**Description of Grounds:** The spectacular formal, landscape gardens were designed by Miss Choate and landscape architect Fletcher Steele

**Best Season to View House:** Late June-early fall

**Style of Architecture:** Norman shingle style summer mansion

**Number of Yearly Visitors:** 12,500

**Number of Rooms:** 26

**Year House Built:** 1886

**On-Site Parking:** Yes **Wheelchair Access:** Yes

## Description of House

The Naumkeag Museum was designed by Stanford White as a summer home for Mr. and Mrs. Joseph Choate. Joseph Choate was a noted attorney who practiced in New York City, and served as Ambassador to the Court of St. James from 1899 to 1905. Mrs. Choate, Caroline Dutcher Sterling, born in Cleveland was studying art in New York where she met Mr. Choate. They were married in 1861 and celebrated their fiftieth anniversary at Naumkeag. Mabel Choate, their youngest daughter, inherited the house in 1929 and created the existing gardens from 1929 to 1956. Mabel died in 1958 and bequeathed the house to the Trustees of Reservations. The house today appears exactly as she left it.

Naumkeag is one of three Berkshire cottages open to the public where the visitors can enjoy the atmosphere of a bygone era. This simple house is constructed of brick and stone and stands on Prospect Hill overlooking the Berkshire hills. All of the furnishings were originally owned by the Choates.

## Notable Collections on Exhibit

Stanford White helped Mrs. Choate purchase part of the collection of 19th-century furnishings and English porcelain for Naumkeag. Miss Mabel Choate later added her own collection of Oriental rugs and Chinese export porcelain.

## Additional Information

To get to the house (which may be difficult for visitors) take Pine Street off Main in Stockbridge. Bear left at the fork and proceed one half mile to the house.

# *Mary Baker Eddy Historic House*

133 Central Street
Stoughton, MA 02702
(617) 344-3904

**Contact:** Longyear Museum and Historical
Society
**Open:** May-Oct., Tues.-Sat. 10 a.m.–4 p.m.;
Sun. 2–4 p.m.
**Admission:** $1.50. Guided tours.

**Suggested Length of Time to View House:**
30 minutes
**Facilities on Premises:** Gift area
**Description of Grounds:** Yard
**Year House Built:** c. 1850
**On-Site Parking:** Yes   **Handicap Access:** No

## *Description of House*

In 1868, at the invitation of Mr. and Mrs. Alanson Wentworth, Mary
Baker Eddy (then Mrs. Patterson) moved into their home. For the next two
years she spent most of her time writing down her ideas on the spiritual
significance of the Scriptures, which led to the completion of her
manuscript, *The Science of Man.* The furnishings are collected and appropriate to the period. A separate and fully equipped cobbler shop of the
period may also be seen on the grounds.

# Old Sturbridge Village

Old Sturbridge Village Road
Sturbridge, MA 01566
(508) 347-3362

**Contact:** Old Sturbridge Village

**Open:** May-Oct., daily 9 a.m.–5 p.m.;
Nov.-April, Tues.-Sun. 10 a.m.–4 p.m.;
closed Christmas and New Year's Day

**Admission:** Adults $14; children (6-15) $7;
under 6 free. 20 minute introductory slide
presentation, year round special events.

**Suggested Time to View House:** 3 hours

**Facilities on Premises:** Gift shop,
restaurant, lodging, book store

**Description of Grounds:** 200 acre living
history museum with over 40 restored
buildings from the 19th century

**Best Season to View House:** All year

**Year House Built:** 6 houses ranging from
early 18th to early 19th centuries

**Number of Rooms:** Varies

**Number of Yearly Visitors:** 500,000

**Style of Architecture:** Vernacular New
England

**On-Site Parking:** Yes  **Wheelchair Access:** Yes

## Description of House

Old Sturbridge Village was first opened to the public in 1946. Today, it is the largest living history museum where visitors can explore and experience the life, work, and celebrations of an early 19th-century New England Community. There are six completely restored historic houses in addition to a water-powered sawmill, a blackshop, tavern, a cider mill, and other shops essential to the community. At the Freeman Farm, visitors can see a reenactment of typical activities on a New England Farm. Everything from the birth of animals in the spring to the hard work of preparing for the long winter is represented through activities at the farm.

Each house is furnished to illustrate an interpretive scenario of use for the period 1825 through 1840. Furnishings include furniture, ceramics, glass, and metalwares. There are also accurately reproduced treatments for textile installations on windows, beds and upholstery.

## Notable Collections on Exhibit

The collections equal about 100,000 objects made or used in New England prior to 1840 of which approximately 20 percent are on exhibit. The J. Cheney Wells Clock Gallery exhibits over 100 early American clocks and time pieces that sound on the hour year round. This collection represents developments in wood and brass movements, and includes tall case, wall, and shelf clocks made in New England between 1750 and 1840.

## Additional Information

Sturbridge Village is noted for its recreations of events and celebrations of the early 19th century including an 1830s Fourth of July and a traditional Thanksgiving celebration. The village also includes one of the most extensive herb gardens in New England.

# *Parson Capen House*

1 Howlett Street
Topsfield, MA 01983
(508) 887-3998

**Contact:** Topsfield Historical Society
**Open:** June-mid Sept., Wed., Fri., Sun.
1–4:30 p.m.
**Admission:** Donations accepted. The
Priscilla Capen Herb Society serves tea
every Wed. from 2–4 p.m. during summer
months; guided tours.
**Suggested Time to View House:** 30 minutes
**Facilities on Premises:** Gift shop, library

**Description of Grounds:** One acre site on
rise overlooking the Topsfield Common
and includes an herb garden
**Best Season to View House:** Summer-fall
**Number of Yearly Visitors:** 1000-2000
**Year House Built:** 1683
**Style of Architecture:** Vernacular
Elizabethan
**Number of Rooms:** 5
**On-Site Parking:** Yes **Wheelchair Access:** No

## Description of House

The house was built by the Town of Topsfield for Joseph Capen, a
minister and Harvard graduate. Capen was minister during the infamous
1692 witchcraft tragedy, and unsuccessfully spoke on behalf of three women
from his congregation who were ultimately hanged.

The Parson Capen House is an outstanding example of an early colonial
period home. The structure is framed by the original oak beams and posts.
The house is probably one of the finest surviving examples of Elizabethan
architecture in America. The second story of the house overhangs the first
in the front, the third story overhangs the second at its ends, all overhangs
are supported by decorative wooden brackets. Some of the furnishings are
appropriate to the period, the rest date from a later period. The house was
designated a National Landmark in 1960.

## Notable Collections on Exhibit

Several paintings of the Capen family are on exhibit, as well as a food
hutch (c. 1675), an oak chest (c. 1670), and a 1708 chair inscribed "P Capen,"
believed to have been a wedding gift from Joseph to his daughter, Priscilla.

# Gore Place

52 Gore Street
Waltham, MA 02154
(617) 894-2798

**Contact:** Gore Place Society
**Open:** Apr. 15-Nov. 15, Tues.-Sat.
10 a.m.–5 p.m. and Sun. 2–5 p.m.
**Admission:** Tours: adults $4; seniors and students with valid ID $3; children (12 and under) $2. Grounds are open free of charge. Guided tours; Sheepshearing Day last Sat. in April; Christmas open house.
**Suggested Time to View House:** 1 hour
**Facilities on Premises:** Gift shop with many books for sale

**Description of Grounds:** The house is situated on 40 acres of cultivated fields, woodlands and gardens. There is also a carriage house and flock of sheep.
**Number of Yearly Visitors:** 8,000
**Year House Built:** Broke ground in 1805, completed in 14 months
**Style of Architecture:** Neo-palladian
**Number of Rooms:** 22
**On-Site Parking:** Yes **Wheelchair Access:** No

## Description of House

Christopher Gore (1758-1827), the son of a Boston heraldic painter of carriages and signs, graduated from Harvard College in 1776 and became a lawyer, diplomat and statesman. In 1783, he married Rebecca Amory Payne, the daughter of a wealthy maritime insurance agent and bank founder. Gore became a very successful mercantile lawyer and within 10 years of marriage, he had acquired a handsome fortune. As a diplomat, Gore served in London on the Jay Commission from 1796 to 1804. He became the seventh governor of Massachusetts in 1809 and later served in the U.S. Senate.

This is one of the finest examples of Federal architecture in New England. Gore Place is a 185 foot long brick structure with a carriage front on a central block. It has an oval saloon with a bow front and a 25 foot high spiral stair and a marble paved reception hall. The first floor of the central block contains the State suite of rooms, the upper floor contains the family living quarters.

The house is filled with fine early American, European, and Oriental furnishings. Approximately five percent of the collection belonged to the Gores, the remainder is appropriate to the period.

The structure of the house is special because of the hyphen arcades and Greek temple form of of the end pavillions.

### Notable Collections on Exhibit

The mansion is furnished with a fine collection of Federal period furniture, china, silver, textiles and paintings. Notable furniture includes an Adam Haines shield back chair, a 7½-foot diameter drop-leaf library table, a step chair, a Baltimore secretary with satinwood inlay and eglomise panels, and numerous clocks. Notable textiles include Gore's diplomatic court uniform and a Gore bed hung with a reproduction of a pillar print.

### Additional Information

In 1935, Gore Place Society was formed to save the mansion from destruction and to research, restore and refurnish the house and the remaining portion of the estate to the period of the Gore's occupancy. A book called *The House Servant's Dictionary*, originally published in 1827 by Gore's butler, Robert Roberts, has been reproduced by the society in a facsimile edition and is available for purchase in the museum shop.

# Lyman Estate, Vale House

185 Lyman Street
Waltham, MA 02154
(617) 891-7232

**Contact:** Soc. for the Preservation of New
Engalnd Antiquities

**Open:** Greenhouse open Mon.-Sat.
9:30 a.m.–3:30 p.m.; groups of 10 or more
may visit both house and greenhouse by
appointment

**Admission:** House $3; Greenhouse $2;
groups by appointment. Camellia Days
in Winter; spring, summer and fall plant
sales; a Christmas open house and plant
sale; and plant and crafts workshops.

**Year House Built:** 1793

**Style of Architecture:** Federal

## Description of House

The house was designed in 1793 by the Salem architect Samuel McIntire for a wealthy Boston merchant and entrepreneur, Theodore Lyman.

The Lyman Estate, known as the Vale, is one of the finest examples in the United States of a country estate laid out according to the principles of 18th-century English naturalistic design. In 1882, the house was substantially enlarged with the addition on the third floor, and in 1917 it was remodeled to reflect its 18th-century origins. The house is now furnished with many reproductions.

The historic greenhouses are evidence of a fascination with horticulture common among the Boston gentry in the early years of the Republic. They contain century-old camellia trees and grapevines, along with tropical and subtropical plants, herbs, and other potted plants. The 1804 Grape House contains grapevines grown from cuttings taken from Hampton Court in England in 1870.

# Grout-Heard House

P.O. Box 56
Wayland, MA 01778
(508) 358-7959

**Contact:** Wayland Historical Society

**Open:** April-June, Sept.-mid Dec., Wed.
10 a.m.–12 p.m. and by appointment

**Activities:** Guided tours, slide and tape programs, monthly meetings

**Suggested Time to View House:** 40 minutes

**Description of Grounds:** Simple, natural grounds

**Best Season to View House:** Spring-fall

**Year House Built:** 1740

**Style of Architecture:** Georgian

**Number of Rooms:** 8

**On-Site Parking:** Yes **Wheelchair Access:** No

## Description of House

Jonathan Grout was the owner of the property at the time the house was built. His marriage in 1743 would have been ample reason to expand the existing structure. Several other generations of the family lived on the property, including Jonathan's daughter, Jerusha, and her husband, Merwell Heard, a local proprietor.

The oldest part of the Grout-Heard House, as determined by architectural studies, was built around 1740. To the original four front rooms and lean-to, subsequent owners added the rear rooms of the first floor and a second floor and attic. The furnishings are local objects which have been donated since 1954.

## Notable Collections on Exhibit

On display are furniture, china, toys, dolls, costumes, quilts, farm tools, maps, documents, and photographs.

# Dadmun-McNamara House

229 Washington Street
Wellesley Hills, MA 02181
(617) 235-6690

**Contact:** Wellesley Historical Society

**Open:** Mon. and Sat. 2–4:30 p.m.

**Admission:** Free; donations accepted.

**Suggested Time to View House:** 20 minutes

**Facilities on Premises:** Gift shop (only during month before Christmas)

**Description of Grounds:** Flower borders and small herb garden

**Best Season to View House:** Spring-fall

**Number of Yearly Visitors:** 500

**Year House Built:** 1824

**Style of Architecture:** Simple, early New England farmhouse

**Number of Rooms:** 8

**On-Site Parking:** Yes  **Wheelchair Access:** Yes

### Description of House

Daniel Dadmun built this simple farmhouse in 1824 at the intersection of two major roads where he worked as a toll taker. The first floor has a 19th-century parlor, two rooms devoted to changing exhibitions and one for varied uses. Rooms on the second floor are used for work, study and storage of archives, artifacts and photographs. The basement is climate controlled and has storage of other archival materials, books, costumes, textiles and natural history specimens.

The east parlor is set up as a period room with furnishings ranging from 18th to late 19th century.

### Notable Collections on Exhibit

Exhibits frequently display artifacts from Wellesley's past as well as art work by Wellesley artists. Recent art showings have included the work of Charles Aiker and Mary Brewster Hayalton and a special exhibition devoted to the original illustrations of William Lodd Taylor, Wellesley's noted period illustrator from 1900.

# Claflin-Richards House

132 Main Street
Wenham, MA 01984
(508) 468-2377

**Contact:** Wenham Museum
**Open:** Mon.-Fri. 11 a.m.–4 p.m.; Sat.
1–4 p.m.; Sun. 2–5 p.m.; closed major
holidays
**Admission:** Adults $3; seniors $2.50;
children (6-14) $1; group rates by
reservation. Guided tours, use of
17th-century room and fireplace for 3rd
grade program on colonial households.

**Suggested Time to View House:** 30 minutes
**Facilities on Premises:** Gift shop
**Description of Grounds:** Two 19th-century
"10-footer" shoe shops
**Number of Yearly Visitors:** 12,000
**Year House Built:** c. 1660

## Description of House

The Claflin-Richards House has had many owners during the more than 300 years it has stood on its Main Street lot in the center of town. As one of the oldest houses in town (built in 1660), the house has been the home of a farmer, minister, cordwainer, of blacksmiths, and of widows. The men held town offices from deer reeve to selectman. During the American Revolution, Captain Friske drilled his company on the nearby training field. Daniel Webster is known to have visited the house and Kossuth, the Hungarian patriot, stopped to drink the excellent water from the well. The house is named for the first known owner and occupant, Claflin, and the last, Richards.

The Claflin-Richards house has many English architectural features adapted by the early settlers: the heavy frame construction; a high pitched roof; the overhanging second story; and small, leaded casement windows with diamond shaped panes, or "quarrels." Today visitors can still see the original one-over-one floor plan with end chimney and the two-and-a-half story addition made twelve years later.

The furnishings reflect various periods in house's history from the mid 1660s to the early 1700s and mid 1800s. All furnishings were collected and donated.

## Notable Collections on Exhibit

The house exhibits a large quilt collection (including a bed rug dated 1724); a costume collection (1800 to present); and tin and woodenware. The nearby museum contains a world-famous doll collection (5,000 items) begun by Elizabeth Richards Horton, who lived in the Clafin-Richards House. Other museum collections are lead soldiers, doll houses, antique toys, and miniature rooms.

# The Potter Mansion

1305 Memorial Avenue
West Springfield, MA 01089
(413) 787-0136

**Contact:** Storrowton Village Museum
**Open:** June-Aug., Mon.-Sat. 11 a.m.–3:30
p.m.; Oct.-Nov., Feb.-June, guided tours
by appointment
**Admission:** Adults $3; children $2; under 6
free. Guided tours of historic houses,
programs throughout the year, craft
workshops, summer day camp, "Taste of
History" tour and dinner, free concerts
**Suggested Time to View House:** 90 minutes
(entire village)

**Facilities on Premises:** General Store,
gift/book shop
**Description of Grounds:** Part of Storrowton
Village Museum
**Best Season to View House:** Summer and
fall
**Number of Yearly Visitors:** 12,000
**Year House Built:** 1776
**Style of Architecture:** Colonial Mansion
**On-Site Parking:** Yes **Wheelchair Access:** No

## Description of House

Captain John Potter served as an officer in the Army during the Revolutionary War and was a survivor of Valley Forge. A skilled mechanic and
master of seven trades, Potter built this magnificient home by himself, with
the exception of the plastering. The home was occupied by five generations
of Potters until it passed out of the hands of the family in 1920. The Potter
Mansion moved to Storrowton Village in 1928.

Potter made all the nails, latches and hinges and fashioned all the
elaborately ornamented wood for this elegant dwelling. The mansion was
built over a smaller house. A large room to the left of the main entrance has
a huge fireplace with a brick bake oven and cabinets across the chimney.
Upstairs, Potter created a large hall that was used for dancing and public
gatherings. The "ballroom" has an arched ceiling and is ornamented with
double dentil work. Outside, the wood sheathing is grooved to represent
stone (an unusual feature). Interior rooms contain fireplaces, mantels and
interesting woodwork of the era.

## Additional Information

The mansion is part of Storrowton Village Museum, an authentic,
recreated village of nine 18th and 19th-century buildings from Massachusetts and New Hampshire. They are assembled around a traditional
town green. A tour of Storrowton offers an intimate look at early American
living. While remaining small enough to allow for a relaxing visit, the village
has all the ingredients for a meaningful historic experience.

# The Phillips House

1305 Memorial Avenue
West Springfield, MA 01089
(413) 787-0136

**Contact:** Storrowton Village Museum
**Open:** June-Aug., Mon.-Sat.
11 a.m.–3:30 p.m.; Oct.-Nov.,
Feb.-June, guided tours only
**Admission:** Adults $3; children $2; under 6
free. Guided tours of historic houses,
programs throughout the year, craft
workshops, summer day camp, "Taste of
History" tour and dinner, free concerts
**Suggested Time to View House:** 90 minutes
(entire village)

**Facilities on Premises:** General Store,
gift/book Shop
**Description of Grounds:** Part of Storrowton
Village Museum
**Best Season to View House:** Summer and
fall
**Number of Yearly Visitors:** 12,000
**Year House Built:** 1767
**Style of Architecture:** Colonial
**On-Site Parking:** Yes **Wheelchair Access:** No

## Description of House

Occupied by more than a dozen families over the years, the Phillips House originally stood on High Street in Taunton, Massachusetts.

Built in 1767, the gambrel-roofed house is the oldest building in Storrowton Village and is a beautiful example of early workmanship. Sills and beams of oak were hand-hewn, partitions were reinforced with hand-split laths, nails were hand-forged and each brick in the chimney and fireplaces was molded by hand.

Built-in cupboards, a spacious kitchen, fireplaces in all the main rooms and interesting woodwork are among the many fine features of this home.

## Additional Information

The Philips House is part of Storrowton Village Museum, an authentic, recreated village of nine 18th and 19th-century buildings from Massachusetts and New Hampshire. They are assembled around a traditional town green.

# *Winslow Crocker House*

**250 Route 6A**
**Yarmouth Port, MA 02675**
**(508) 362-4385**

**Contact:** Soc. for the Preservation of New
England Antiquities
**Open:** June 1-Oct. 15, Tues., Thurs., Sat.,
Sun. 12–5 p.m.; tours on the hour

**Admission:** $4. Guided tours.
**Year House Built:** c.1780
**Style of Architecture:** Colonial Cape Cod

## *Description of House*

This was originally the house of a wealthy 18th-century trader and land speculator. In 1936, Mary Thacher, an antiques collector moved the house to Yarmouth Port and used it to display her collection.

In 1936, the house was moved to its present location by Mary Thacher, an avid collector of antiques. Considering that Cape Cod in the 18th century was a region of small farms and fishing ports, the house is surprisingly elaborate, with rich paneling in every room. Thacher took a non-historical approach to its restoration, because her primary goal was to provide a backdrop for the display of her collection. Woodwork was stripped, smaller-paned windows installed, and a fireplace rebuilt to contain a beehive oven. The result is a colonial Cape Cod with a 20th-century flavor.

Thacher's collection of furniture, accented by colorful hooked rugs, ceramics, and pewter, presents a thorough survey of early American styles, from Jacobean, William and Mary, and Queen Anne to Chippendale.

# New Hampshire

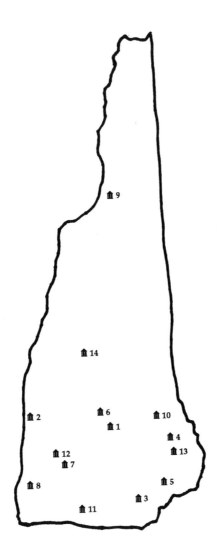

1. **Canterbury**
   *Canterbury Shaker Village*

2. **Cornish**
   *Aspet*

3. **Derry**
   *Robert Frost Farm*

4. **Dover**
   *John Parker Hale House*

5. **Exeter**
   *Gilman Garrison House*

6. **Franklin**
   *Daniel Webster Birthplace*

7. **Hillsboro**
   *Franklin Pierce Homestead State Historic Site*

8. **Keene**
   *Wyman Tavern*

9. **Lancaster**
   *John Wingate Weeks Historic Site*

10. **Milton**
    *Jones Farm*

11. **New Ipswich**
    *Barrett House—Forest Hall*

12. **Newbury**
    *The Fells—John Hay National Wildlife Refuge*

13. **Portsmouth**
    *Governor John Langdon House*
    *John Paul Jones House Museum*
    *Rundlet-May House*
    *Strawberry Banke Museum*
    *Wentworth-Coolidge Mansion*

14. **Rumney**
    *Mary Baker Eddy Historic House*

# Canterbury Shaker Village

288 Shaker Road
Canterbury, NH 03224
(603) 783-9511

**Contact:** Canterbury Shaker Village, Inc.

**Open:** May-Oct. 31, Mon.-Sun.
10 a.m–5 p.m.; Sun. noon–5 p.m.;
April, Nov.and Dec., Fri.and Sat.
10 a.m–5 p.m.; Sun. 12–5 p.m.

**Admission:** Adults $7; children $3.50;
group rates available. Guided tours,
special events, craft demonstrations,
exhibits.

**Suggested Time to View House:** 90
minutes

**Facilities on Premises:** Gift shop,
restaurant

**Description of Grounds:** 690 acres
with a nature trail around Shaker
dug pond

**Best Season to View House:** May-Oct.

**Number of Yearly Visitors:** 60,000

**Year House Built:** 1792 (Meeting
House)

## Description of House

Canterbury Shaker Village was founded in the 1780s, the sixth of nineteen Shaker communities. At its peak in 1860, 300 people lived, worked and worshipped in 100 buildings on 4,000 acres. These hard-working people made their living from farming, selling seeds and herbs, manufacturing medicine, and making crafts.

The twenty three buildings in Canterbury Shaker Village are all original to the site and completely furnished. With the exception of the brick Trustees building, all of the living and working structures have simple clapboard construction. The furnishings are from the original Shakers who lived here and are partially augmented with Shaker acquisitions from other communities.

## Notable Collections on Exhibit

The most noteworthy collection on exhibit is the beautiful and functional furniture which comes from the original residents and from other Shaker communities. Some of the items on display include tall chests, sewing desks, work tables, beds, chairs, peg rails, benches, stoves, oval boxes, and Shaker baskets. For the first time, the Injarmary with original 1848 to 1890 furnishings is now open to the public.

# Aspet

RR 3, Box 73<br>Cornish, NH 03745<br>(603) 675-2175

**Contact:** Saint-Gaudens National Historic Site

**Open:** Memorial Day-Oct. 31

**Admission:** Adults (17-61) $1; all others free. House tours, walking tours, studio talks, demonstrations, concerts and exhibitions, walking trails.

**Suggested Time to View House:** 2 hours

**Facilities on Premises:** Gift shop and book store

**Description of Grounds:** Grounds with sculpture garden

**Best Season to View House:** Summer and fall

**Number of Yearly Visitors:** 40,000

**Year House Built:** c. 1800

**Number of Rooms:** 11 (only 4 rooms open to the public)

**Style of Architecture:** Georgian-Federal

**On-Site Parking:** Yes  **Wheelchair Access:** Yes

## Description of House

This stately house and scenic grounds were the final home of noted sculptor Augustus Saint-Gaudens. Beginning in 1891, the property was first rented by Saint-Gaudens from a friend as a summer resort. The sculptor made certain alterations to the house that year and many more after he purchased the property in 1895. In 1897, he went abroad to live for three years. He gave up his New York residence, but he kept his home in Cornish. When he returned, he lived there the remainder of his life. After Saint-Gaudens's death in 1907, his widow and son, Homer Saint-Gaudens, provided for the preservation of the property.

Constructed of brick, Aspet's elegant symmetry is enhanced by a gable roof surmounted by a pair of parapeted brick chimneys and two porches along the west and east elevations, The symmetry is broken only by a glazed second story porch off the east side of the master bedroom where one can almost picture Saint-Gaudens sitting and breathing in the fresh air to improve his health. In addition to large white shuttered windows, decorating the facade is an arching trellis over the front doorway. All furnishings are from the original residents.

## Notable Collections on Exhibit

The grounds feature a striking collection of over 200 pieces of sculpture by Saint-Gaudens. Aspet also houses an exhibit of several paintings by acquaintances of the sculptor known as the Cornish Colony artists: George Deforest Brush, Thomas Dewing and John LaFarge.

# Robert Frost Farm

**Route 28, P.O. Box 856**
**Derry, NH 03302**
**(603) 432-3051**

**Contact:** New Hampshire Div. of Parks and Recreation

**Open:** Memorial Day-Labor Day, 10 a.m.–6 p.m.

**Admission:** Adults $2.50; under 18 free (with adult supervision), children's groups by reservation. Guided tours, audio visual presentation, poetry/nature walks.

**Suggested Time to View House:** 1 hour

**Facilities on Premises:** Frost books for sale

**Description of Grounds:** Half mile nature trail which passes by Hyla Brook and Mending Hall

**Best Season to View House:** Late spring, summer, fall

**Number of Yearly Visitors:** 5000

**Year House Built:** 1884

**Style of Architecture:** New England Farmhouse

**Number of Rooms:** 8

**On-Site Parking:** Yes  **Wheelchair Access:** Yes

## Description of House

Robert Frost moved into the Derry farm in 1900 with his wife Elinor and their daughter Lesley. On the farm, Frost found the peace and tranquility he needed to write his poetry. Frost wrote nearly all the poems for his first two volumes of poetry: "A Boy's Will" and "North of Boston" on and about the Derry farm. Places, events, and things from the Derry farm have been immortalized in Frost's poetry.

This typical turn-of-the-century New England farmhouse, where Frost lived for ten years, has white clapboard siding and an attached barn. When the poet moved here in 1900, the house had with it thirteen acres of land. Visitors can still see the original land holdings plus an additional forty seven which were added more recently.

Most of the furnishings represent what was in the Frost home during that period. Smaller items are original Frost family items donated to the state by his eldest daughter, Lesley Frost Ballentine.

# *John Parker Hale House*

190 Central Avenue
Dover, NH
(603)742-1038

**Contact:** The Woodman Institute

**Open:** Tues.-Sat. 2–5 p.m. Closed in Feb. and March and major holidays.

**Admission:** Free admission, donations accepted. Free public lectures. Please call ahead for additional information.

**Suggested Time to View House:** 90 minutes

**Facilities on Premises:** Book store

**Best Season to View House:** Spring-fall

**Number of Yearly Visitors:** 4,000

**Year House Built:** 1813

**Style of Architecture:** Three-story brick

**On-Site Parking:** No **Wheelchair Access:** No

## Description of House

John P. Hale was a famous abolitionist U.S. Senator from 1840 until his death in 1872. His widow made her home here until she passed away in 1903. The property was acquired by the institute trustees in 1915.

The John P. Hale House is the third structure in the three building complex. Furniture includes one of the first Chickering pianos which has been in the building for over 130 years. There are also several pieces of black and gold furniture that the Hales brought home from Spain where John Hale served as Minister of the Court of Spain from 1865 to 1869.

## Notable Collections on Exhibit

Extensive historical collections are shown in the house. The first floor contains nearly forty glass cases containing hundreds of items relating to the Dover historical background. Tools, engraved powder horns, pewter, political items and old fire-fighting equipment are to be seen. A large number of navigational equipment and scrimshaw is also shown. The second floor houses an interesting display of antique furniture and oil paintings, some pieces being of exceptional value and interest.

## Additional Information

The John P. Hale House forms part of a three building complex which also contains a museum of natural history. Of particular interest is the Garrison House built in 1675. It is one of the few, if not the only garrison of that era with its original exterior intact. The house has port-holes where guns could fire at attacking Indians should they penetrate the stockade that surrounded the building. The building was used as a residence until after the Civil War. The third building is the Woodman House. This was the residence of Annie E. Woodman, the donor of the Institute trust fund.

# *Gilman Garrison House*

12 Water Street
Exeter, NH 03883
(603) 436-3205

**Contact:** Soc. for the Preservation for New England Antiquities
**Open:** June-mid Oct., Tues., Thurs., Sat.-Sun. 12–5 p.m.
**Admission:** $4. Guided tours on the hour.

**Suggested Time to View House:** 1 hour
**Year House Built:** c. 1690
**Style of Architecture:** Colonial
**On-Site Parking:** Yes

## Description of House

From the first English settlements of the 1630s to the Treaty of Paris in 1763, the frontier towns of New England lived with the threat of Indian attack. The Gilman Garrison, known after 1700 as "the old logg house", was built as a fortified house, strategically sited to protect the valuable sawmills and water power sites owned by John Gilman.

The interior of this unique building reveals walls constructed of massive sawn logs, an interior strong room, and a system of pulleys used to operate a portcullis, or heavy door that could be dropped down behind the main entrance. The huge squared-off logs were held together by dovetail joints which formed impenetrable and fire-resistant walls. In 1772, Peter Gilman, John Gilman's Tory grandson, substantially remodelled the house. He added a new wing to accomodate the Royal Governor during his periodic visits to Exeter. Ironically, this fashionable refurbishing, with rich interior paneling in honor of the king's emissary, was completed only four years before the Revolution. The house has been restored to reflect its appearance during this period.

# Daniel Webster Birthplace

Route 127, P.O. Box 856
Franklin, NH 03235
(603) 934-5057

**Contact:** New Hampshire Div.of Parks and
Recreation

**Open:** Memorial Day-Labor Day,
10 a.m.–6 p.m.

**Admission:** Adults $2.50; under 18 free
(with adult supervision); N.H. senior
citizens, free. Guided tours, special
programs.

**Suggested Time to View House:** 30 minutes

**Description of Grounds:** Nature trail and
picnic grounds

**Best Season to View House:** Summer

**Number of Yearly Visitors:** 3000

**Year House Built:** c. 1750

**Number of Rooms:** 2

**Style of Architecture:** Frame

**On-Site Parking:** Yes  **Wheelchair Access:** No

## Description of House

Daniel Webster (1782-1852), the renowned orator and lawyer, was born in this simple frame dwelling in rural New Hampshire on January 18, 1782. His father, Ebenezer, a farmer and sawmill operator, had recently built the two room house to replace a log cabin which had grown too small for his growing family. Although Daniel Webster was a frail and sickly child, he built up his physical strength during the time he lived on the farm, and also developed a love for literature. After graduating from Dartmouth College in 1801, he began his long career as a lawyer and statesman in the service of his country. He served in the Congress as a representative from both New Hampshire and Massachusetts, and as Secretary of State under Presidents Harrison, Tyler and Fillmore.

Today, visitors can see the humble dwelling where this famous statesman spent his early years. Much of the house is believed to be original, despite having been moved several times over the years. The fireplace was rebuilt using the original handmade bricks and hearthstone. The attached woodshed and well enclosure are reconstructions. The foundations of Webster's father's mill can still be seen among the trees behind the house. The original mill was for wood, but Ebenezer also mills for grain and cider.

Furnishings such as the flax spinning wheel and kitchen utensils, are typical of a rustic farm of this period; other items on display belonged to Daniel Webster later in his life.

## Additional Information

The old Salisbury cemetery is on the same road as the Webster birthplace. His father and mother are buried here along with many other Webster family members.

# *Franklin Pierce Homestead State Historic Site*

Route 31, P.O. Box 856
Hillsboro, NH 03244
(603) 271-3254

**Contact:** New Hampshire Div.of Parks and Recreation
**Open:** Memorial Day-Labor Day, 10 a.m.–6 p.m.
**Admission:** Adults $2.50; children (under 18) free (with adult supervision). Guided tours.
**Suggested Time to View House:** 1 hour
**Facilities on Premises:** Small shop

**Description of Grounds:** Grounds are suitable for picnics
**Best Season to View House:** Summer
**Number of Yearly Visitors:** 3000
**Year House Built:** 1804
**Style of Architecture:** Federal
**Number of Rooms:** 15 plus
**On-Site Parking:** Yes **Wheelchair Access:** No

## *Description of House*

Franklin Pierce, the fourteenth president of the United States, spent his childhood in this mansion in Hillsboro. Like Pierce's father, who was elected twice as governor of New Hampshire, Franklin entered politics. He held several state offices and was both a U.S. Congressman and Senator. He was also a distinguished war hero, serving as brigadier general in the War of 1812. He returned to New Hampshire after the war to practice law. In 1852, Pierce reluctantly ran for president during a time when the country was struggling with the issue of slavery. Pierce's attempt to smooth over differences in the democratic party, and his opposition to the impending Civil War, made him unpopular in the North and South. He was not nominated for a second term.

This Federal style mansion, built by Franklin Pierce's father, has recently been restored to reflect the graciousness of affluent living in the 1800s.

# Wyman Tavern

339 Main Street, P.O. Box 803
Keene, NH 03431
(603) 352-1895

**Contact:** Historical Society of Cheshire County

**Open:** June 1-Labor Day, Thur.-Sat. 11 a.m.–4 p.m.; or by appointment

**Admission:** Adults $2; under age 12 free. Guided tours, school visitation program.

**Suggested Time to View House:** 1 hour

**Description of Grounds:** Period gardens
**Best Season to View House:** Summer
**Number of Yearly Visitors:** 500
**Year House Built:** 1762
**Style of Architecture:** Georgian-Colonial
**Number of Rooms:** 10
**On-Site Parking:** No **Wheelchair Access:** No

## Description of House

This tavern holds a unique place in American history as it was the meeting place of Keene's Minutemen before their historic march on Lexington and Concord in April of 1775. The leader of the march, Captain Isaac Wyman (1762-1792), was also the co-owner and innkeeper of this establishment together with the Congregational minister Zedekiah S. Barstow (1818-1873). The tavern also housed a school attended by the noteworthy pupil Salmon P. Chase, Secretary of the Treasury (he is pictured on the $10,000 bill) and Chief Justice of the U.S. Supreme Court.

This typical colonial tavern features a restored taproom, two parlors, a ballroom, kitchen, study, and two bedrooms. There are two small wings which were added to each end (c. 1820). The two story structure has a center chimney and five fireplaces.

Wyman Tavern is furnished as a period house with some furnishings of the original residents but most collected and appropriate to the period 1760 to 1820.

## Notable Collections on Exhibit

Wyman Tavern is furnished as period house with most of furnishings collected and appropriate to the period 1770 to 1820.

# John Wingate Weeks Historic Site

Route 3, P.O. Box 856
Lancaster, NH 03584
(603) 788-4004

**Contact:** New Hampshire Div.of Parks and Recreation

**Open:** Memorial Day-Labor Day, 10 a.m.–6 p.m.

**Admission:** Adults $2.50; Children (under 18) free (with adult supervision); N.H .senior citizens free. Guided tours.

**Suggested Time to View House:** 1 hour

**Description of Grounds:** The house is on the summit of Mt. Prospect, hiking trails are available as well as an auto road

**Best Season to View House:** Summer and fall

**Number of Yearly Visitors:** 5000

**Year House Built:** 1910

**Number of Rooms:** 8

**Style of Architecture:** Gable roof

**On-Site Parking:** Yes  **Wheelchair Access:** No

## Description of House

Built as a summer retreat and as a testament to Weeks's affection for the locale of his ancestry and birth, the Mt. Prospect estate typifies a spirit of private land conservation often seen in New Hampshire at the turn of the century. The estate is one of the best preserved of many grand summer homes built in New York during this period. The main house, the lodge, is built of fieldstone and stucco; its gable roof is covered with red terra cotta tiles. The plan of the house is mostly original and its architectural style is not easily defined. The furnishings are appropriate to the period of Weeks's residency.

John Wingate Weeks (1860-1926) was born and raised on this picturesque farm in Lancaster. Following several years in local government, he was elected to the U.S. congress in 1904, and to the Senate in 1910. Weeks is best known for his work as a conservationist and his efforts to establish the eastern National Forest System. The "Weeks Act" in 1911 authorized the federal government to purchase lands to be permanently reserved, held and administered as national forest lands.

The most outstanding feature of the house is a 30 foot by 70 foot living room which makes up the entire second floor. Its many large picture windows are most unsual for the era. Balconies take full advantage of the lodge's mountain top setting, providing dramatic views of the surrounding scenery.

# Jones Farm

Route 125, Plummer's Ridge
Milton, NH 03851
(603) 652-7840

**Contact:** New Hampshire Farm Museum, Inc.

**Open:** June-Labor Day, Tues.-Sun.
10 a.m–4 p.m.; Labor Day-mid. Oct.,
Sat.- Sun. 10 a.m–4 p.m.

**Admission:** Adults $4; children $1
(exception: Old Time Farm Day—Adults
$4.50; children $1.50). Guided tours,
special displays, exhibits, visual
presentations, special events every
Sat.and Sun., demonstrations and
"hands on" activities.

**Suggested Time to View House:** 2 hours

**Best Season to View House:** Summer
and fall

**Number of Yearly Visitors:** 8,000-9,000

**Style of Architecture:** Several styles
represented on the farm: Colonial, Federal,
Greek Revival, and American Gothic

**Year House Built:** 1780

**Number of Rooms:** 12 in house

**On-Site Parking:** Yes  **Wheelchair Access:** Yes

## Description of House

The most noteworthy resident of this charming farm and tavern was Levi Jones who, despite his humble beginnings, was to become "one of the wealthiest men in Milton and for years one of the most influential". After moving to New Hampshire from Maine, Jones was hired to work at the tavern by the owner, Joseph Plummer, and soon after married Plummer's daughter. By 1815, Jones had become the owner of the tavern, following the death of his wife and her father.

The Jones Farm is actually a collection of buildings with different architectural styles. This eclectic group of structures include the original house built in the 1780's, a two-and-a-half story structure built as a tavern c. 1810, an early 19th-century barn; an ell built between 1830 and 1850 with attached pigshed, a large 100 foot barn with attached watering shed, and a cobbler shop. The Jones Farm buildings have a unique appearance because they are all connected and are oriented in an east to west direction at right angles to the main road. This distinguished farm is listed in the National Register of Historic Places. All of the furnishings are collected and appropriate to the period.

## Notable Collections on Exhibit

An exhibit of spinning and weaving artifacts and a collection of children's toys from the late 1800s are on display in the museum in the main structure. In addition, the cobbler shop houses an excellent collection of cobbler tools which include an extensive variety of hammers spanning a hundred year period. Visitors interested in the history of dairy farming can also see an exhibit of milking artifacts: cream separators, bottles, butter making churns and jars.

# Barrett House—Forest Hall

Main Street
New Ipswich, NH 03071
(603) 878-2517

**Contact:** Soc. for the Preservation of New England Antiquities

**Open:** June 1-Oct. 15, Thurs.-Sun.; tours at 12 p.m., 1 p.m., 2 p.m., 3 p.m., 4 p.m.

**Admission:** $4. An open house coincides with the Memorial Day parade.

**Description of Grounds:** The extensive grounds contain a carriage shed and a Gothic Revival summer house.

**Year House Built:** 1800

**Style of Architecture:** Federal

## Description of House

New Ipswich was a flourishing mill town at the beginning of the 19th century and, and the Barrett House (also known as Forest Hall) is one of several mansions in the vicinity reflecting the prosperity of the era. In later years, the town fell into economic decline when the railroad bypassed the area; yet this situation had the beneficial side effect of preserving the historic character of the town. According to tradition, the mansion was built as a wedding gift for Charles Barrett and his bride by his father. The house's grand scale was encouraged by the bride's father, who promised to furnish it in as lavish a manner as it could be built. The interiors are, indeed, elegantly furnished, and must have presented a fine backdrop for the couple.

The Barrett House is a grand, three-story clapboard mansion constructed using a Federal style of architecture. The house features a large ballroomon the top floor well-suited for elegant entertaining. In addition to the fine furnishings, the house displays a number of family portraits and a carriage house on the grounds holds special exhibitions.

## Additional Information

The Merchant-Ivory film of Henry James's *The Europeans* was shot at the Barrett House.

# The Fells—John Hay
# National Wildlife Refuge

Route 103A, P.O. Box 856
Newbury, NH 03255
(603)-271-3254

**Contact:** New Hampshire Div.of Parks
and Recreation

**Open:** Memorial Day-Labor Day,
10 a.m.–6 p.m.

**Admission:** Adults $2.50; under 18 free
(with adult supervision); N.H. senior
citizens free. Guided tours,
environmental education programs.

**Suggested Time to View House:** 45 minutes

**Description of Grounds:** 838 acres open to
the public with extensive hiking trails,
and designed landscape and gardens

**Best Season to View House:** Spring and
summer

**Number of Yearly Visitors:** 5000

**Year House Built:** 1891 to 1897

**Number of Rooms:** 35

**Style of Architecture:** Dutch-Colonial Revival
**On-Site Parking:** Yes  **Wheelchair Access:** Yes

## Description of House

The distinguished diplomat and author, John Hay (1838-1905), sought refuge at this scenic cottage situated on an extensive tract of land. At the age of twenty-two, he was chosen to be private secretary to President Abraham Lincoln. He also had a noteworthy career as a foreign statesman, serving in Paris, Vienna, and Madrid, as well as achieving diplomatic eminence as ambassador to Great Britain, and Secretary of State under Presidents McKinley and Theodore Roosevelt. As an author, he wrote a definitive biography of Lincoln as well as essays and novels.

The Fells was constructed over a period of years until it attained the form that visitors see today. Construction began in 1890, and in 1891 the Hay family moved in to the partially completed gambrel roofed cottage with servants' kitchen wing and Doric porch. In 1897, a "twin" cottage was built along with a low hallway to connect the two structures. After Hay died in 1905, his son Clarence Hay inherited the house and hired the architect Prentice Sanger to make alterations. These included the construction of a broad gambrel roof cross hall for passage between the two cottages, and elaborate Colonial woodwork in the downstairs interior.

## Notable Collections on Exhibit

The Fells contains two libraries of note: one devoted to history and the other to contemporary natural history.

## Additional Information

The house is surrounded by extensive formal gardens and a naturalized Alpine garden as well as an abundant outdoor statuary.

# *Rundlet-May House*

364 Middle Street
Portsmouth, NH 03801
(603) 436-3205

**Contact:** Soc. of the Preservation of
NewEngland Antiquities
**Open:** June 1-Oct. 15, Wed.-Sun.; tours at
12 p.m., 1 p.m., 2 p.m., 3 p.m., 4 p.m.
**Admission:** $4. The Rudlet-May House
participate in the annual Candlelight
Tour in August.
**Description of Grounds:** Formal gardens
**Year House Built:** 1807

## *Description of House*

The merchant James Rundlet was a self-made man. To proclaim his success, he built this expansive mansion.

Merchant James Rudlet built this mansion on a terraced rise above the street and filled it with the finest furnishings available. He imported his wallpapers from England and purchased his furniture from local cabinet-makers, whose work was noted for its fine craftsmanship and striking use of veneer. Rudlet also saw to it that his house was equipped with the latest technologies. The kitchen boasts both a Rumford roaster and Rumford range, as well as a set kettle and an elaborate venting system that serivces a smoke room on the third floor. There is an early coal-fired central heating system and an indoor well. The formal gardens, orchards, and attached outbuildings (including two privies) remain as designed by Rudlet.

The house is shown as it was turned over to the society from Rundlet's descendants, with most of its original furnishings, as well as some pieces added by later generations.

# John Paul Jones House Museum

43 Middle Street
P.O. Box 728
Portsmouth, NH 03801
(603) 436-8420

**Contact:** Portsmouth Historical Society

**Open:** May 15-Oct. 15, Mon.-Sat.
10 a.m.–4 p.m.; July-Sept., Sun.
12–4 p.m.

**Admission:** Adults $4; children $2;
senior citizens and groups have
special rates.
Guided tours, candlelight tour third
Fri. in Aug.

**Suggested Time to View House:**
45 minutes

**Description of Grounds:** Lovely
gardens are open to the public at no
charge.

**Best Season to View House:** June-Sept.

**Number of Yearly Visitors:** 6,000

**Year House Built:** 1758

**Number of Rooms:** 12 open to the public

**Style of Architecture:** Georgian

**On-Site Parking:** Yes  **Wheelchair Access:** Yes

## Description of House

This impressive structure was built by Captain Gregory Purcell and was run as a genteel boarding house for gentlemen by his widow after his death. It takes its name, however, from its most famous resident, John Paul Jones, known to most as the "father of the U.S. Navy". This hero of the American Revolution resided here while his ships, the Ranger and America, were being outfitted for service in the war. Although only a boarder, Jones considered Portsmouth his home in the United States. The Portsmouth Historical Society obtained the house in 1920 and opened it to the public in 1923.

The John Paul Jones House is a magnificent example of American colonial Georgian architecture. The building now serves as a museum celebrating Portsmouth's historic past.

The house displays the country's best collection of "Portsmouth built" furniture according to the Society for the Preservation of New England Antiques. Almost all of the pieces are from the original house and date from the 18th and 19th centuries.

## Notable Collections on Exhibit

In addition to the outstanding furniture display, the house also exhibits original portraits by Samuel F. B. Morse and other painters of the 19th century. The collection also contains various memorabilia of Portsmouth's illustrious history and a fine jewelry and 18th-century needlework collection.

# Governor John Langdon House

143 Pleasant Street
Portsmouth, NH 03801
(603) 436-3205

**Contact:** Soc. for the Preservation of New England Antiquities

**Open:** June 1-Oct. 15, Wed.-Sun.; 12–5 p.m.

**Admission:** $4. Guided tours on the hour.

**Description of Grounds:** The handsome garden dating from the same era features restored perennial beds, a rose and grape arbor, and a gazebo.

**Year House Built:** 1784

## Description of House

John Langdon rose from modest origins to become a merchant, ship-builder, Revolutionary leader, signer of the United States Constitution, and three-term Governor of New Hampshire.

The house was built by Governor John Langdon and expresses his status as Portsmouth's leading citizen. It was praised by George Washington, who visited here in 1799. The dwellings reception rooms—of a grand scale suited to ceremonial occasions—are ornamented by elaborate wood carving in rococo style. Another feature of the house is the 1905 wing designed by McKim, Mead, and White, which contains a formal dining room in the Colonial Revival style.

Today the house contains furnishings assembled from the society's collection that illustrate the evolution of taste and the social history of the Portsmouth area in the 18th and 19th centuries.

# *Wentworth–Coolidge Mansion*

Little Harbor Road
Portsmouth, NH 03801
(603) 436-6607

**Contact:** State of New Hampshire Parks and Recreation

**Open:** May 23-June 20 and Labor-Columbus Day, Sat.- Sun. 10 a.m.–5 p.m.; June 20-Labor Day, daily 10 a.m.–5 p.m.

**Admission:** Adults $2.50; children (under 18) and New Hampshire residents over 65 free. Guided tours and picnicking permitted on grounds.

**Suggested Time to View House:** 30–45 minutes

**Description of Grounds:** Waterfront property with view of Little Harbor including two small islands and a garden.

**Best Season to View House:** Early summer

**Number of Yearly Visitors:** 1,500

**Year House Built:** 1750

**Style of Architecture:** Colonial

**Number of Rooms:** 42

**On-Site Parking:** Yes  **Wheelchair Access:** Yes

## *Description of House*

Benning Wentworth was appointed Royal Governor by King George II in 1741 following New Hampshire's separation from the Massachusetts Bay Colony in 1679. The mansion he built is one of the few existing colonial governors' residences to survive almost unchanged. From the Council-Chamber, Went worth signed the charters that incorporated towns over a wide territory including present day New Hampshire and Vermont (Bennington, Vermont is named after him). Following his death in 1770, his widow, Martha, married a retired British Army Colonel and accomplished musician. The house was passed on to their daughter, Martha.  In 1816, Martha and her husband sold the house to successful merchant Charles Cushing.

The mansion's unusual appearance is a reflection of an a typical construction history. An early 18th century shop or warehouse was presumably moved to the site and converted into a kitchen wing about 1750. That same year two homes were also moved to the site and attached to the warehouse. The main residential section, built from 1750 to 1755, contains elaborate woodwork and wallpaper. Part of this structure was originally covered by a flat deck which provided a view of the formal garden laid out on the lawn below. Between 1759 and 1764 a Council Chamber wing was added, containing a monumental carved mantelpiece. The design was derived from an English guidebook of the 1700s. The house is not fully furnished, however the existing furniture is appropriate to the period. The house has many unusual built in features such as a spy closet overlooking the waiting room, which enabled former residents to screen visitors. There is also a smoking chamber (used to prepare meats) built into the chimney on the second floor.

## Notable Collections on Exhibit

The house contains an interesting collection of furnishings including a Sheraton server (c.1800) decorated with inlay, birdseye maple veneer and painted columns; a Longman & Broderip inlaid harpsichord (c.1780); and Langley Boardman federal sidechairs. Paintings and photographs of former residents of the house are also on display.

# Strawberry Banke Museum

P.O. Box 300
Portsmouth, NH 03802
(603) 433-1100

**Contact:** Strawberry Banke Museum

**Open:** May-Oct. and first 2 weeks in Dec., 10 a.m–5 p.m.

**Admission:** Adults $9; seniors $8; children $5; group rates available; tickets valid for 2 consecutive days. Daily tours, craft shops.

**Suggested Time to View House:** 2 hours–1 day

**Facilities on Premises:** Gift shop

**Description of Grounds:** Several period gardens and a display garden for the Daffodil Society of America (with over 100 varieties) are open to the public.

**Best Season to View House:** May-Oct.

**Number of Yearly Visitors:** 56,000

**Year House Built:** 1695-oldest

**Style of Architecture:** Varied

**On-Site Parking:** Yes **Wheelchair Access:** Yes

## Description of House

The complex known as Strawberry Banke Museum provides a fascinating glimpse of over three centuries of change in one urban neighborhood, Portsmouth's South End. First settled in 1630 by the English, this area was named Strawberry Banke until 1653, when the city name was officially changed to Portsmouth. During the 17th and 18th centuries the site became a thriving economic center as a waterfront neighborhood and one of the nation's most important seaports. By the late 19th century this prosperous waterway, which was then called Puddle Dock, had become choked with debris, rotten wharves, and by the early 20th century the channel had become filled in. Recognizing that the homes and buildings in this area had served the needs of Portsmouth people in four different centuries, a group of local citizens banned together in 1958, to save the neighborhood from urban renewal and establish Strawberry Banke Museum.

With forty-two houses on over ten acres of land, Strawberry Banke provides a rare view of New England's past with its magnificently maintained houses, and craft exhibitions which range from pottery to boat building. Each of the eight furnished houses have a story to tell through their well-preserved architecture and handsome furnishings. The Goodwin Mansion (c. 1811), portrays the lives of New Hampshire's Civil War era Govenor, Ichabod Goodwin, and his family who lived here for over fifty years. In contrast, the Wheelwright house (c. 1780) depicts the lives of a mariner's family during the post-Revolutionary depression. The Chase House with furniture and decorative arts owned by the Wendell family of Portsmouth in the early 1800s suggests the appearance of a merchant's house just after the War of 1812.

Many of the houses display exhibitions illustrating historical themes such as the Lowd House with its fascinating array of early tools and craftsmanship, the Sherburne House with its exhibit of early 17th-century construction techniques, and the Jones House with its unusual collection of archeological artifacts and pottery. Other houses are currently under restoration and are available for exterior viewing only.

### Notable Collections on Exhibit

The museum collection includes approximately 25,000 examples of decorative arts and household furnishings, architectural fragments, tools, boat patterns, and other objects, ranging in date from the 17th to the 20th century; the strengths are in ceramics and furniture. About 700,000 archeological fragments, excavated from the local sites, have been catalogued and stored at the museum's Jones House Archaeology Center. The museum's Thayer Memorial Reference Library consists of about 5,000 books and periodicals on regional history, architecture, decorative arts and material culture, landscape, archeology, and other topics.

### Additional Information

One of the most enjoyable features for visitors to Strawberry Bank is the extensive variety of gardening styles which adorn the houses. The Goodwin House is surrounded by an elaborate Victorian garden while the Thomas Bailey Aldrich garden, laid out in 1907 as a memorial to the 19th-century writer and poet, is a wonderful example of a Colonial Revival garden complete with sundial, brick paths, and colonial urns on arbors. An excellent example of an 1830s urban backyard garden with a workyard and reconstructed privy can be seen at the Rider-Wood House.

# *Mary Baker Eddy Historic House*

on Lake Road
Rumney, NH 03266
(603) 786-9943

**Contact:** Longyear Museum and Historical
Society
**Open:** May-Oct., Tues.-Sat 10 a.m.–5 p.m.;
Sun. 2 p.m.-5 p.m.
**Admission:** $1.50.  Guided Tours.
**Suggested Time to View House:** 30 minutes

**Facilities on Premises:** Gift area
**Description of Grounds:** Yard
**Year House Built:** c. 1850
**On-Site Parking:** Yes
**Wheelchair Access:** No

## *Description of House*

Mary Baker Eddy, discoverer of Christian Science and founder of the
Christian Science Church, lived in the house from 1860 to 1862. At that time
she was Mrs. Daniel Patterson, and was beginning to search for means to
bring about her own healing of a longstanding illness. Her health and spirits
improved. She was soon writing again, following closely the intensity of
feeling between the North and South. Her poem "Major Anderson and Our
Country," was written and published on February 14, 1861. The furnishings
are collected and appropriate to the period.

# Rhode Island

1. **Block Island**
   *Woonsocket House*

2. **Bristol**
   *Blithwood Mansion*
   *Coggeshell Farm Museum*

3. **Little Compton**
   *Wilbor House*

4. **Newport**
   *The Breakers*
   *Chateau-sur-Mer*
   *The Elms*
   *Hunter House*
   *Kingscote*
   *Marble House*
   *Rosecliff*

5. **Pawtucket**
   *Sylvanus Brown House*

6. **Providence**
   *Governor Henry Lippitt House Museum*
   *The Nightingale-Brown House*

7. **Warwick**
   *John Waterman Arnold House*

# Woonsocket House

Corner of Old Town Road
and Ocean Avenue
Block Island, RI
(401) 466-2481

**Contact:** Block Island Historical Society
**Open:** July-Aug., daily 10 a.m.–4 p.m.
**Admission:** Adults $2; seniors and children (12 and over) $1. Various activities, changing historical exhibits, and slide talks.
**Suggested Time to View House:** 30–60 minutes

**Facilities on Premises:** Gift/book shop
**Best Season to View House:** Summer
**Number of Yearly Visitors:** 4,500
**Year House Built:** 1870s
**Style of Architecture:** Victorian
**Number of Rooms:** 12
**On-Site Parking:** No   **Wheelchair Access:** No

## Description of House

Originally a seaside boarding house, this Victorian structure with a mansard roof was purchased and opened to the public in 1942 by the Block Island Historical Society. The house is now a museum with period rooms and furnishings. There is also an exhibit space with changing installations on Block Island history. Most pieces of furniture on display were collected and donated and are appropriate to the 1850s to 1870s.

## Notable Collections on Exhibit

Victorian furniture comprises the majority of the permanent collection with a few earlier, primitive pieces. There are also paintings, clothing, ship models, historic photographs and decorative arts on exhibit.

# *Blithewolde Mansion*

101 Ferry Road, P.O. Box 716
Bristol, RI 02809-0716
(401)253-2707

**Contact:** Blithewold Gardens and Arboretum

**Open:** April-Oct., Tues.-Sun. Closed Mon. and holidays.

**Admission:** Adults $6; children (6-15) $2; special group rates available. Guided tours and horticultural and historical programs thoughout the year.

**Suggested Time to View House:** 45 minutes

**Facilities on Premises:** Gift shop

**Description of Grounds:** 33 landscaped acres overlooking Narragansett Bay which are open all year for guided tours

**Best Season to View House:** Spring, summer and early fall

**Number of Yearly Visitors:** Approx. 20,000

**Year House Built:** 1908

**Style of Architecture:** Styled after 20th-century English country manor

**Number of Rooms:** 45

**On-Site Parking:** Yes   **Wheelchair Access:** Yes

## Description of House

This elegant mansion was originally the summer home of Pennsylvania coal baron Augustus Van Wickle. The last owner, Marjorie Van Wickle Lyon was the daughter of the original owners. She died in 1976 and bequeathed the property to the Heritage Trust of Rhode Island.

Blithewold Mansion was designed by the Boston architectural firm of Kilham and Hopkins with a stone and stucco exterior styled along the lines of a 17th-century English country manor. There is a deliberate interplay between the indoors and outdoors by the use of porches, a terrace and large windows. A porte-cochere over a circular drive marks the front entrance. A second floor sleeping porch off the master bedroom overlooks the ten-acre great lawn and Narragansett Bay, and features a hanging bed. The interior, with elaborate woodwork, ceilings and stairways in Colonial Revival style, offers visitors a glimpse of the gracious summer lifestyle of a bygone era.

## Notable Collections on Exhibit

The original furnishings on display reflect the Van Wickle family's interest in travel; they include a 17th-century Brittany bed box, a Beidermeier desk, Renaissance tables, Delft plates, Tiffany glass, and Chinese Rose medallion urns.

## Additional Information

Blithewold is known for its spectacular garden, with exotic and native plants not commonly grown elsewhere in New England, and an arboretum where the largest sequoia tree east of the Rockies stands.

# *Coggeshell Farm Museum*

Colt Drive (P.O. Box 562)
Bristol, RI 02809
(401) 253-9062

**Contact:** Coggeshell Farm Museum
**Open:** Will open to general public in 1994
**Activites:** Guided tours for groups (mostly school) from March-Oct.
**Description of Grounds:** A 1790s salt marsh farm, barns, sheep shed, church, weaving shed, blacksmith shop, workshop/carriage shed-across from the marsh

**Best Season to View House:** All
**Year House Built:** 1750 to 1790
**Style of Architecture:** Cape
**Number of Rooms:** 4
**On-Site Parking:** Yes   **Handicap Access:** No

## Description of House

The original owner of this modest, saltbox home built in the 1790s is unknown. The house was named after Chandler Coggeshell, who was born and lived here as an adult. He was a founder of the college that is now known as the University of Rhode Island.

Coggeshell Farm is a living, historical farm museum representing an 18th-century Rhode Island salt marsh farm and the surrounding community. The main living structure has high ceilings, a central chimney, three fireplaces and one oven. Most doors and all of the molding, with the exception of the windows, appears to be original. At various periods in its history, Coggshell was used as a tenant farm.

## Notable Collections on Exhibit

The collection includes early agricultural and wood working tools appropriate for the time period (1790s), and a mid to late 18th-century lock-colten plow.

# *Wilbor House*

548 West Main Road
Little Compton, RI 02837
(401) 635-4559

**Contact:** Little Compton Historical Society

**Open:** Mid June-mid Sept., Tues.-Sun.

**Admission:** Adults $2.50; children $.75.
  Guided tours.

**Suggested Time to View House:** 1 hour

**Description of Grounds:** Small green
  garden with holly, box, and shrubs

**Best Season to View House:** Summer

**Year House Built:** 1680

**On-Site Parking:** Yes

**Style of Architecture:** 18th-century
  farmhouse

**Number of Yearly Visitors:** 250

**Number of Rooms:** 10

**Wheelchair Access:** No

## *Description of House*

Samuel Wilbore built the original two room house in 1860. Since then, eight generations of Wilbors (variously spelled Wilbore, Wilbor, Wilbour, Wilber and Wilbur) continuously occupied the house until after 1900.

Wilbor House today maintains the features of a 17th-century New England farmhouse. Nearly all the early details of the house survived, including beamed ceilings, feather-edge boards, and original plaster. Where necessary, some doors, floor boards, and mouldings, were obtained from contemporary local houses being demolished. Some millwork was copied from remnants in place.

Many of the furnishings in the house are loans or gifts from residents of Little Compton and span the four centuries that the house has been occupied.

## *Notable Collections on Exhibit*

This modest home exhibits simple local furnishings, paintings, ceramics, fabrics and embroidery of the 17th, 18th and 19th centuries. In addition, a barn museum, built in 1850, maintains an excellent collection of farm implements and vehicles. The second story of the barn museum houses the Portuguese Room with a unique exhibit devoted to the cultural contributions and traditions of the Azoreans who immigrated to Little Compton over 100 years ago.

# Chateau-sur-Mer

118 Mill Street
Newport, RI 02840
(401) 847-1000

**Contact:** The Preservation Society of
Newport County

**Open:** April 4-May 1 and Oct. 1-Nov. 1,
weekends 10 a.m.–5 p.m.;
May 2-Sept. 30, daily 10 a.m.–5 p.m.;
Nov. 2-March 31, weekends and holidays

**Admission:** Adults $6; children (6-11) $3;
combination tickets available. Guided
tours, lectures, special events.

**Suggested Time to View House:** 1 hour

**Best Season to View House:** May-June,
summer and early fall

**Number of Yearly Visitors:** 800,000

**Year House Built:** 1852

**Style of Architecture:** Victorian

**On-Site Parking:** Yes  **Wheelchair Access:** No

## Description of House

William Shepard Wetmore began his business career with the Providence China trade firm of Carrington & Co. In 1820 at the age of nineteen, he sailed to Canton as supercargo of one of the company's merchantmen. Three years later, he joined in establishing a trading company in Valparaiso, Chile which became the port's exclusive agent for British and American trade and made the fortunes of its founders. His success continued with other trade and banking ventures and retired to live Chateau-sur-Mer in 1852.

Chateau-sur-Mer is a fascinating Victorian amalgam: a product of two periods, the 1850s and the 1870s, and a bridge between the other architectural styles found in Newport: the human-scale "retreat" architecture of Kingscote and the palatial aspect of Marble House and its Gilded Age successors. It combines the work of a Newport contractor, Seth Bradford, with later modifications by architect Richard Morris Hunt whose work in the 1880s and 1890s would help change the face of New York City's Fifth Avenue as well as that of Newport. One of the most impressive features of the house is a staircase designed by Hunt which is enhanced by stained glass windows and French bronze figurines. The acreage on which the rough-cut granite retreat, brownstone carriage house, and porter's lodge are situated provide a magnificent view of the ocean.

## Notable Collections on Exhibit

The house is completely furnished with period originals and reproductions. There are also a number of extraordinary 19th and 20th-century paintings and drawings and a collection of 18th-century European porcelains on display.

# *Hunter House*

118 Mill Street
Newport, RI 02840
(401) 847-1000

**Contact:** The Preservation Society of
Newport County

**Open:** April 4-May 1 and Oct. 1-Nov. 1,
weekends 10 a.m.–5 p.m

**Admission:** Adults $6; children (6-11) $3;
combination tickets available. Guided
tours, lectures, special events.

**Suggested Time to View House:** 1 hour

**Description of Grounds:** A pretty colonial
garden overlooking Narragansett Bay

**Best Season to View House:** May-June,
summer and early fall

**Number of Yearly Visitors:** 800,000

**Year House Built:** 1748

**Style of Architecture:** 18th-century
residential

**On-Site Parking:** Yes  **Wheelchair Access:** No

## *Description of House*

Hunter House was built by the prosperous ship owner and entrepeneur Jonathan Nichols. A native Newporter with large landholdings in nearby Portsmouth, Nichols had a house, a wharf, and warehouses built on the Washington Street (then Water Street) site to accommodate his shipping enterprises. In the course of his career, Nichols held several posts in the colonial government. At the time of his death in 1756, he was deputy governor of Rhode Island.

Hunter House is prized for the quantity and quality of its faithfully restored interior decorations. The carved paneling, black and gold faux-marbre Corinthian pilasters and baseboards, shell carvings and small polychromed cherub heads of the northeast parlor show the detail that went into the interior design of the house. In addition, the main staircase makes striking use of its turned Santo Domingan mahogany balusters of three alternating designs. Paint colors throughout Hunter House approximate those used, according to expert paint analysis, during the 1760s and 1770s, when the Wanton family occupied the house. The pine paneling of the southeast parlor is "grained" or painted to resemble walnut.

## *Notable Collections on Exhibit*

One of the country's finest collections of Townsend and Goddard furnishings made in 18th century Rhode Island, other parts of New England, and Great Britain are gracefully displayed in the house.

## *Additional Information*

The efforts to restore Hunter House marked the beginnings of the Preservation Society of Newport County; they are responsible for the restoration of Kingscote and The Breakers as well as other Newport mansions.

# Kingscote

118 Mill Street
Newport, RI 02840
(401) 847-1000

**Contact:** The Preservation Society of
Newport County

**Open:** April 4-May 1 and Oct. 1-Nov. 1,
10 a.m.–5 p.m.; May 2- Sept. 30, daily
10 a.m.–5 p.m.

**Admission:** Adults $6; children (6-11) $3;
combination tickets available. Guided
tours, lectures, special events.

**Suggested Time to View House:** 1 hour

**Description of Grounds:** One city block of
lawn, large old trees, and shrubs

**Best Season to View House:** May-June,
Summer and early Fall

**Number of Yearly Visitors:** 800,000

**Year House Built:** 1839

**Style of Architecture:** Gothic Revival

**On-Site Parking:** Yes   **Wheelchair Access:** No

## Description of House

The construction of Kingscote in 1839 helped to establish Newport as America's premier summer resort. The house's original owner was George Noble Jones of Savannah, Georgia. He commissioned Richard Upjohn, a major promoter of the Gothic Revival style in the U.S., to design the cottage for his personal summer use. The outbreak of the Civil War forced him to leave the house in 1861 to return south. William King, a successful trader and friend of the Jones family, purchased the house in 1863 and evenutally settled there permanently.

Kingscote's exterior surface of horizontal matched boards was originally covered with beige paint mixed with sand to resemble masonry. With its assymetry and variety of textures; its gables, dormers, pendants, bargeboards, dripmouldings, and lattices, Kingscote is an outstanding example of "stick style" Gothic Revival architecture. It is, in fact, one of the few surviving wooden structures of its size, style and period in the U.S. The interplay of design and setting is particularly evident in Kingscote's twin drawing rooms where large French windows open onto a veranda facing the shaded east lawn. A magnificent dining room, large enough to serve as a ballroom, distinguishes the interior of the house. The walls and ceiling of the room are covered with a herringbone pattern of cork acoustic tiles, among the first used in decorating. Louis C. Tiffany and Co. (later known as Tiffany studios) of New York produced the opalescent glass bricks and tiles and the dahlia mosiacs over the Italia Siena marble fireplace.

### Notable Collections on Exhibit

In addition to its architectural significance, Kingscote is also a museum of period interiors and decorative objects—from fine Oriental rugs to distinctive porcelains—commissioned or collected by five generations of the King family and preserved exactly as they left them.

### Additional Information

During the 1950s and 1960s, Maud Armstrong, a descendant of the King family, resisted the city government's efforts to buy and demolish Kingscote and replace it with a school. The house stands today, skirted by two modern shopping centers, as a monument to her foresight and endurance.

# Marble House

118 Mill Street
Newport, RI 02840
(401) 847-1000

**Contact:** The Preservation Society of
Newport County

**Open:** April 4-Sept. 30 and Oct. 1-
Nov. 1, daily 10 a.m.–5 p.m.; Nov. 2-
March 31, weekends and holidays
10 a.m.–4 p.m

**Admission:** Adults $6; children (6-11)
$3. Guided tours, lectures, special
events.

**Suggested Time to View House:** 1 hour

**Facilities on Premises:** Gift shop

**Description of Grounds:** Large lawn
with a Chinese Tea House, a colorful
Oriental-style pavilion set on the
cliffs behind the house

**Best Season to View House:** May-June,
summer and early fall

**Number of Yearly Visitors:** 800,000

**Year House Built:** 1892

**Style of Architecture:** Neoclassical

**On-Site Parking:** Yes

**Wheelchair Access:** Yes

## Description of House

In 1888, William Kissam Vanderbilt, grandson of the shipping and railroad magnate, asked Richard Morris Hunt to design for him "the very best living accommodations that money could buy." Marble House was the result, the most ornate and expensive summer house in Newport when it was built in 1892. William, like his older brother Cornelius, and his father William Henry Vanderbilt, served on the board of the family's New York Central and other railroads. An avid yachtsman, William co-sponsored a number of America's Cup yachts. He also sponsored early auto races on Aquidnick Island and Long Island, and he indulged a life-long interest in raising race horses in the United States and France.

Marble House's designer, Richard Hunt, trained at France's Ecole des Beaux Arts, and was committed to neoclassical principles. His plan for Marble House, derived from that of the Petit Trianon at Versailles, is an academic example of the Beaux Arts classicism that shaped American taste during the 1880s and 90s. The house's white marble exterior is a prelude to its richly colored and decorated interiors. The interior design of Marble House is the epitome of what was implied in the term "gilded age". The Louis XIV motif of the Gold Ballroom with its gilt surfaces, mirrors and lights prompted a guest in the 1890s to liken it to a jewel box, "far ahead of any palace I have ever seen...or dreamed of." Other noteworthy rooms include the dining room which replicates the Salon of Hercules at Versailles.

Each of the rooms in Marble House contains the original Vanderbilt furnishings ranging from solid bronze chairs made in Paris by Allard to two matching cabinets in the style of 17th-century designer A.C. Boule with ebony frames inlaid with tortoise shell and etched brass, and bronze cherubs gilded with mercury.

### Notable Collections on Exhibit

Alongside original 18th-century tapestries and magnificent chandeliers, visitors will also see an exhibit of family portraits, yachting memorabilia, and decorative arts.

# The Breakers

118 Mill Street
Newport, RI 02840
(401) 847-1000

**Contact:** The Preservation Society of
Newport County
**Open:** April 4-Nov. 1, daily 10 a.m.–5 p.m.;
July 4-Labor Day, Sat. 10 a.m.–6 p.m
**Admission:** Adults $7.50; children (6-11)
$3.50; combination tickets available.
Guided tours, lectures, special events.
**Suggested Time to View House:** 1 hour
**Facilities on Premises:** Gift shop

**Description of Grounds:** 12 acres including
a formally landscaped terrace
surrounded by Japanese yew, Chinese
juniper and dwarf hemlock
**Best Season to View House:** May-June,
summer and early fall
**Number of Yearly Visitors:** 800,000
**Year House Built:** 1895
**Style of Architecture:** Renaissance Revival
**Number of Rooms:** 70
**On-Site Parking:** Yes **Wheelchair Access:** Yes

## Description of House

The Breakers, designed by Richard Morris Hunt, after northern Italian palaces, was built in 1895 for Cornelius Vanderbilt. Cornelius Vanderbilt II was born in 1843, the oldest of nine children of William Henry and Louisa Kissam Vanderbilt. Serious and hardworking, he was a favorite of his grandfather Cornelius, the self-made shipping and railroad magnate whose consolidation of the Harlem, Hudson and Central New York Railway Lines made him America's richest man. Cornelius II began his working life at the age of sixteen as a messenger for the New York Shoe and Leather Bank; at nineteen he joined Kissam Brothers banking firm, and at twenty four he became assistant treasurer of the Vanderbilt owned New York and Harlem Railroad. When his father died in 1885, he left Cornelius and William equal shares of his enormous fortune and management of the family business.

The original wood and brick Breakers cottage was destroyed by fire in 1892 and the impressive structure that stands today was built to replace it. In the Breakers, the architecture and design trends of the Gilded Age reached a pinnacle. The largest of the period's Newport "cottages" is also its most perfectly realized product—a Renaissance revival structure built without limitations of scale or expense. The seventy-room cottage had grand-scale reception rooms on the first floor and bedrooms on the second and third, several of those on the upper story were for children. The thirty-three rooms set aside to accommodate resident staff members as well as the maids and valets of guests will give visitors an idea of the magnitude of the house and the entertaining which took place here.

Because of its incendiary history, The Breakers was made as fireproof as possible. The structure has no wooden parts; a steel skeleton supports the masonry and exterior Indiana limestone blocks. An enormous heating plant beneath the caretaker's cottage was joined to the basement of the house by a wide tunnel. Several hundred tons of coal could be stored at once in the underground boiler room.

## Notable Collections on Exhibit

An eclectic variety of furnishings and objects are on display including 16th-century style chairs, settes, and table (reproductions of pieces in Venice's Palazzo Cornaro); a bronze bust of William Henry Vanderbilt III and a marble bust of his father Cornelius II, both by American sculptor John Q.A. Ward; china and glassware original to the house; a hand-woven 19th-century Savonnerie carpet, from the famous French rug works begun by Henry IV in the 17th century.

# The Elms

118 Mill Street
Newport, RI 02840
(401) 847-1000

**Contact:** The Preservation Society of
Newport County

**Open:** April 4-May 1, weekends
10 a.m.–5 p.m.; May 2-Sept. 30, daily
10 a.m.–5 p.m.; Oct. 1-Nov. 1, daily
10 a.m.–5 p.m.

**Admission:** Adults $7; children (6-11) $3;
combination tickets available. Guided
tours, lectures, special events.

**Suggested Time to View House:** 1 hour

**Description of Grounds:** 11 acre grounds
with a formal sunken garden with
hundreds of pink and white begonias and
ornamental parterre patterns composed
of [more]

**Best Season to View House:** May-June,
Summer and early Fall

**Number of Yearly Visitors:** 800,000

**Year House Built:** 1901

**Style of Architecture:** French Neoclassical

**On-Site Parking:** Yes **Wheelchair Access**: Yes

## Description of House

Edward J. Berwind was the son of German immigrants who worked in
the manufacture of pianos. In 1865, seventeen year old Edward was named
by President Lincoln to the U.S. Naval Academy at Annapolis. He served in
the Franco-Prussian War and was for a time a naval aide to President Grant.
He left his military career for the coal business in 1875, eventually ac-
cumulating the fortune that would bring a French chateau to Bellevue
Avenue in Newport, Rhode Island.

The Elms is an early 20th-century copy of the Chateau d' Asnieres, a few
miles from Paris. The house, designed in 1899 by architect Horace Trumbauer, is a near exact replica of the chateau designed by Mansart for the
Marquis d'Argenson in 1750. The cottage has a rounded central section
flanked by wings of equal size creating a simple classical plan of balanced
proportions. Trumbauer concealed the extensive staff quarters the Berwinds
required behind a third floor balustrade and arranged the kitchen, laundry
and other workrooms in a deep cellar. The Elms is also raised above the
ground level situation of its model and set on a broad balustraded terrace
above expansive lawns.

The interior decoration of the Elms is eclectic, borrowing from a number of styles, in typical turn-of-the century fashion.

### Notable Collections on Exhibit

The house displays a magnificent collection of family owned pieces including a pair of Louis XV-style gilt console tables with purple Breccia tops; a pair of ormolu-mounted Chinese vases in oxblood porcelain; 19th-century blue and tan dragon rug; four marble sculptures personifying the seasons; a series of large English landscape paintings; and a large number of stone, marble, and bronze statues and fountains.

### Additional Information

The Elms and its park-like grounds are imposing reminders of the turn-of-the century impulse to bring the European past to life in America.

# Rosecliff

118 Mill Street
Newport, RI 02840
(401) 847-1000

**Contact:** The Preservation Society of Newport County

**Open:** April 4-Sept. 30 and Oct. 1-Nov. 1, daily 10 a.m.–5 p.m

**Admission:** Adults $6; children (6-11) $3; combination tickets available. Guided tours, lectures, special events.

**Suggested Time to View House:** 1 hour

**Description of Grounds:** Garden of 200 hybrid tea rose bushes and everblooming climbers

**Best Season to View House:** May-June, summer and early fall

**Number of Yearly Visitors:** 800,000

**Year House Built:** 1902

**Style of Architecture:** Neoclassical

**On-Site Parking:** Yes  **Wheelchair Access:** No

## Description of House

Among the undisputed leaders of the Newport summer colony was Theresa Fair Oelrichs. Born in Virginia City, Nevada, to a family of ordinary means, she grew into one of the most celebrated debutantes of her day and reached her apex in society as mistress of Rosecliff. Theresa was an ambitious, energetic woman whose intelligence and drive were channeled into the avenue of high society—of calling cards and invitations, dinners and balls, gowns and jewels. Everything from the elegant daumount that carried her in Central Park's fashionable afternoon carriage procession, to Rosecliff, her regal summer house, mirrored her position and power.

Created as a showcase for extravagant summer entertainments, Rosecliff was modelled after the Grand Trianon, a neoclassical pleasure palace built in the great park at Versailles for Louis XIV. Architect Stanford White designed the white terra cotta house to suit his client's turn-of-the-century requirements while preserving much of the 18th-century detail of its model. White's own commitment to graceful effect and beautiful sculptured ornament, evident in the Rosecliff, was well-known in New York and Newport circles when Theresa Fair Oelrichs commissioned her new summer cottage in 1898. The numerous French doors and windows, Ionic pilasters and columns, entablature, and modelled floral decoration of the house are all replicated from the Grand Trianon.

## Additional Information

Some of the splendor of Rosecliff's Gilded Age past was recreated when the house was used as a setting for scenes from the films *The Betsy* (1978) with Sir Laurence Olivier and *The Great Gatsby* (1974) with Robert Redford.

# Sylvanus Brown House

P.O. Box 727
Pawtucket, RI 02862-0727
(401) 725-8638

**Contact:** Slater Mill Historic Site
**Open:** Closed Dec. 15 to Mar. 1
**Activities:** Guided tours of 3 on-site historic buildings slide/tabe show "Pawtucket—Cradle of Industry"
**Suggested Time to View House:** 90 minutes
**Facilities on Premises:** Gift shop, historic machine shop, water wheel and main exhibit

**Description of Grounds:** 5.5 acres includes a riverside park, view of two dams, seating and picnic table
**Best Season to View House:** Spring and summer
**Number of Yearly Visitors:** 16,000
**Year House Built:** 1758
**Style of Architecture:** Gambrel-roofed cottage
**Number of Rooms:** 8
**On-Site Parking:** Yes **Wheelchair Access:** Yes

## Description of House

The house was built to be shared by blacksmith Nathan Lenks and his brother Ebenezer Lenks. The building was located on Quaker Lane (now East Avenue) in Pawtucket. By 1784, Sylvanus Brown, a millwright and carpenter, purchased half the dwelling which he shared with a tenant of Eliphalit Slack and Nathan Lenk's widow. By 1796, Brown owned the entire dwelling and property including a carpenter's shop on the banks of Sargeant's trench. From 1789 through 1791, a business relationship between Brown and Samuel Slater was solidified by Slater's need for Brown's expertise in pattern making. The building was moved to the present site in 1942 and opened for tours in 1975.

The house is a two-and-a-half story gambrel-roofed structure with two dormers in the back. Of the eight rooms, five are currently opened to the public. A central staircase links the floors and a single entrance allows access to the top two stories of the building. The building has a single chimney and four operating fireplaces. The house rests on a foundation built during the 70s in an area landscaped to simulate the house's original surroundings. All of the furnishings are collected and appropriate to the period.

## Notable Collections on Exhibit

The house exhibits an unusual collection of hand textile processing equipment and utensils for open hearth cooking.

# The Nightingale-Brown House

357 Benefit Street
Providence, RI 02903
(401) 272-0357

**Contact:** The John Nicholas Brown Center
**Open:** By appointment only
**Activities:** Guided tours of the first floor
**Suggested Length of Time to View House:**
30 minutes including grounds
**Description of Grounds:** ½ acre designed
after one by Olmsted in 1890

**Best Season to View House:** Spring
**Number of Yearly Visitors:** 100
**Year House Built:** 1792, with additions in
1853, 1858, 1863 and 1922
**Style of Architecture:** Georgian
**Number of Rooms:** 23
**On-Site Parking:** No   **Handicap Access:** No

## Description of House

The Nightingale-Brown House was built by Colonel Joseph Nightingale, whose heirs sold it to Nicholas Brown in 1814. The structure was owned and occupied by memebers of this family until it was deeded to the John Nicholas Brown Center in 1985. The Browns were among the early settlers of Rhode Island and since the 17th century have been closely intertwined with the cultural and economic development of not only Rhode Island, but of the nation.

The Nightingale-Brown House is thought to be the largest wood frame house surviving from 18th-century America. The structure stands three stories tall, capped with a two-story attic. The fifty-five foot wide clapboard facade is broken by a central pavillion rising three stories to the cornice, by heavy bevelled quoins at the corners, and rusticated window surrounds.

The first floor, which is used for public functions, contains original furnishings of the Brown family of Providence.

## Notable Collections on Exhibit

The decorative arts of New England, including a reproduction of the desk made for Nicholas Brown in 1763, probably by Newport, cabinetmaker John Goddard, and sold at auction by the John Nicholas Brown Center in 1989 to fund the restoration of this National Historic Landmark property.

## Additional Information

The importance of the Nightingale-Brown House lies primarily in its architectural history. It was built in 1791 for Col. Joseph Nightingale, an entrepreneur in the American China Trade who, like many of his contemporaries, committed much of his fortune to building a monumental residence on a scale essentially without precedence in America. In style, it summarizes and concludes that period of late Georgian architecture in Providence. In size and quality it is distinguished even among its neighboring structures, which one authority has called "one of the great groups of early post-Republican houses in the country." The house is now used as a center for visiting scholars. The second floor is used for offices and the third floor is a private apartment.

# Governor Henry Lippitt House Museum

199 Hope Street
Providence, RI 02906
(401)453-0688

**Contact:** Heritage Trust of Rhode Island
**Open:** Tues.-Fri. 10 a.m.–4 p.m;
   Sat. 1–4 p.m; closed holidays
**Admission:** Adults $3; students and
   children $1. Guided tours, lectures and
   workshop series, concert series.
**Suggested Time to View House:** 45 minutes
**Year House Built:** 1862 to 1865
**Style of Architecture:** Renaissance Revival,
   High Victorian
**Number of Rooms:** 8 rooms currently open
   to public
**On-Site Parking:** No
**Wheelchair Access:** Yes

## Description of House

Many generations of Rhode Island politics live on in this Victorian mansion in the heart of downtown Providence. Governor Henry Lippitt, the namesake of the house, governed the state from 1875 to 1877. His son, Charles, also served as governor and a great-grandson, John Chaffee, today serves as U.S. Senator from the state.

Built between 1862 to 1865, the Governor Henry Lippitt House Museum is undoubtedly one of the finest mid 19th-century houses in Providence open to the public. The house's Renaissance revival style traditional architectural forms with an interior decorative scheme that is the essence of high-style Victorian. The interior craftmanship includes richly carved woodwork, colorful stenciling, faux marble and dazzling stained and etched glass windows. All furnishings are from the original Lippitt family.

## Notable Collections on Exhibit

Each room on the first floor has highly detailed chandeliers, one of which just returned from the United States Treasury in Washington D.C., where it was on loan to be re-cast for the Andrew Johnson Presidential suites.

## Additional Information

The house sponsors an informative series of workshops on gilding, faux finishes, and wall stenciling.

# *John Waterman Arnold House*

25 Roger Williams Circle
Warwick, RI 02888
(401) 467-7641

**Contact:** Warwick Historical Society

**Open:** Wed. 9 a.m.–1 p.m. and by
appointment

**Admission:** Donations accepted. Speakers
on the third Thur. of each month.

**Suggested Time to View House:** 90 minutes

**Facilities on Premises:** Book store

**Description of Grounds:** Historic village
and colonial gardens

**Best Season to View House:** Spring,
Summer and Fall

**Number of Yearly Visitors:** 600

**Year House Built:** 1760

**Style of Architecture:** Farm house with
central chimney

**Number of Rooms:** 6

**On-Site Parking:** Yes  **Wheelchair Access:** No

### *Description of House*

The John Waterman Arnold House stands on the grounds of a former fifty-nine acre farm owned by Israel Arnold. Arnold was one of the first settlers in Pawtuxet. He bought the land from its original Native American owner in 1600. This plot of land, where the house now stands was passed down from father to son for six generations. John W. Arnold, Israel's son, was the last of the family to live on the land.

This is an exceptional example of a Colonial farmhouse with a central chimney. It stands on the site of an earlier house, which was part of a large working farm. The Colonial period design is evident in the six by six windows, panelled doors, H & L hinges and thumb latches. In 1825, the front staircase was renovated into a semi-circular position. That same year an ell was added. The furnishings are collected and appropriate to the colonial period. The kitchen has a unique beehive oven.

### *Notable Collections on Exhibit*

The house exhibits various textiles and clothing; a collection of Rhode Island books is available in the research center.

# Vermont

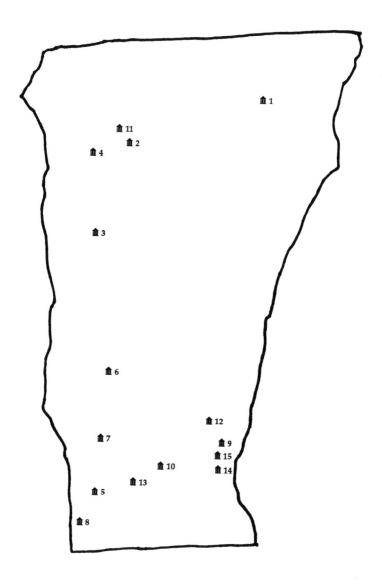

1. **Brownington**
   *Old Stone House*

2. **Fairfield**
   *President Chester A. Arthur
   Historic Site*

3. **Ferrisburgh**
   *Rokeby Museum*

4. **Grand Isle**
   *The Hyde Log Cabin*

5. **Manchester**
   *Hildene*

6. **Middlebury**
   *Judd-Harris House of the
   Sheldon Museum*

7. **Middleton**
   *Adams House and Museum*

8. **North Bennington**
   *The Park-McCullough House*

9. **Norwich**
   *Taylor-Hutchinson House*

10. **Plymouth Notch**
    *Plymouth Notch Historic District*

11. **Saint Albans**
    *St. Albans Historical Museum*

12. **Strafford**
    *Justin Smith Morrill Homestead*

13. **Weston**
    *Farrar-Mansur Museum*

14. **Windsor**
    *The Old Constitution House*

15. **Woodstock**
    *Dana House*

# *Old Stone House*

Brownington, VT 05860
(802) 754-2022

**Contact:** Orleans County Historical
  Association
**Open:** May 15-June 20 and Sept. 1-Oct. 15,
  Fri.-Tues. 11 a.m–5 p.m.

**Admission:** Adults $3; Orleans County
  residents $2; children (under 12) $1;
  special rates for student groups
**Year House Built:** 1830s
**Number of Rooms:** 30

### Description of House

The Old Stone House provides a fascinating glimpse of early American education. Built as a school dormitory in the 1830s, this four story structure was designed and erected by a man believed to be America's first black college graduate and first black legislator, Reverend Alexander Twilight. Stone by stone, Twilight and his neighbors split and hauled granite blocks until the building reached its full height. Once it was complete, Twilight spent the next two decades instructing and inspiring the region's school children within its thick walls.

### Notable Collections on Exhibit

The former school today houses a regional museum displaying tools and kitchenware, needlework and crafts, furniture and art related to local history. Reverend Twilight's desk and Bible are also on exhibit.

### Additional Information

The Old Stone House is part of the Brownington Village Historic district and is listed in the National Register of Historic Places.

# President Chester A. Arthur Historic Site

**Route 36**
**Fairfield, VT 05609-1201**
**(802) 828-3226**

**Contact:** Vermont Division for Historic Preservation

**Open:** Memorial Day-Columbus Day, Wed.-Sun. 9:30 a.m.–5:30 p.m.

**Admission:** Admission by donation, $1 recommended

**Suggested Time to View House:** Less than 1 hour

**Description of Grounds:** There are picnic areas on the 36 acres surrounding the historic site.

**Best Season to View House:** Memorial Day-Columbus Day

**Number of Yearly Visitors:** 1,000

**Year House Built:** 1829 (reconstructed in 1953)

**Style of Architecture:** Rural Cottage

**Number of Rooms:** 2

**On-Site Parking:** Yes

**Wheelchair Access:** No

## Description of House

This small Vermont cottage stands as a historic memorial to Chester A. Arthur, the twenty-first President of the United States. Arthur's father William, an emigrant from Ireland, came to Fairfield as a Baptist minister. The future President was born in 1829 and began to live in this humble cottage in 1830. From these poor beginnings, Arthur later went on to become a school teacher and a lawyer, before assuming the Presidency after Garfield's assassination in 1881.

The parsonage is actually a reconstruction of the one-and-a-half story story wood frame house to which the family moved when Arthur was only one month old. William Arthur preached at the brick Baptist church on a nearby ledgy hillside which is also open to visitors. Both the house and church are maintained by the Vermont Division for Historic Preservation.

## Notable Collections on Exhibit

The house is not furnished as a historic house, but instead offers a pictorial exhibit covering Chester Arthur's life and career.

# Rokeby Museum

R.R. 1, Box 1540
Ferrisburgh, VT 05456-9711
(802) 877-3406

**Contact:** Rowland Evans Robinson Memorial Association

**Open:** May 15-Oct. 15, Thur.-Sun. 11 a.m.–2 p.m.

**Admission:** Adults $2; students $1; seniors and children $.50. Guided tours, research facilities, special events, off-site exhibits and presentations.

**Suggested Time to View House:** 60–90 minutes

**Description of Grounds:** Complete complement of farm outbuildings surrounded by 85 acres

**Best Season to View House:** May-Sept.

**Number of Yearly Visitors:** 1,250

**Year House Built:** Built in 3 phases—1780s, 1814, 1893

**Style of Architecture:** Colonial, Transitional Greek Revival, Victorian

## Description of House

The Robinsons came to Rokeby in 1791 from Rhode Island. Rokeby became a prosperous sheep farm and orchard in the 19th century. The second and third generations of the family were actively involved in issues of regional and national importance. Rowland Thomas Robinson (1796-1879) was influential in the national abolitionist movement and worked with leading anti-slavery advocates including Wendell Phillips and William Lloyd Garrison. Rowland Evans Robinson was Vermont's best known and most-beloved writer in the late 19th century. He was an artist, a storyteller and an early cautionary environmentalist.

Overlooking the Champlain Valley, Rokeby holds an unusual place in Vermont history. Because of the Robinsons's political activities in the abolitionist movement, Rokeby served as a stop on the Underground Railroad and provided safe haven for slaves fleeing the South. All of the furnishings, artwork, costumes and ephemera in Rokeby belonged to the Robinsons, the original owners, between 1791 and 1961.

The house is being conserved to illustrate evolutionary aspects of life in a single building which contains wallcoverings, furnishings, and fixtures from various periods of occupancy. The collection of outbuildings is very complete and creates a unique agricultural setting—few Vermont farms currently resemble Rokeby. Innovative work with wood preservatives and masonry and plaster stabilization has helped make Rokeby an important preservation site in Vermont.

## Notable Collections on Exhibit

Rokeby exhibits nearly 200 years of family and architectural history including a large collection of early 19th-century Vermont-made furnishings. There is also an important collection of manuscripts and books detailing all aspects of life on a Vermont farm.

# The Hyde Log Cabin

Route U.S. 2
Grand Isle, VT 05609-1201
(802) 828-3226

**Contact:** Vermont Division for Historic
Preservation

**Open:** July 4th-Labor Day, Wed.-Sun.
9:30–5:30 p.m.

**Admission:** $1. Self-guided tours with a
host/hostess available to answer
questions and to provide information.

**Suggested Time to View House:** 30 minutes

**Best Season to View House:** Late summer

**Number of Yearly Visitors:** 2,000

**Year House Built:** 1783

**Style of Architecture:** Log cabin

**Number of Rooms:** 1

## Description of House

After fighting in the American Revolution, Jebediah Hyde, Jr. and his father, Captain Jebediah Hyde, travelled to Grand Isle in the summer of 1783 to work as surveyors. Four years earlier, Ira and Ethan Allen had modestly named the Island "The Two Heroes" and, with Governor Chittendon, had parcelled out grants to the Green Mountain Boys. Most of the grantees sold their rights and Captain Hyde purchased several in the part that would later be called Grand Isle. In 1783, Jebediah, Jr. built a cabin on his father's property which served as home to various members of the Hyde family for nearly 150 years.

The Hyde Log Cabin is a one story structure with a steeply pitched gable roof sheathed in cedar shingles. Constructed of cedar logs fourteen to eighteen inches in diameter, the cabin consists of a single room with a massive fireplace at one end and an overhead loft. Hyde Cabin is typical of the log structures built by the early settlers of Vermont and is considered one of the oldest log cabins in the United States. In 1945, the Vermont Historical Society acquired the cabin and moved it about two miles to its present location for restoration.

## Notable Collections on Exhibit

The cabin houses an exhibit of maps of the county's original grants, furnishings from the cabin and other homes of the county, agricultural and household implements from the area, and other items related to the history and settlement of Grand Isle. Many of the furnishings are representative of those found in other frontier settlements near the Canadian border in Vermont.

# *Hildene*

Historic 7A South, P.O. Box 377
Manchester, VT 05254-0377
(802) 362-1788

**Contact:** Friends of Hildene, Inc.

**Open:** Mid May–Oct. 31, daily 9:30 a.m.–4 p.m.

**Admission:** Adults $6; children $2; under 6 free; group rates $4; students and school groups $1. Guided tours preceded by audiovisual presentations; numerous special activities.

**Suggested Time to View House:** 90 minutes

**Facilities on Premises:** Gift shop

**Description of Grounds:** Formal gardens included in guided tour; picnic facilities

**Best Season to View House:** May-Oct.

**Year House Built:** 1904

**Number of Rooms:** 24

**Number of Yearly Visitors:** 85,000

**Style of Architecture:** Georgian Revival

**On-Site Parking:** Yes  **Wheelchair Access:** No

## Description of House

Robert Todd Lincoln, the only son of Abraham Lincoln who survived adulthood, built Hildene for his family's summer residence in 1904. After the assassination of his father, Robert Lincoln became a successful lawyer and then served as Secretary of War under President Garfield. Lincoln also made his mark in business as president and chairman of the board of the Pullman Company. In 1902, at the height of his corporate career, Lincoln sought refuge in the mountains, and selected Manchester as the site for Hildene or "hill and valley" and spent more than twenty summers here. Descendants of the Lincoln family continued to live in the house until 1975.

This majestic twenty four room Georgian Revival mansion sits on a grassy promontory with a panoramic view of the Green and Taconic mountain ranges and the Battenkill valley below. In addition to serving as a summer retreat, Lincoln also ran the Pullman Company's business out of two of the rooms for six months of the year. The office still contains many of his original files and personal papers, and the books in the library are almost exactly where he left them at the time of his death in 1926. The property also contains a completely refurbished plank school house from 1848 and an observatory built to house a telescope manufactured to Lincoln's detailed specifications. Most of the furnishings on display belonged to the Lincoln family including the late Victorian parlor furniture and the Queen Anne dining room set.

## Notable Collections on Exhibit

Visitors to Hildene will see and the oldest residential Aeolian pipe-organ, with over 1000 pipes and 242 rolls, still in working order in the United States. The complete house tour includes an exhibition of furniture, books, paintings, toys, and needlework typical of early 20th-century homes of well-to-do families. Mementos of Lincoln's wide-ranging experiences as Secretary of War, as minister to Great Britain under President Harrison, and as president of the Pullman Company are also on display.

# *Judd-Harris House*
# *of the Sheldon Museum*

**1 Park Street**
**Middlebury, VT 05753**
**(802) 388-2117**

**Contact:** The Sheldon Museum

**Open:** June-Oct., Mon.-Fri. 10 a.m–5 p.m.;
Nov.-May, Wed.-Fri. 1–4 p.m.

**Admission:** Adults $3.50; seniors and
students $3; children $.50. Guided tours,
special exhibits.

**Suggested Time to View House:**
30–45 minutes

**Facilities on Premises:** Museum shop and
research center

**Description of Grounds:** Garden with
historic perennials

**Best Season to View House:** Summer
and fall

**Number of Yearly Visitors:** 4,500

**Year House Built:** 1829

**Number of Rooms:** 15

**Style of Architecture:** Federal (brick)

**On-Site Parking:** No **Wheelchair Access:** Yes

## Description of House

The house was built by the founders of a local marble business, Eben Judd and Lebeus Harris in 1829. A later occupant named Henry Sheldon lived as a boarder in the house for many years until he converted the house into a community history museum, the Sheldon Museum, in 1882. His extraordinary collections form the basis of the current holdings both in the house and in the research center of local history.

The Judd Harris House heated the cold Vermont winters with six fireplaces made of local black marble produced in the owners factory. There is also an impressive beehive oven in the kitchen. The furnishings are collected and appropriate to period. The house displays a unique collection of Vermont paintings, furniture and decorative arts.

## Notable Collections on Exhibit

The research center has an outstanding collecton of local diaries, photographs, business records, letters and newspapers.

# Adams House and Museum

On the Green
Middleton, VT 05757
(802) 235-2376

**Contact:** Middletown Springs Historical
Society
**Open:** Memorial Day-mid Oct., Sun.
2–4 p.m.; or by appointment
**Admission:** Donation. The society
sponsors many annual events such as
the Maple Festival, the Strawberry
Festival, the Antique Transportation
Festival, and the Springs Park Picnic,
call for schedule.
**Suggested Time to View House:**
30–60 minutes
**Description of Grounds:** Museum is
located one quarter of a mile from a
historic mineral springs and public park.
**Best Season to View House:** Year round
**Year House Built:** c. 1800
**Number of Rooms:** 10

**Number of Yearly Visitors:** 500–1,000
**Style of Architecture:** Federal
**On-Site Parking:** Yes **Wheelchair Access:** No

## Description of House

In the early part of the 19th century, Middleton was a thriving community
with a large population of visitors who would come for therapeutic treatment
at the nearby mineral springs. The Adams family, prominent business owners
in the community, lived and worked in this attractive Federal-style home
during this period. They ran an unusual assortment of businesses from the
home ranging from a millenery shop to an undertaking business. In the 1920s,
the town suffered a devastating fire which destroyed many of the downtown
buildings. The Adams House survived and became the new home for the local
grocery store and an auditorium where townspeople would gather for every
conceivable event—from town meetings to basketball games. In 1969, the
house, which had been neglected for many years, was given to the recently
established historical society for restoration.

The six by two bay, two-and-a-half story clapboard Adams House is
considered one of the most significant buildings in the Middleton Springs
historic district. The house is both a focal point on the town green and the
only surviving commercial structure from the town's pre-1811 period of
prosperity due to the nearby mineral springs.

## Notable Collections on Exhibit

The museum houses a fascinating town history exhibit related to
Middleton's more prosperous years. These include artifacts from the former
grand hotel with over 300 rooms where visitors would come to use the
mineral springs. Items on display include furniture, china, and photographs
of the now destroyed hotel. In addition, there are exhibits on the manufacture of horsepower farm implements and other local industries.

# The Park-McCullough House

P.O. Box 366
N. Bennington, VT 05257
(802) 442-5441

**Contact:** The Park-McCullough House
Association

**Open:** May 4-Oct. 31 and Dec. 7-21,
10 a.m.–3 p.m.

**Admission:** Adults $4; seniors $3.50;
children (12-17) $2.50; under 11 free.
Guided tours, special events.

**Suggested Time to View House:** 45 minutes

**Facilities on Premises:** Museum shop

**Description of Grounds:** A children's
playhouse, carriage barn, and beautiful
Victorian and Colonial gardens are open
to the public.

**Best Season to View House:** Summer
and fall

**Number of Yearly Visitors:** 14,000

**Year House Built:** 1865

**Number of Rooms:** 35

**Style of Architecture:** French Second Empire

**On-Site Parking:** Yes   **Wheelchair Access:** Yes

## Description of House

The Park-McCullough home was the summer home of Trenor and Laura Hall Park. Completed in 1865, the house remained occupied by their descendants until 1965. Laura and Trenor were Bennington natives who went to California from 1852 to 1863 to seek their fortune. Trenor, an attorney, amassed a fortune in enterprise realty and in the management of the gold mines of the "Great Pathfinder", General John S. Fremont. Returning to Vermont, they commissioned architects to design this important early example of American Summer Architecture. The generations who have called this house home made history including two of Vermont's governors: Hiland Hall and and John McCullough.

This thirty-five room Victorian mansion is a classic example of French Second Empire style. Visitors will find rooms with fourteen foot ceilings opening onto a gracious central hall with a sweeping staircase. The house contains the finest details: oak and walnut paneling, handsome parquet floors, and bronze chandeliers (supplied with gas from a gas-making machine). The second floor consists of large, airy bedrooms, and a beautiful stained glass skylight. All of the furnishings and decorative objects are from the original residents.

## Notable Collections on Exhibit

Park-McCullough House exhibits an extensive collection of family portraits, American and European landscape paintings, and genre paintings by Henry Siddons Mowbray and Gustave Jacquet among others. In addition to the art exhibit, the museum also holds an estimated 100,000 pieces in its collection including a 37,000 piece family archive of letters, diaries and invoices.

# *Taylor-Hutchinson House*

Church Street, P.O. Box 284
Norwich, VT 05055
(802) 649-2711

**Contact:** Norwich Historical Society
**Open:** Wed. 2:30–4:30 p.m.
**Admission:** Free. Open house.
**Suggested Time to View House:** 30 minutes
**Best Season to View House:** Summer

**Number of Yearly Visitors:** 100
**Year House Built:** 1825
**Style of Architecture:** Cape
**Number of Rooms:** 7
**On-Site Parking:** Yes

### Description of House

Little is known of the original residents of this quaint house located in a small Vermont village. The Taylor-Hutchinson house, a one and half story cape style structure with three bay windows, is located on its original site in the historic district of Norwich village. The building is listed in the National Registry of Historic Places. The furnishings are collected and span the period from 1870 to the present.

### Notable Collections on Exhibit

Visitors to the house will see a small collection of clothing, textiles manuscripts and photographs on display. There are also genealogical resources available to those attempting to research relatives from Norwich.

# Plymouth Notch Historic District

Route 100-A
Plymouth Notch, VT 05056
(802) 672-3773

**Contact:** Vermont Division for Historic
Preservation

**Open:** Memorial Day-Columbus Day, daily
9:30 a..m.–5:30 p.m.

**Admission:** $3.75. Hostess/hosts located in
each of the buildings in the historic
district.

**Suggested Time to View House:** 3 hours

**Facilities on Premises:** Gift shop, book store

**Description of Grounds:** An entire
preserved village centered around the
life of Calvin Coolidge

**Best Season to View House:** Memorial
Day-Columbus Day

**Number of Yearly Visitors:** 50,000

**Year House Built:** 1840 to 1874

**Number of Rooms:** 12

**Style of Architecture:** Rural Vermont

## Description of House

Plymouth Notch has been called the best preserved Presidential
birthplace in the nation. The birthplace and boyhood home of Calvin
Coolidge (1872) distinguishes this small village where Coolidge returned
time and time again during his busy public life. The Coolidge Homestead
holds an unusual historical significance for being the site of Coolidge's
swearing in as the Thirtieth President of the United States in 1923. Never
before or since, has a President taken the oath of office from his own father,
in his own home, and within such unique surroundings.

Calvin Coolidge was born in an unpretentious wood frame house with
an attached general store. At the age of four, the family moved to the larger
residence known as the homestead where Coolidge's father, Colonel John
Coolidge, lived the rest of his life. In addition to the birthplace and homestead, visitors to Plymouth Notch may also visit the childhood home of
Coolidge's mother, Victoria Josephine Moore. The yellow clapboard house,
known as the Wilder House, was built in 1830 and originally operated as a
tavern. This rural village also has a functioning cheese factory, originally
built in 1890 by Col. Coolidge and several other local farmers.

The Coolidge birthplace is furnished as it was in 1872 at the time of his
birth and the Homestead as it was at the time of the swearing in in 1923.

## Additional Information

Other notable sites to visit in the village include the Union Christian
Church, a Greek Revival structure build in 1840 as a meeting house and
formally dedicated as a Congregational church in 1842. One can also visit
the gravesite of Calvin Coolidge in Plymouth Cemetery where he is buried
along with six generations of Coolidges and neighbors and friends.

# St. Albans Historical Museum

Church Street
St. Albans, VT
(802)-527-7933

**Contact:** St. Albans Historical Museum
**Open:** June-mid. Oct., Tues.-Sat. 1–4 p.m.,
other times by appointment
**Admission:** Adults $1; Groups donation.
Monthly programs, Victorian teas.
**Suggested Time to View House:** 1 hour
**Year House Built:** 1861
**Style of Architecture:** Italianate
**On-Site Parking:** Yes

## Description of House

Located near Lake Champlain, this impressive Italianate structure today houses an eclectic array of collections devoted to regional history. Although the building served as a school over the years, the furnished period rooms and display give parts of it a house-like quality.

The Beaumont Room contains an unusual medical display related to Dr. William Beaumont, a former resident of St. Albans. This "doctor's office" is arranged as it was represented in a Norman Rockwell painting. The Margaret Armstrong Room, showcases a lovely display of furniture, china, pottery, miscellaneous antiques, and paintings, including some portraits of early residents of St. Albans. The Military Room contains photos, guns, and uniforms dating from the Civil War to the present day while the C.V. Railway Room is devoted to artifacts and paraphernalia of the railroads. The Children's Room houses a unique collection of antique toys, dolls, and furniture. A special reference room on the second floor holds maps, photos, and genealogical records, which supplement the other holdings in local history. Visitors to the St. Albans Historical Museum will have a rare experience of Vermont's past.

# Justin Smith Morrill Homestead

Strafford, VT 05609-1201
(802) 828-3226

**Contact:** Vermont Division for Historic
Preservation

**Open:** Memorial Day-Columbus Day,
Wed.-Sun. 9:30 a.m.–5:30 p.m.

**Admission:** $2. Guided tours.

**Suggested Time to View House:** 2 hours

**Description of Grounds:** The grounds are
landscaped and reflect the Gothic
Revival period of the house.

**Best Season to View House:** Memorial
Day-Columbus Day

**Number of Yearly Visitors:** 1,000

**Year House Built:** 1849 to 1850

**Number of Rooms:** 15

**Style of Architecture:** Gothic Revival

## Description of House

Senator Justin S. Morrill, author and chief sponsor of the acts establishing land grant colleges, constructed this distinctive homestead between 1848 and 1851. It is ironic that this this proponent of historic educational reform was forced to leave school at the age of fifteen. He worked his way up from merchant clerk to successful businessman. Morrill designed and built the house during a brief retirement period before he started on his new career in politics. A self-taught architect, Morrill borrowed and adapted the forms and details of the Gothic Revival style to suit his own particular needs and vision.

The Morrill Homestead is an outstanding example of a Gothic Revival Cottage, a style of architecture popular in rural America in the mid-19th century. The two-and-a-half story house incorporates much of the stone-like detail—actually rendered in wood—that is the hallmark of the style. The exterior flush board siding is painted the original rosy pink color, Morrill's attempt to imitate the appearance of cut sandstone. There are seven agricultural outbuildings including a blacksmith shop and several barns which are open for viewing. The house is furnished entirely with the Morrill family possessions dating from 1849 to 1890. Most are original to the house, however, some were brought from the Senator's home in Washington, D.C. following his death.

There is an imported French window in the library painted especially for Morrill which depicts the picturesque and crumbling ruins of Scotland's famed Holyrood Chapel. The first floor also features a clever, yet aesthetic, measure of privacy with hand-painted window screens illustrated with romantic landscapes which allow a view out, but not in.

## Additional Information

The walkways and gardens surrounding the house are in the best tradition of the romantic landscape movement in America. Today much of the original plantings made by Morrill survive, including species from Europe and the Orient.

# Farrar-Mansur Museum

P.O. Box 247
Weston, VT 05161
(802) 824-6781

**Contact:** Weston Historical Society

**Open:** Memorial Day-Columbus Day,
weekends; July and Aug., weekdays;
closed Tuesdays

**Activities:** Guided tours

**Suggested Time to View House:** 1 hour

**Best Season to View House:** June 1-Oct. 15

**Number of Yearly Visitors:** 900

**Year House Built:** 1797

**Style of Architecture:** Federal

**Number of Rooms:** 10

**On-Site Parking:** Yes

**Wheelchair Access:** No

## Description of House

In 1795, Oliver Farrar of Concord, Massachusetts and his wife Polly purchased the land and adjacent saw mill and built this home. Polly gave birth to thirteen children in the house. The next occupants, John and Dolly Mansur, bought the house in 1857. Four generations of Mansurs lived in the house until 1932 when the house was given to the Weston Community Club to convert to a historic house museum.

The house and its contents reflect or describe life in a Vermont village throughout the 19th century. In keeping with the period, this two story, post and beam framed, Federal-style house has a granite block foundation, clapboard siding, and a slate roof. Inside, the house has a unique "I" shaped kitchen with a beehive chimney and a large second-story ballroom. There is also a tavern building addition at the rear of the house with a taproom adorned by original grills. The ladies parlor is decorated with rare wall murals painted by WPA artist Roy Williams in 1936.

All furnishings were owned or used by Weston families. Some are of the same period of the house and locally made, while others are authentic 19th century.

## Notable Collections on Exhibit

The house exhibits outstanding early 19th-century portraits including some of national signifigance. A wide collection of personal belongings such as quilts, costumes, spinning and weaving equipment, open hearth cooking utensils, lighting devices, dolls, toys, guns, pewter are also on display as well as genealogical records, family Bibles, and a photo collection.

## Additional Information

The adjacent Mill Museum holds a fine collection of Vermont crafts and industries of the 19th century, displaying tools, farm implements, and a granary.

# The Old Constitution House

Route U.S. 5
Windsor, VT 05609
(802) 828-3226

**Contact:** Vermont Division for Historic
Preservation

**Open:** Memorial Day-Columbus Day,
Wed.-Sun. 9:30 a.m.–5:30 p.m.

**Admission:** $1. Self-guided tours with a
host/hostess available to answer
questions and to provide information.

**Suggested Time to View House:** 90 minutes

**Description of Grounds:** A small village lot
with gardens

**Best Season to View House:** Memorial
Day-Columbus Day

**Number of Yearly Visitors:** 5,000

**Year House Built:** 1774

**Style of Architecture:** Georgian, Federal,
Colonial Revival

**Number of Rooms:** 8

**On-Site Parking:** Yes  **Wheelchair Access:** Yes

## Description of House

While no individual was ever born here, this tavern can rightly be called
the birthplace of the republic of Vermont as the state's first constitution was
written and adopted here on July 8, 1977. Vermont was an independent
republic for fourteen years before joining the union to become the fourteenth
state in 1791. Vermont's constitution was the first in America to prohibit
slavery and to establish universal manhood suffrage, thereby rejecting
property ownership or specific income as voting requirements. It was also
the first Constitution to establish a state wide system of public schools.

This two and a half story wood frame house was originally built as a
tavern and was owned by Elijah West at the time of the signing of the
constitution. The building operated as a tavern until it was converted into
a tenement house. The structure was moved off of Main Street and converted
to shops for merchandising and small manufacturing in 1870. In 1914, the
historic importance of the building was fully recognized and it was moved
to its present location.

The various rooms of the tavern are furnished to reflect the period and
the uses of the building. Many come from collections donated to the state,
and although many are appropriate to the period, there are also Victorian
furnishings.

## Notable Collections on Exhibit

The 20th-century tea room has a mounted interpretive exhibit on the
Vermont constitution and the events which led up to the establishment of
the republic of Vermont.

# Dana House

26 Elm Street
Woodstock, VT 05091
(802) 457-1822

**Contact:** Woodstock Historical Society
**Open:** Mid May-late Oct.; weekends in Dec.
**Admission:** Adults $3.50; seniors $2.50;
    13-18 $1, children (12 and under) free.
    Guided tours, monthly lecture series,
    bus tours to other sites.
**Suggested Time to View House:** 50 minutes
**Facilities on Premises:** Museum shop,
    research library
**Number of Yearly Visitors:** 3,000
**Year House Built:** 1807
**Style of Architecture:** Federal
**Number of Rooms:** 14

**On-Site Parking:** No **Wheelchair Access:** Yes

## Description of House

The house was built in 1807 for Charles Dana, a local dry goods merchant. Of his eight children, two became prominent in the area: Henry, the author of a history of the town of Woodstock and Joseph who founded the Elm Tree Press. His grandson, John Cotton Dana, was a well known early librarian and museum professional. He is nationally known for introducing new concepts of library and museum usage—making services more accessible to the public. Another grandson, Charles Loomis Dana, was a pioneering neurologist, professor at the Cornell University Medical College in New York City and president of the New York Academy of Medicine.

This graceful brick and frame house on Elm Street represents Vermont's most productive and exhilarating years of youthful growth. The Federal house has fourteen rooms exquisitely decorated and detailed with the personal touches of its owners and other furnishings given to the society as gifts. The house has its original kitchen with fireplace and oven. The original barn now houses exhibitions and a museum shop. Furnishings date from 1740 to 1900 and are appropriate to the various periods portrayed in the house. Some of the furnishings are from the Dana family.

## Notable Collections on Exhibit

Dana House has a complete collection of Woodstock memorabilia ranging from town charters to Woodstock-made silver. There is also a large collection of engravings by John Taylor Arms and paintings, including portraits by Thomas Ware (one spectacular portrait is unique in American art). In addition, Dana House displays a variety textiles such as coverlets, quilts and historic clothing, a large collection of antique dolls and toys, Woodstock Railroad artifacts, a sleigh belonging to Frederick Billings, and an extensive photograph collection.

# $\mathscr{Index}$

## 🏛 *Connecticut*

## 🏛 Maine

## 🏛 Massachusetts

# 🏛 New Hampshire

# 🏛 Rhode Island

# 🏛 Vermont

## 🏛 Connecticut

| | Photo or illustration courtesy of |
|---|---|
| 1640 Lt. Walter Fyler House | The Windsor Historical Society, Inc. |
| 1765 Dr. Hezekiah Chaffee House | The Windsor Historical Society, Inc. |
| Amasa Day House | Antiquarian and Landmarks Society |
| Bates-Scofield Homestead | Charles Miller/Darien Historical Society |
| Bowen House, Roseland Cottage | J. David Bohl/ Soc. for the Preservation of New England Antiquities |
| Bradley Wheeler House | Westport Historical Society |
| Butler-McCook Homestead | Antiquarian and Landmarks Society |
| Buttolph-Williams House | Antiquarian and Landmarks Society |
| Capt. Elisha Phelps House | Gerald Mason/Simsbury Historical Society |
| Enoch Kelsey House | Newington Historical Society & Trust, Inc. |
| Florence Griswold Museum | Florence Griswold Museum, Inc. |
| Gen. William Hart House | Thomas Eppleby/Old Saybrook Historical Society |
| Glebe House Museum | Glebe House Museum & Gertrude Jekyll Gardens |
| Gunn Historical Museum | Gunn Historical Museum |
| Nathaniel Hale Homestead | Antiquarian and Landmarks Society |
| Nathaniel Hempsted House | Antiquarian and Landmarks Society |
| Hatheway House | Antiquarian and Landmarks Society |
| Henry Whitfield State Historical Museum | Connecticut Historical Commission |
| The Holley-Williams House Museum | Hugh McMillan |
| Hotchkiss-Fyler House | Torrington Historical Society, Inc. |
| Hurd House | Louise Keating/Old Woodbury Historical Society Inc. |
| Isham-Terry House | Antiquarian and Landmarks Society |
| Jonathan Dickerman House | Hamden Historical Society |
| Joshua Hempsted House | Antiquarian and Landmarks Society |
| Keeler Tavern Museum | Keeler Tavern Preservation Society, Inc. |
| Kellogg-Eddy House | Newington Historical Society |
| King House Museum | Suffield Historical Society |
| Lockwood-Mathews Mansion Museum | Lockwood-Mathews Mansion Museum |
| Noah Webster House | Historical Society of West Hartford, Inc. |
| Prudence Crandall Museum | Connecticut Historical Commision |
| Samuel Parsons House | D. Lyons/Wallingford Historical Society |
| Shaw-Perkins Mansion | New London County Historical Society |
| Silas Deane, Joseph Webb & Isaac Stevens Museum | Webb-Deane-Stevens Museum |
| Sloan-Raymond-Fitch House | Wilton Historical Society |
| Smith-Harris House | Town of East Lyme |
| Stanley-Whitman House | Stanley-Whitman House |

## 🏛 Massachusetts

| | |
|---|---|
| 1830 Brick Dwelling | Hancock Shaker Village |
| Adams National Historic Site | U. S. Dept. of the Interior, National Park |
| Alcott/Orchard House | Louisa May Alcott Memorial Association |
| Amherst History Museum and 18th Century Garden | Amherst Historical Society |
| Amos Blanchard House and Barn Museum | Andover Historical Society |

| | |
|---|---|
| *Arrowhead* | Berkshire County Historical Society |
| *Ashley House* | Susan Ryan |
| *Atwood House* | Chatham Historical Society |
| *Beauport-Sleeper-McCann House* | J. David Bohl/ Soc. for the Preservation of New England Antiquities |
| *Clara Barton Birthplace Museum* | Clara Barton Camp for Girls with Diabetes |
| *Codman House-The Grange* | J. David Bohl/ Soc. for the Preservation of New England Antiquities |
| *Coffin House* | J. David Bohl/ Soc. for the Preservation of New England Antiquities |
| *The Col. John Ashley House* | N. Scott/The Trustees of Reservations |
| *Conant House Museum* | Falmouth Historical Society |
| *Cushing House* | Historical Society of Old Newbury |
| *Dadmun-McNamara House* | Wellesley Historical Society |
| *Derby House* | Salem Maritime National Historic Site |
| *General Sylvanus Thayer Birthplace* | Braintree Historical Society |
| *Glen Magna* | Danvers Historical Society |
| *Gore Place* | Gore Place Society |
| *Gropius House* | J. David Bohl/ Soc. for the Preservation of New England Antiquities |
| *Grout-Heard House* | Wayland Historical Society |
| *Hancock-Clarke House* | Lexington Historical Society |
| *Harlow Old Fort House* | Plymouth Antiquarian Society |
| *Hedge House* | Plymouth Antiquarian Society |
| *Historic Deerfield* | Susan Ryan |
| *Hooper-Lee-Nichols House* | George Taloumus/Cambridge Historical Society |
| *Hoxie House* | Town of Sandwich |
| *Indian House* | Rupert Miles |
| *Iron Works House* | Saugus Ironworks National Historic Site |
| *Jeremiah Lee Mansion* | Marblehead Historical Society |
| *John Cabot House* | Beverly Historical Society and Museum |
| *John F. Kennedy National Historic Site* | National Park Service |
| *John Greenleaf Whittier Home* | Whittier Home Association |
| *The Julia Wood House* | The Falmouth Historical Society |
| *Longyear Family Mansion* | Longyear Museum and Historical Society |
| *Lyman Estate, Vale House* | Soc. for the Preservation of New England Antiquities |
| *Mary Baker Eddy Historic House (Amesbury)* | Longyear Museum and Historical Society |
| *Mary Baker Eddy Historic House (Stoughton)* | Longyear Museum and Historical Society |
| *Mary Lincoln House* | Centerville Historical Society & Museum |
| *Merwin House-Tranquility* | J. David Bohl/ Soc. for the Preservation of New England Antiquities |
| *The Naumkeag Museum and Gardens* | Wallert Scott/The Trustees of Reservations |
| *Nichols House* | W. H. Pear/Nichols House Museum, Inc. |
| *Old State House* | The Bostonian Society |
| *Old Sturbridge Village* | Donald Eaton/Old Sturbridge Village |
| *Parson Capon House* | Topsfield Historical Society |
| *The Paul Revere House* | The Paul Revere Memorial Association |
| *The Pierce-Hichborn House* | The Paul Revere Memorial Association |
| *Plimoth Plantation* | Plimoth Plantation |

| | |
|---|---|
| Porter-Phelps-Huntington Historic House Museum | Porter-Phelps-Huntington Foundation, Inc. |
| Quincy Homestead | The National Society of Colonial Dames. |
| Rebecca Nurse Homestead | Danvers Alarm List Company |
| Rotch-Jones-Duff House and Garden Museum | Rotch-Jones-Duff House and Garden Museum, Inc. |
| Spencer-Pierce-Little Farm | J. David Bohl/ Soc. for the Preservation of New England Antiquities |
| Spooner House | Plymouth Antiquarian Society |
| Wells Thorne House | Rupert Miles |
| William Clapp House | Dorchester Historical Society |
| William Cullen Bryant Homestead | The Trustees of Reservations |
| Winslow Crocker House | J. David Bohl/ Soc. for the Preservation of New England Antiquities |

## 🏛 Maine

| | |
|---|---|
| The Black House | Hancock County Trustees of Public Reservation |
| Dr. Moses Mason House | Bethel Historical House |
| Farnsworth Homestead | Farnsworth Art Museum |
| Harrington House | Freeport Historical Society |
| Hamilton House | J. David Bohl/ Soc. for the Preservation of New England Antiquities |
| Joshua L. Chamberlain House | Pejepscot Historical Society |
| Marrett House | J. David Bohl/ Soc. for the Preservation of New England Antiquities |
| Nickels-Sortwell House | J. David Bohl/ Soc. for the Preservation of New England Antiquities |
| Nordica Homestead | Nordica Memorial Association |
| Nott House-White Columns | Kennebunkport Historical Society |
| Pettengill Farm | Freeport Historical Society |
| Sarah Orne Jewett House | J. David Bohl/ Soc. for the Preservation of New England Antiquities |
| Sayward-Wheeler House | J. David Bohl/ Soc. for the Preservation of New England Antiquities |
| The Shaker Museum | The United Society of Shakers |
| Skolfield-Whittier House | Pejepscot Historical Society |
| Tate House | Lois Orazand/National Society of Colonial Dames in Maine |
| The Taylor-Barry House | The Brick Store Museum |
| The Victoria Mansion | Victoria Society of Maine |
| Thomas A. Hill House | Bangor Historical Society |
| Thomas Ruggles House | Laurietta Austin/Ruggles House Society |

## 🏛 New Hampshire

| | |
|---|---|
| Aspet | Saint-Gaudens National Historic Site |
| Barrett House—Forest Hall | J. David Bohl/ Soc. for the Preservation of New England Antiquities |
| Canterbury Shaker Village | Canterbury Shaker Village, Inc. |
| Daniel Webster Birthplace | New Hampshire Div. of Parks and Recreation |

| | |
|---|---|
| Franklin Pierce Homestead State Historic Site | New Hampshire Div.of Parks and Recreation |
| Gilman Garrison House | J. David Bohl/ Soc. for the Preservation of New England Antiquities |
| Governor John Langdon House | J. David Bohl/ Soc. for the Preservation of New England Antiquities |
| John Paul Jones House Museum | Portsmouth Historical Society |
| John Wingate Weeks Historic Site | New Hampshire Div.of Parks and Recreation |
| Jones Farm | New Hampshire Farm Museum, Inc. |
| Mary Baker Eddy Historic House (Rumney) | Longyear Museum and Historical Society |
| Robert Frost Farm | New Hampshire Div.of Parks and Recreation |
| Rundlet-May House | J. David Bohl/ Soc. of the Preservation of New England Antiquities |
| Strawberry Banke Museum | David Mendleshon/Strawberry Banke Museum |
| The Fells—John Hay National Wildlife Refuge | New Hampshire Div.of Parks and Recreation |
| Wentworth-Coolidge Mansion | State of New Hampshire Parks and Recreation |
| Wyman Tavern | Historical Society of Cheshire County |

## 🏛 Rhode Island

| | |
|---|---|
| Coggeshell Farm Museum | Coggeshell Farm Museum, Inc. |
| Blithwood Mansion | Blithewold Gardens and Arboretum |
| Chateau-sur-Mer | The Preservation Society of Newport County |
| Governor Henry Lippitt House Museum | Mary Kocol/Heritage Trust of Rhode Island |
| Hunter House | The Preservation Society of Newport County |
| John Waterman Arnold House | Warwick Historical Society |
| Kingscote | The Preservation Society of Newport County |
| Marble House | The Preservation Society of Newport County |
| Rosecliff | The Preservation Society of Newport County |
| The Breakers | The Preservation Society of Newport County |
| The Elms | The Preservation Society of Newport County |
| The Nightingale-Brown House | Barnaby Evans/The John Nicholas Brown Center |
| Woonsocket House | Block Island Historical Society |

## 🏛 Vermont

| | |
|---|---|
| Adams House and Museum | Middletown Springs Historical Society |
| Dana House | Woodstock Historical Society |
| Farrar-Mansur Museum | Robert Cranshaw/Weston Historical Society |
| Hildene | Friends of Hildene, Inc. |
| The Hyde Log Cabin | Vermont Division for Historic Preservation |
| Judd-Harris House of the Sheldon Museum | The Sheldon Museum |
| Justin Smith Morrill Homestead | Vermont Division for Historic Preservation |
| The Old Constitution House | Vermont Division for Historic Preservation |
| Old Stone House | Orleans County Historical Association |
| The Park-McCullough House | The Park-McCullough House Association |
| Plymouth Notch Historic District | Vermont Division for Historic Preservation |
| President Chester A. Arthur Historic Site | Vermont Division for Historic Preservation |
| St. Albans Historical Museum | St. Albans Historical Society |
| Taylor-Hutchinson House | Norwich Historical Society |